About the Editors

Dr Malcolm MacLachlan is Senior Lecturer in Psychology and a Fellow of Trinity College Dublin, the Psychological Society of Ireland and the Royal Anthropological Institute. His major interests are in the interplay between culture and health, acculturation experiences and embodiment. He has published over 100 academic papers and book chapters, authored two books — *Culture and Health* (Wiley, 1997) and *Psychology of Aid* (Routledge, 1998) — and edited several volumes, including the recently published, *Cultivating Health: Cultural Perspectives on Promoting Health* (Wiley, 2000). He is currently chairperson of the National Committee for the Economic and Social Sciences.

Dr Michael O'Connell is lecturer in social psychology at University College Dublin. His research interests are in the areas of inter-group relations, media representations, crime and social deprivation. He has published papers in leading journals as well as co-editing a recent volume entitled *Crime and Poverty in Ireland* (Round Hall, Sweet and Maxwell, 1998).

CULTIVATING PLURALISM

Psychological, Social and Cultural Perspectives on a Changing Ireland

Edited by
Malcolm MacLachlan
Michael O'Connell

Oak Tree Press
Dublin

Oak Tree Press
Merrion Building
Lower Merrion Street
Dublin 2, Ireland
www.oaktreepress.com

A catalogue record of this book is
available from the British Library.

ISBN 1 86076 192 5

Printed in the Republic of Ireland by Colour Books Ltd.

CONTENTS

Part Three: The Sojourn Experience

Reflection

About the Contributors

Joe Barry is a Specialist in Public Health Medicine in the Eastern Regional Health Authority and Senior Lecturer in Public Health in the Department of Community Health and General Practice, Trinity College Dublin. His research interests include addiction, Traveller health, prisoner health and general inequalities in health.

John Berry was formerly Professor of Psychology at Queen's University, Kingston, and is now engaged in independent consultancy work. He is a past Secretary-General, past President, and Honorary Fellow of the International Association for Cross-Cultural Psychology. He is the author or editor of over 20 books in the areas of cross-cultural, social, and cognitive psychology, and is particularly interested in the application of cross-cultural psychology to public policy and programmes in the areas of acculturation.

Steven Bochner is currently a Visiting Professor in the School of Psychology at the University of New South Wales. He has had a continuing interest in both the theory as well as the practical consequences of culture contact, publishing widely in the field. Some of his books include *Culture Shock* (with Adrian Furnham), *The Psychology of Culture Shock* (with Colleen Ward and Adrian Furnham), *The Mediating Person*, and *Cultures in Contact*.

Gerry Boucher is currently a Research Fellow at the Employment Research Centre at Trinity College Dublin and is completing a PhD in Sociology at TCD on Ireland's national, British, European and global integration. He is now working on UNIREG, a European study on the role of Universities in regional development.

Sinéad Casey completed her degree in Psychology at the Psychology Department, Trinity College Dublin. Her Masters degree research examined the experience of prejudice among minorities. She has also studied and published in the area of the public perception of crime seriousness.

Mary Corcoran is a Senior Lecturer in Sociology at the National University of Ireland, Maynooth. Her research interests include urban culture, social change in the city, ethnicity and migration.

Philip Curry received his PhD from the Psychology Department, Trinity College Dublin. He currently teaches research methods at the Department of Sociology, National University of Ireland, Maynooth. His research interests include majority attitudes towards minorities as well as changing political values.

Michael Fitzgerald is a Consultant Psychiatrist and Henry Marsh Professor of Child and Adolescent Psychiatry at Trinity College Dublin. His research interests concern the epidemiological aspects of child psychiatry.

Adrian Furnham MSc Econ, DPhil, DSc, DLitt is Professor of Psychology at University College London. He has lectured widely abroad and held scholarships and professorships at, amongst others, the University of New South Wales, the University of the West Indies and the University of Hong Kong. He has written over 400 scientific papers and 25 books including *Culture Shock* (1994), *The New Economic Mind* (1995), *Personality at Work* (1994), *The Myths of Management* (1996) and *The Psychology of Behaviour at Work* (1997). He is a Fellow of the British Psychological Society and is on the editorial board of a number of international journals, as well as the board of directors of the International Society for the Study of Individual Differences. He is also founder director of Applied Behavioural Research Associates (ABRA), a psychological consultancy.

Treasa Galvin is a lecturer in the Sociology Department, Trinity College Dublin. Her teaching and research interests are development, ethnic and racial studies and migration with a specific focus on Zimbabwe and Ireland.

Sinead Glennon is an Assistant Psychologist in Edinburgh and a graduate of the Psychology Department, Trinity College Dublin.

Katrina Goldstone is a researcher, critic and broadcaster. She researched and co-scripted the RTE documentary "No More Blooms", which described Irish wartime policy towards Jewish refugees. She has written and lectured on anti-Semitism and attitudes to ethnic minorities.

Sally Heron is currently an Addiction Worker at Wandsworth Prison, London. Prior to researching Traveller women's health she was employed as a Research Assistant on a project concerning ADHD in the Psychiatry Department of Trinity. She has a Masters degree from the Psychology Department in Trinity College Dublin.

Olga Horgan is a Research Assistant in the Department of Psychology, Trinity College Dublin. She has degrees in Communication from Dublin City University and Psychology from Trinity. She is currently working on phantom experiences amongst people who have had limb amputations.

Anna Keogh studied Social Anthropology in Queen's University Belfast, and continued her studies in Ethnicity and Racial Studies in Trinity College Dublin. She has worked on research reports with Pavee Point Travellers' Centre. Her special interests are in cross-cultural issues and minority ethnic group rights.

Cathal O'Regan is Training and Development Liaison Officer for the Fastrack to Information Technology initiative (FIT), which re-skills long-term unemployed people for careers in the IT industry. As a research psychologist, he has worked on social, educational, and vocational issues for various Government departments, private companies and community organisations, including as Project Director on the Refugee Settlement Research Project.

David Orr is a graduate of the Psychology Department of Trinity College Dublin and is currently an Assistant Psychologist in Elderly Mental Health, North Tees Hospital, Stockton-on-Tees, England.

David Walsh is a Garda Sergeant attached to Harcourt Square in Dublin. He has recently taken over responsibility for the operation of the newly formed Garda Racial and Intercultural Office, which has been established to deal with the policing issues raised by racial and ethnic diversity.

ACKNOWLEDGEMENTS

We are grateful to our friends, students and colleagues at Trinity College Dublin, University College Dublin and further abroad who have supported and participated in researching the still fledgling area of pluralism in Ireland. Many of them are contributors to this volume. We are also most grateful to David Givens, Brian Langan, Leonie Lawler and Maureen McDermott at Oak Tree Press for the professionalism, warmth and efficiency of their service.

To our families

Chapter One

A State of Diversity?

Malcolm MacLachlan and Michael O'Connell

"It is not possible to walk through a door that is locked and the door to integration in Ireland is locked." — Ms Hope Hanlan, UNHCR, 23 March 2000

". . . the more people who are on the margins the weaker is the centre . . . we all have a stake in building a future which respects and celebrates diversity — a generous, sharing Ireland that encompasses many traditions and cultures and creates space for all its people." — President Mary McAleese, 24 February 2000

Interviewer: "Councillor Cahill, when you say that you've had decent and genuine people with you looking for loans, are you suggesting Travellers aren't?

Michael Cahill: I am not suggesting that for one moment. But what I am saying is that it's in their nature to cause trouble. It's in their nature to steal, you know, quite simply. And that, you know, is not something that I alone state from time to time. It's in their nature to cause trouble. It's in their nature to try and do the system, as you and I well know.

Interviewer: Is that something of a generalisation?

Michael Cahill: I do believe that, yes, the general public is of that opinion.

> *Interviewer:* No, I'm asking is your claim that they cause trouble and they steal, is that not a generalisation?
>
> *Michael Cahill*: That claim is based on fact. I mean just go to Puck Fair, for example, any day or during the three days, and just stand there with your hands in your pockets and you can see it all happening around you and it's all itinerants. Who's stealing from the elderly people?"
>
> [Extract from an interview by Niall Madigan, on Radio Kerry's *Kerry Today*, with Mr Michael Cahill, Kerry County Councillor and Chairman, Southern Regional Health Board, reproduced in *The Irish Times*, 24 March 2000]

Ireland is changing. In a recent editorial in *The Irish Times* (1 April 2000), citing figures comparing January 2000 with the same month in the previous year — car sales up 50 per cent, retail sales up 17 per cent, and the underlying level of borrowing up 29 per cent — the government was called on to face up to:

> . . . tackling what might be termed the *problems of success* — congestion, a flood of immigrants and soaring house prices. . . recognising that the old policy priorities of maximising economic growth and job creation will, in many cases, no longer apply (p. 17, italics added).

The historical hallmarks of the Irish psyche are changing. Amongst these are perhaps the "factual" experiences of colonialism, the civil war and more recent terrorism, the influence of the Catholic church, and of Ireland being a small island on the fringes of Europe, yet achieving great literary and artistic fame. Also, the more mythical accounts of the Irish being rooted in Celtism, of them being heavy drinkers, lawless, violent and sexually repressed (see Halliday and Coyle, 1994; MacLachlan, 1998) have receded into a historical context. The "new" Ireland of the late 1990s, a software hothouse, of *Riverdance*, e-commerce and property speculators, with its cosmopolitan cities and an increasingly self-confident, agnostic, entrepreneurial and worldly youth, has leapt into a future unimagined, and certainly unanticipated, in the doldrums of a decade ago.

Part of the new Ireland is an increasing recognition of, and an increasing number of, minority groups within Ireland. Cultivating pluralism is about finding ways to enhance social inclusion, for all members of our society. As President McAleese (2000) has stated:

> The basic building block of social inclusion is respect for every human being, not just those you like, not just those who share our views and identity, but for everyone who shares this island with us.

This volume takes a particular interest in ethnic minority groups. Thus, other forms of social inclusion in modern Ireland — for instance, increasing tolerance of different political and religious traditions within the island; or increasing disabled people's access to and civil rights to participant fully in society; or increasing the rights of older people to comprehensive health and social support — while beyond the scope of this volume, are also consistent with an ethos of cultivating pluralism in Ireland. In one sense, what we are arguing is that through social inclusion, through tolerance for difference, through accepting and working with "others", the whole of our society can be greater than simply the sum of its parts. The goals of social inclusion can be realised through cultivating an ethos of pluralism in our society.

Hope Hanlan's metaphor of the door to integration being locked in Ireland, given as part of her address at a conference on the *Integration of Refugees in Ireland*, is a telling metaphor because it not only conjures up the hopes of an "open door", and perhaps a warm Irish welcome on the other side of it, but it also hints at the perceived dangers of an "open door" policy to immigration being perhaps too lax, and even "opening the floodgates". The Department of Justice now has 20,000 asylum-seekers on its books, with 1,000 more arriving each month. To house some of these people, at the end of March 2000, the Cabinet sanctioned the building of thousands of permanent and temporary accommodation spaces for asylum-seekers, including 1,000 spaces in the controversial "flotels". "Flotels", are perhaps, so controversial because they both metaphorically and literally embody marginalisation, imply a "work camp" ethic, and keep immigrants "offshore", at a safe distance. This is not even to question the economic necessity, social appropriateness, or general expediency of them, but to illustrate the sort of problems that success has brought us.

This country of emigrants, with a diaspora of tens of millions, now wants 200,000 immigrants by the year 2006. However, Ms Mary Harney, the Tanaiste, has stated that:

> You can't have a situation where, as people come in, they're entitled to work because then you have an open door. We can't have a completely open door. We wouldn't be able to cope . . . employers would import cheaper labour and displace Irish workers. (*The Irish Times*, 31 March 2000, Business This Week 1 supplement, p. 2).

Ireland needs immigrant labour to implement its National Development Plan, but also fears the possible consequence that such labour may bring. Mr Brendan Butler, IBEC's director of social policy, asks:

> What does that mean for the entire fabric of Irish infrastructure? It has the potential to solve the labour shortage, but it also has the potential to affect the quality of life not only of people arriving here, but also the existing population (*The Irish Times*, 31 March, 2000, Business This Week 1 supplement, p. 2).

There are indeed problems with success, but they should be welcome ones. The paradoxical aspect of rapid economic success is that it has been perceived in such a negative manner (noted above). This is demonstrated in reactions to the by-products of growth, such as housing and transport demands, but also in the way in which minorities have been viewed. In one respect, it is puzzling that the idea of minorities coming to Ireland should be a source of anxiety for the dominant population. For most of this century, many of Ireland's citizens felt forced to leave the country and suffered much merely for an opportunity to start elsewhere and a chance to build a decent life. Few from outside wished to come here. This population haemorrhage sapped national self-confidence and left its scar on the collective memory of all but the most recent generation. One might then have reasonably assumed that the concept of people actually wanting to come to live in the country's towns and cities would be welcomed as the sign of a new, prosperous and attractive identity. But that does not seem to have happened. The Irish, having in the past accused themselves of begrudging the success of others, little realised that they would ultimately begrudge their own success.

The severity and negativity of the reactions to minorities cannot be understated. It is depressing just how far *back* the clock has been turned. In the late 1980s, Micheál MacGréil gathered data on Irish attitudes to various social groups, which was published as *Prejudice in Ireland Revisited* (1996). This analysis allowed the reader an overview of the way in which Irish attitudes towards minorities had changed over time since the same questions had been asked by MacGréil in his earlier (1977) work *Prejudice in Ireland.* The results did not depict the Irish in any way as being wholly without prejudice, but the positive aspect of the longitudinal work was the fact that tolerance appeared to be generally on the increase (apart from some worryingly hostile reactions to socially excluded groups such as drug-users), and responses regarded as revealing very high levels of racial prejudice were far less prevalent than in the original study from the 1970s.

But that trend towards greater tolerance appears to have been reversed. Many students of public opinion speak of "modern" or "symbolic" racism (McConahay, 1986), in contrast to so-called "old-fashioned racism" with its notions of white superiority, segregation and formal discrimination. "Modern" racism, it is argued, is subtle and often involves resentment rather than active hostility towards minorities. Modern racism is still potent but the implication is that at least blatant prejudice is no longer acceptable and at some level this is an improvement on the old-fashioned ideology. But what is one to make of these comments made to an *Irish Times* journalist by residents of the port town of Rosslare? One man, who asked not to be named, said:

> feelings are fairly strong. A lot of people in the area work away . . . if it was your wife and kids and you were away for two weeks at a time, how would you feel? (Reported on 8 April 2000, p. 9)

Another retired businessman, who did not object to being named, argued that Wexford rather than Rosslare would be better able to cope with asylum-seekers who were liable to "come in with AIDS".

This is rancid stuff, with little of the "modern" about it. All the traditional virulent weapons in the racist armoury are there — the vulnerability of white women to vicious sexual assault, the cultural threat to our children and the outsider as symbolic and actual plague. Of course, these comments were made by two individuals, selected by a single journalist, and it is difficult to assess their generalisability. But to many observers, there is an increasingly hysterical reaction among large sections of the Irish population, which is tangible even if it has not been adequately measured in an empirical way. It is interesting to note that one fairly crude correlate of public concern such as the frequency of newspaper articles appearing with the term "refugee" in the *Irish Times* Irish news section averaged just 9 per month in 1998, 16 per month in 1999 and 28 per month from January to March 2000.

To understand prejudice in its traditional form, one looks to the traditional psychological theories. Allport (1954), in a classic treatment of the topic, first proposed the *contact hypothesis*: this is the idea that at the core of much intergroup hostility is ignorance and that increased contact between groups should lead to an increase in knowledge about each other and therefore a reduction in hostile attitudes and behaviour. Has the Irish experience refuted Allport's theory, whereby increased contact between ethnic minorities and the dominant population has appeared to generate more rather than less hostility, or at the very least to make salient previously latent attitudes? Not necessarily. Allport qualified his hypothesis and suggested that contact was only likely to be positive if the group members were of equal status, pursuing common goals and their interaction was backed by institutional support. It is clear that, in this case, those conditions are not met since minorities coming to Ireland have been effectively stigmatised, stereotyped and labelled in many ways. Rather than being portrayed as pursuing the same goals as Irish society, they have to deal with a population which often perceives them as a drain and a parasite on resources, rather than being potential partners and fellow citizens.

Furthermore, while institutional support in Ireland has at times been positive towards supporting and building acceptance of minorities, at other times, sections of the establishment, through their political, religious and media elites, have been ambivalent or downright shameful in their treatment of and reaction to minorities. The comment cited at the beginning of this chapter is interesting in that it reflects the uses to which a member of a political elite (an elected councillor) can put the media. On a local radio station, Radio Kerry, he used old-fashioned racism to appeal to his electorate while commenting on the supposed innate criminality of Travellers. On the following day, using the national media, he adopted a more "modern" tone. Teun van Dijk (1992) has spoken about the use of denials of prejudice as a necessary precursor to expressions of modern racism, such as "I'm not racist but . . ." These denials were all employed by the councillor in his more modern mode of expression the following day — denial he had said it, denial he had intended it, denial he had control over the statement (e.g. interviewers putting words in mouth), and finally denial of the consequences of this type of language.

The authors therefore regard Allport's message as all the more important, since his book on prejudice appeared at a time when the US was beginning its transition from widespread old-fashioned racism to systematic modern racism. Unfortunately, there is all too much anecdotal and actual evidence to suggest that this is where Irish society is currently "at" in its intergroup dynamics, where both old-fashioned and modern racism are at work. The authors recognise, as Allport did, the importance of understanding the different ways in which groups can have contact with one another. Centrally we accept, as he suggested, that ignorance is rarely helpful and thus the first and foremost purpose of this volume is to gather information so that knowledge on minorities can be disseminated. Of course, it is not alone in doing that and this edited volume seeks to complement other research in the area, which has been primarily theoretically and policy driven, by providing some *empirical basis* for decision making in the years ahead.

In this edited volume, we present a range of chapters divided into three sections: The Minority Experience, The Majority Experience and The Sojourn Experience. Each section culminates in an *International Commentary*, reflecting on how the Irish context and research reported here, relates to similar issues internationally. Each of our three international commentators, drawn from North America, Europe and Australia, are world authorities in their area of expertise. Below we outline some of the important issues addressed in the following chapters.

The Minority Experience

The first section of the book focuses on the experiences of minority groups in Ireland. Ethnic minority individuals in Ireland form an easily identifiable minority group and therefore are vulnerable to prejudice due to their distinctiveness. The specific experience of prejudice based on skin colour has not previously been empirically examined in Ireland. In Chapter Two, "Pain and Prejudice", Sinead Casey and Michael O'Connell investigate four aspects of this experience: mental health, the salience of ethnicity in self-concept, perceptions of racism in Irish society and actual experience of racism and discrimination. Perhaps surprisingly, ethnicity was not found to be a particularly salient aspect of the self-concept, but Casey and O'Connell argue that this may be because of the difficulty in achieving identities which challenge the dominant concept of "Irishness". Despite this, ethnic minority individuals displayed lower levels of psychological well-being than found in the Irish sample studied here. One reason for this may be the very high levels of racism reported by minority respondents, especially those labelled "Black". Casey and O'Connell also find a strong correspondence between experiencing racism and lower psychological well-being. These were both also strongly related to the perception of prejudice among majority Irish society, reported by minority group members. Casey and O'Connell's major conclusion is that prejudice (both in terms of minorities experiencing it and perceiving it in the environment) is not "simply" a political issue, but also an important determinant of health, especially psychological health.

The third chapter, "Seeking Refuge in Ireland" by Olga Horgan, explores acculturation experiences of refugees and asylum-seekers, and compares them to a group of international students, in terms of acculturation level, psychological distress, social support and discrimination. Clinically significant levels of psychological distress were found in all three groups, with one half of forced migrants (refugees and asylum-seekers) exceeding the cut-off for clinical "caseness". Such psychological distress among refugees and asylum-seekers was significantly associated with lack of employment and lower satisfaction with social support. Furthermore, across the whole sample, reported satisfaction with social support was significantly related to acculturation stress and to experiences of perceived discrimination. Horgan argues that her data suggest a need for procedures to be put in place to counteract discrimination at both the individual and institutional level, and indicate the importance of social support and employment in facilitating the psychological well-being of forced migrants coming to Ireland.

In Chapter Four, Mary Corcoran's "Local Authority Residents" reminds us that minority status and social exclusion are not restricted to migrants, or to those of a "different" ethnic identity. Corcoran argues that the benefits of Ireland's recent economic growth have not been evenly distributed and that socio-economic inequalities are deepening rather than attenuating. This chapter explores the social consequences of this change by focusing on the experiences of local authority residents in Ireland, whom, it is argued, display many of the characteristics of minority groups. The analysis presented here is based on qualitative data gathered from residents in seven housing estates, three located in and around Dublin and one in each of Cork, Limerick, Sligo and Dundalk. While quality of life varies between and even within these estates, there is a certain commonality of experience. That experience crystallises around the idea of minority status with residents perceiving themselves to be "second class citizens", particularly when they compare themselves to residents of neighbouring private housing estates. On a daily basis they contend with poor service provision, lack of security and the pervasive impact of labelling or address effects. On those estates where a drug economy and culture flourish, there are enormous social and psychic costs for the residents. At the same time, residents on every estate take pride in their status as enduring communities — characterised by a high degree of sociability, supportive familial networks and a norm of reciprocity — all features common to minority groups. Where community activism brings success, people's sense of themselves as agents, rather than subjects that are acted upon, is enhanced. However, Corcoran argues that such activism alone cannot provide a mechanism for integrating estate residents into mainstream society.

In Chapter Five, the final chapter in the section on minority experience, Sally Heron, Michael Fitzgerald, Joseph Barry and Malcolm MacLachlan examine "The Psychosocial Health of Irish Traveller Mothers". Much of our thinking about ethnic minority groups is a product of socialisation that implies that these groups come from elsewhere. There is, however, an ethnic minority group, indigenous to Ireland, which has always been a part of Irish society — albeit existing on its margins. This group is the Irish Travelling Community. Previous research has emphasised the poor health status of Travellers in Ireland and Britain. The present study followed up 47 Traveller mothers (and their children) from the (then) Eastern Health Board's ten Community Care Areas, whose health status was examined in 1987 (Barry, Herity and Solan, 1989). Almost one-half of mothers interviewed were found to have a clinically significant level of psychological distress. Psychological stressors identified included environmental hazards, the level of social support available, and the types of health behaviours engaged in by the individual. Heron et al. discuss the implication of these findings for service provision and Traveller culture.

In Chapter Six, Adrian Furnham, our distinguished international commentator, compares and contrasts the Irish experiences reported here with those in other parts of the world, highlighting some key issues which the chapters in the first section point up.

The Majority Experience

The second section of the book deals with the majority response to minority groups within Ireland. Anna Keogh, in Chapter Seven, explores "Talking about the Other". Keogh studied transition year students from four secondary schools in order to understand not only the attitudes of these pupils toward refugees and asylum-seekers, but also their sources of knowledge and the process through which their attitudes were social constructed. Adopting this social constructivist perspective, Keogh argues that constructions of "otherness" reflect much about the self, and in the present context, about "Irishness". Keogh's suggestion that negative constructions of refugees and asylum-seekers reflect shortcomings in the construction of Irish identity and ethnicity, calls for an in-depth review of our education curriculum and the role of media portraying refugees and asylum-seekers.

Chapter Eight, by Philip Curry, ". . . she never let them in", builds on the previous chapter by exploring the attitudes of adults in Dublin towards indigenous and foreign minority groups. Of particular interest in Curry's study was the level of hostility towards some newly arrived foreign groups (Romanians, Bosnians, Spaniards, African and Arabs) compared to an indigenous minority group (Travellers). Adopting a social distance paradigm — asking people to indicate the degree of physical proximity to which they would be willing to admit a typical member of each of the target groups — produced valuable insights. Travellers were viewed as the most distant group (i.e. the group from which people wanted to keep most distant) and Spaniards as the least distant group, with Africans, Bosnians, Romanians and Arabs being rated as increasingly distant. However, most importantly, the level of distance for all groups was very high. It would seem then that Dubliners harbour significant hostility towards minority group members and, as Curry argues, this should be targeted as a concern before it is allowed to develop its destructive potential.

David Walsh's "Policing Pluralism" (Chapter Nine) examines the provision of a police service — the Garda Síochána — in an increasingly multiethnic and multicultural society. Walsh surveyed members of the Garda Síochána on their attitudes and perceptions concerning cultural diversity and racism in Ireland. He also interviewed ethnic minority group members regarding their attitudes to and perceptions of the Irish police force. Walsh, himself a Garda, concludes that each of his sources points to a clear need for the introduction of anti-racist and cultural diversity training in An Garda Síochána. Walsh recognises that training alone is not enough and that structural and policy changes within the police force may also be necessary. However, he emphasises that the primary source of, and force for change in policing, should be the ethnic minority groups themselves.

In Chapter Ten on "Immigration and Resettlement in Ireland", Cathal O'Regan reports on his study of Bosnian and Vietnamese programme refugees. This project, involving five government departments and two specialist agencies, has provided valuable data on the acculturation process, the motives of refugees, how best to support refugees on their arrival and to facilitate their resettlement. O'Regan argues that integration and empowerment are two of the key principles involved in successful resettlement. Outreach programmes to refugees and other immigrants should not, it is argued, be left to refugee support agencies and charities, but must be incorporated into mainstream service provision. The diverse resettlement needs of refugees (e.g. health, education, housing, employment, language training) challenges interdepartmental communication and co-operation within government. O'Regan calls for us to recognise that integration involves adaptation by both minority and majority group members: immigrants must be afforded the opportunity to develop their own support networks and to participate in Irish society; while mainstream society must be given an opportunity to learn how immigrants can contribute to the betterment of our society.

Treasa Galvin's chapter, "Refugee Status in Exile", focuses on the experience of Africans seeking asylum in Ireland. It explores the process of transition and the social constructions involved in moving from "being" an asylum-seeker to "being" a refugee. Asylum-seekers' transition to the host society involves a change in their status and identity, and ambivalence about being incorporated into a different, and often for them, incomplete social world. Having gone into exile, an individual trades their network of family and friends for other asylum-seekers and possibly members of the host society. Galvin argues that "resource-based" restrictive inclusion, perceived hostility from the Irish, an ambivalent government approach and their own changing status, all combine to produce the asylum experience in Ireland. In Ireland, asylum-seeker is a "dirty word": it creates barriers to social inclusion, prohibits employment and narrows the individual's experience of broader Irish society. The consequence is feelings of loneliness, exclusion and alienation. Is this how we wish the asylum experience to be?

The final chapter in the second section of the volume, Chapter Twelve, by our distinguished international commentator, Steve Bochner, compares the Irish majority response to minority issues with that of other countries and international institutions.

SOJOURNERS

The third and final section of this book looks at a special group of migrants, that of sojourners, and particularly foreign students, or academic sojourners. While the economic boom may have smothered some of the traditional lures of Ireland, the isle of saints and scholars has not taken its eye off the commercial value of the latter, at least! For instance, Cox (1997) states that the proportion of international students in Ireland has risen from three to four per cent of third level students in the late 1980s to almost ten per cent in the mid-1990s. Ireland's continuing economic and cultural boom, its cosmopolitan mix and its strong academic reputation, have meant that we continue to attract large numbers of international students. Aside from the financial assets they provide, as a group which can observe social structure but do not have to commit to it permanently, they bring very useful psychological assets and insights about the society in which they are immersed.

In Chapter Thirteen, "Mixing Multiculturalism, Assimilation and Discrimination", Gerard Boucher summarises the perceptions of international students regarding the degree to which they found Irish culture open to integration. It is interesting that competing and contradictory processes at work emerged from Boucher's analysis of the viewpoints of the students. They found that the insularity of Irish culture can mean increased friendliness towards outsiders but only if those outsiders acted in ways seen as strongly integrationist. Friendliness was withdrawn where individuals and their "foreignness" were perceived as a threat to the homogeneity of Irish culture. A contradiction was also recognised by these students in the behaviour of the Irish state; between formal and abstract policies of equality and non-discrimination enacted in law, but discriminatory behaviour by officials of the Irish state (for example at the border, when seeking visas or permits). Boucher interprets the qualitative data very skilfully to uncover this important lack of fit between reality and official ideology.

Glennon and MacLachlan's chapter, "Stress, Coping and Acculturation of International Medical Students in Ireland", explores the psychological well-being of international students in a medical school (the Royal College of Surgeons in Ireland) whose students are predominantly foreign. Coping styles (Problem Solving,

Seeking Social Support and Avoidance) as well as Berry's framework of acculturation strategies (assimilation, separation, integration and marginalisation), are examined as possible predictors of psychological well-being or distress. A high proportion of visiting students (in comparison to a control group of Irish students) suffered from clinically significant levels of psychological distress. Across the whole sample, an integration acculturation strategy (seeking to identify with the Irish culture and to also maintain identity with the culture of origin) was associated with greater psychological well-being, than a separation acculturation strategy (seeking to retain identity with the culture of origin, but not to identify with the Irish culture). In terms of the personal coping strategies adopted by foreign students, the use of avoidance was associated with more distress, while the use of problem solving was associated with greater well-being, and the degree to which social support was sought was unrelated to reports of psychological distress. These findings, and the fact that problems solving strategies were used to different extents by those adopting different acculturation strategies, illustrates how individualised and more socially based responses to stress interact in complex ways to influence the well-being of foreign sojourners in Ireland.

In Chapter Fifteen, "SOCRATES in Ireland: Field Dependence and Homesickness among International Students", Orr and MacLachlan examine another distressing aspect of the acculturation experience of foreign students — homesickness. While homesickness is usually a rather mild and transitory experience, it may also be quite severe and chronic, and has even been associated with suicide. In the present study, Fisher's (1989) role-change theory is employed as the theoretical framework within which homesickness is examined. Orr and MacLachlan have introduced the idea of field dependence–independence to this literature. This dimension is the assessment of the degree to which an individual feels a separate sense of self from the surrounding environment. The Embedded Figures Test was used to assess field dependence–independence and the dimension was found to be strongly associated with reported homesickness. More specifically, the study found that there was a high degree of homesickness among the sample group of international students but this appeared to be lessened to a certain degree by a high level of field independence or autonomy from the immediate environment. This may be of consequence for the way in which people "fit into" Irish society and more generally may be useful for selecting and preparing students to acculturate effectively.

In Chapter Sixteen, John Berry, our distinguished international commentator, seeks to tease out the nature of the complexities described above and to relate these to international findings elsewhere.

Finally, in a provocative and thoughtful piece, Katrina Goldstone, in the final chapter of this volume, "Rewriting You", asks both authors and readers to reflect on the nature of the work about minorities or the "Other". She considers what the direct and indirect consequences are of researching groups from the outside, as many psychologists, anthropologists and sociologists do (and have done in this volume). Taking the example of understanding Jews in Ireland, Goldstone highlights the problem of imposing homogeneity from "outside" on a group and the reification that results. It is an uncomfortable and difficult issue for researchers to grapple with, since the threat of stereotyping at a further level is very real. As Goldstone says, just as journalists can ring up individuals because they are "doing something about antisemitism" or "doing something about racism", researchers can fall into the dangerous trap of just "doing something about refugees" or "minorities" or "Travellers", *without actually really doing anything*.

This warning is a timely and important reminder, and a suitable one with which to conclude this book. It is our hope that the empirical emphasis of this volume, and the research reported herein, will make a modest, but important, contribution not just to doing something, but to doing *the right things*. To cultivating Ireland as a diverse state, which is tolerant of difference, inclusive of minorities and accepting of pluralism.

References

Allport, G. (1954), *The Nature of Prejudice*. MA: Addison-Wesley.

Cox, W. (1997), "ICOS and International Students", in O. Egan (ed.) *Minority Ethnic Groups in Higher Education*, Proceedings of a conference held on 27 November 1996, in St. Patrick's College, Maynooth. Cork: Higher Education Quality Unit.

Fisher, S. (1989), *Homesickness, Cognition and Health*, Erlbaum: London.

Halliday, A. and K. Coyle (eds.) (1994), "The Irish Psyche", Special Issue, *Irish Journal of Psychology*, Vol. 15, No. 2/3, pp. 243–507.

MacLachlan, M. (1998), "Promoting Health: Thinking through context", in E. McAuliffe and L. Joyce, *A Healthier Future? Managing Healthcare in Ireland*, Dublin: Institute for Public Administration.

McAleese, M. (2000), Remarks by President McAleese to the Tipperary Rural Travellers Project, Anti-Racism Conference, 24 February 2000.

McConahay, J.B. (1986), "Modern Racism, Ambivalence, and the Modern Racism Scale", in J.F. Dovidio and S.L. Gaertner (eds.), *Prejudice, Discrimination, and Racism*, New York: Academic Press.

MacGréil, M. (1996), *Prejudice in Ireland Revisited*, Dublin: Survey and Research Unit, St. Patrick's College, Maynooth.

MacGréil, M. (1977), *Prejudice and Tolerance in Ireland*, Dublin: Research Section, College of Industrial Relations.

Van Dijk, T. (1992), "Discourse and the Denial of Racism", *Discourse and Society*, Vol. 3, pp. 87–118.

Part One

The Minority Experience

CHAPTER TWO

PAIN AND PREJUDICE: ASSESSING THE EXPERIENCE OF RACISM IN IRELAND

Sinéad Casey and Michael O'Connell

INTRODUCTION

The numbers of "naturalised coloured" or "mixed race" people living in Ireland in the past number of decades is virtually impossible to establish, since the Irish census has never asked a question regarding ethnicity. According to the *1992 United Nations Human Development*, there were about 50,000 people in Ireland from outside the EU and possibly 30,000 of these were from the developing world. Robbie McVeigh, in *The Racialization of Irishness* (1996), provides a more recent estimate of the numbers of minority ethnic people living in Ireland through statistics which have been calculated by collating the responses to other census questions, as well as estimates supplied by the minority ethnic communities themselves. He states that:

> People of colour in Ireland have their origins, mostly, in British colonies. In Northern Ireland members of this group are largely of South Asian and Chinese origin; in Southern Ireland, this population also includes a substantial number of people of African origin. There are around 45,000 people of colour in Ireland, north and south. (p. 22)

Given the presence of minorities in Ireland, what has been the experience of discrimination, prejudice or racism? Travellers have experienced consistent and systematic discrimination. The European Committee of Inquiry on Racism and Xenophobia (1991) stated that:

> the single most discriminated against ethnic group is the "travelling people". . . . Like gypsies in other countries, they are considered undesirable neighbours and are usually forced to move out of residential areas.

Discrimination against Travellers takes many forms; it can be personal or institutional, direct or indirect. In overt terms, they are often refused entry into public houses, hotels and other establishments and are frequently shadowed by security guards in shops.

On the other hand, up to the end of the 1980s, prejudice towards minorities of colour has been of a different nature. The *European Parliament Committee of Inquiry on Racism and Xenophobia* (1991) took the view that Ireland was "remarkably free" from racism because "there is not a large presence of foreigners". According to this report:

> The number of known cases of racial harassment or violence is very small compared to other countries. However, precisely because of the insignificant foreign population, the few cases which [the report goes on to mention] are indicative of some racism and xenophobia which could reach more dangerous levels if there were more foreigners, particularly non-Europeans.

It can be argued that this is what has occurred in the 1990s. A refugee woman who had lived in Tallaght in Dublin for a number of years spoke about the abrupt change in her experience of racism to McVeigh and Binchy (1998):

> When I first came here it was what you might call innocent. They came up to you as you were walking along and wanted to touch your hair and things like that but people were more curious than hostile. It all changed with the (General) Election (Summer, 1997). Some politicians said some things about refugees and after that there was a difference — there was a lot more racism (p. 21).

It is worth examining the article by Curry in this volume for more recent measures of social distance (see glossary). His work suggests that prejudice towards ethnic minorities and foreign nationals has increased rapidly in Dublin. One consequence of this of course is more experiences of racism and discrimination by minorities. In the media, anecdotal accounts of these experiences have appeared quite regularly. An example can be found in an excerpt from an article by Sarah Marriott published in *The Big Issues* (August 1998):

> "The first thing I noticed when I arrived in Ireland was the cold," says fourteen-year-old Anna, who came to Dublin from Africa several years ago. Speaking in a soft Dublin accent, she remembers: "People then were very friendly and were always saying 'hi'. In the last year, that's changed and now people in town call me names."(p. 22)

There have also been frequent reports of violent physical attacks in the media.

An important challenge to social scientists is to go beyond the individual tragedies and misery of these stories and provide a more systematic and standardised account of the experience of discrimination and racism by minorities in this country. Thus, it is necessary both to develop a tool to measure comprehensively the negative experiences people have had and also, using that tool, to establish a reliable measure against which international and future comparisons can be made. For example, in the US, Landrine and Klonoff (1996) constructed a Schedule of Racist Events (SRE) in an attempt to assess and quantify the racial discrimination experienced by African Americans in the United States.

As psychologists, we were also interested in assessing the psychological impact that prejudice may have on those suffering its expression. For example, in the Landrine and Klonoff study above, the experience of racism was associated with high levels of stress. Generally, the research regarding the mental health of minority group members does indicate a higher prevalence of mental illness among minority groups compared with the majority population. Harrison et al. (1988) found that black people in the US were twelve times more likely to be diagnosed with schizophrenia than whites. According to Landrine and Klonoff (1996):

> African Americans (regardless of class) experience racism so frequently that depression, tension and rage about racism is the single most common problem presented by African Americans in psychotherapy.

The rationale for the research described in this article is as follows. Although there have been a few studies of the ethnic minority experience in Ireland, these have concentrated quite exclusively on programme refugees and do not allow generalisation. This is despite Ireland's gradual growth towards a more multicultural and multiethnic society in the last few years. Given the issues raised in the research reviewed above, it was decided to approach the ethnic minority experience in Ireland from three angles:

1. The experience of racism and discrimination by minorities in Ireland
2. Levels of mental health of minorities
3. The relationship between the experience of racism and mental health.

To date, there have been no major studies conducted which have examined the experience of racism in Ireland, let alone any that have attempted to explore its possible mental health consequences, indicating an obvious necessity for research in this area. It is important to go beyond shocking but possibly atypical accounts in the media of racism and provide data from a larger sample of minority people living in Ireland. Rather than rely on guesswork, a small-scale survey was designed and carried out gathering data on issues that the international literature as well as common sense suggested would be important. First, looking at people from ethnic minority background, it was important to know the levels of discrimination and prejudice they were experiencing. Once these were measured, their impact on psychological well-being could be ascertained. The focus here was on people of colour as an ethnic group, since they are completely under-researched in Ireland. (By "people of colour", the authors wish to distinguish those individuals perceived by the general Irish population as ethnically distinct or diverse.) Given the excellent work of Pavee Point, Travellers' Support Groups and others, it was felt that attempts to deal with these issues in relation to

Travellers would necessarily be a poor repetition of work done elsewhere. The small-scale nature of the work, as well as the absence of much data on Irish ethnic minorities, means that it is necessarily exploratory in its approach.

METHOD

A survey questionnaire was created to gather information. While its structured format makes it difficult to explore and pursue themes that might emerge, it was thought that the confidentiality and anonymity permitted to respondents were essential.

Questionnaire Items

Assessment of Psychological Health

The General Health Questionnaire was selected as a measure of psychological distress among the participants (see Appendix 1). The GHQ is a standardised and widely used method of assessing levels of psychological well-being which has been normed on a variety of populations, including Irish and adolescent samples. It has also been used with ethnic minority groups in Ireland, as mentioned above, and in many other studies worldwide (Goldberg and Williams, 1991). The GHQ-28, which was developed by Goldberg and Hillier (1979), was chosen as it can be broken down into four subscales which can be used for separate analyses. These subscales are:

- Somatic symptoms
- Anxiety and insomnia
- Social dysfunction
- Severe depression.

The Experience of Racial Abuse

This section in the questionnaire attempted to encompass and measure the range of potential racial abuse, from the verbally offensive (derogatory assumptions about people's origins and name-calling) to the physically abusive (threats or experiences of racially motivated attacks), in a type of "checklist" form (see Appendix 2). From the literature, the following areas were identified and a question devised for each:

1. Outright racist insults
2. Racist jokes or snide remarks
3. Racist phone calls or mail
4. Deliberate damage to property
5. Feelings of avoidance
6. Feelings of being snubbed
7. Persistent verbal harassment
8. Threats of physical violence
9. Physical attacks.

For the majority of these incidences, the respondents were asked to indicate the frequency of the abuse, that is whether the incidences occurred "Rarely", "Sometimes", "Often" or "All the time". They were also asked to indicate the identity of the perpetrator of the abuse, i.e. whether it was "Strangers", "Class/Work Mates", "Friends" or "Others".

The final part of the checklist section detailed different areas of life where people might experience discrimination. These situations included gaining entry to pubs, clubs or restaurants, shopping, using public transport, finding accommodation, dealing with landlords, the Social Welfare, doctors, schools or colleges, banks, the police and finding a job. Participants were asked to indicate whether they had experienced racial discrimination in any of these areas "Ever" and "In the last six months".

Demographics

The final section of the questionnaire asked for some basic demographic information and was varied depending on whether the respondents were older or younger. The demographics also included questions regarding the ethnicity of the respondents' parents in a multiple choice format for ease of analysis while the person was also given the opportunity to describe their own ethnicity as they wished.

Accessing the Sample

The Younger Sample

It was decided that the best way to access a fairly representative younger sample was to approach them through the educational system. Permission was received from the Department of Education to conduct this research through the secondary school system. Twenty-five schools in the Dublin area were selected. The main criterion for selection was the number of pupils in the school, as it was thought that the larger schools would be more likely to have minority students. A further three schools were approached due to the fact that one had a specific department catering for international students and the other two were recommended by third parties as having many suitable students.

A letter was sent to the principals asking them to forward a letter to parents of ethnic minority children (e.g. children of Afro-Caribbean, African, Asian, Arabic or Oriental extraction) asking for permission to send a questionnaire on. If parental consent was received, we sent the questionnaire by post and provided a SAE for its return. A number of schools declined to participate because there were no minority students or because they feared offending parents or because they felt the questionnaire items were inappropriate. The remaining thirteen schools participated in the survey.

The selection of the sample from Dublin does bias the findings, but the research was carried out before the government began to systematically move some asylum-seekers outside the capital and obtaining a reasonable number of respondents would have been very difficult if schools had been selected on a national basis.

Accessing the Adult Sample

The adult sample was approached through a variety of methods. A number of groups which work with minorities in Ireland, as well as a number of anti-racist organisations, were approached, as well as some English-language schools for adults. Those who facilitated the study included the Islamic Centre, the African Cultural Project,

Harmony, the African Refugee Network and LSB College. Questionnaires were left with these organisations and collected when completed at a later time.

There was a risk of potential bias in contacting anti-racist organisations, but respondents obtained through these made up a very small minority of adult respondents. There was a trade-off between the desire to be representative and the need for an adequate number of responses to make meaningful comment.

The Participants

Following a pilot study, 146 people participated in the survey (33 per cent being adults and 67 per cent under 18). There were 121 participants of minority ethnicity (40 per cent being adults with the remainder being under 18) and there was a comparison group of 25 other respondents. The minority group sample was made up of people of black (African/Afro-Caribbean), South Asian, Oriental or Arabic origin and those of mixed race. The minority group sample was further divided into an adult sub-sample and a school sub-sample. The school sub-sample ranged in age from 12 to 21, the average age being 16. The adult sub-sample ranged in age from 18–25 to 46–55, the median age-group being 26–35. The comparison group consisted of non-Irish white students. The ages of the comparison group members ranged from 14 to 21 with an average age of 16.

Due to the diversity of the sample, it was deemed necessary to sub-divide the minority group. This was done on the basis of ethnic similarity. Although this may seem relatively crude, the aim of the research was to examine the experience of people who fall victim to prejudice due to their relative distinctiveness. This breakdown therefore facilitated comparisons between different ethnic/racial groups who are distinctive in different ways. The first group was the Black sub-group, which consisted of people of African and Afro-Caribbean origin who described both of their parents as being Black. The second group, referred to as the Asian sub-group, consisted of people of South Asian (Indian or Pakistani) and Arabic origin. The next group consisted of those of East Asian extraction (for example Chinese, Japanese and so forth) and was called the Oriental group. The final group was the Mixed Race group — the backgrounds varied, but each had one white parent. It must be emphasised that these names are merely *labels* to facilitate the comparison of large amounts of data. It is not being implied that, for example, Chinese and Japanese experiences are identical or that these groups should be treated similarly. The diverse nature of the sample necessitated some form of breakdown to make it more manageable.

FINDINGS

Checklist of Racial Abuse

The items on the checklist were first examined to establish the basic frequencies of each of the events. The type of racial abuse and the percentage of the minority sample that experienced each type of abuse are presented in Table 2.1. These percentages are further broken down to account for the adult and youth sub-samples.

The most common form of abuse reported by the sample was "outright racist insults", which had been experienced by 64.2 per cent of people. "Racist jokes or snide remarks" was the next most frequent type of abuse, with 45.8 per cent of the sample having experienced this type of harassment at some time in Ireland. These were followed by "feelings of being avoided" (37.5 per cent) and "feelings of being snubbed" (20.8 per cent). "Persistent verbal harassment" (17.5 per cent) and "actual physical attacks" (16.7 per cent) ranked next in the order of frequency, while "threats of physical violence" (13.3 per cent) and "deliberate damage to property" (10.0 per cent) were experienced relatively infrequently. The lowest incidence of racist abuse was "racist phone calls or mail" which was reported by only 5.8 per cent of the sample.

Age Differences in the Experience of Racial Abuse

The adult sub-group scored consistently higher than the youth sub-group on all of the items. More than five times more adults than youths had experienced deliberate damage to property, 21.3 per cent compared with 4.2 per cent. More than twice as many adults as youth had felt they were snubbed, 34.0 per cent versus 12.7 per cent, and adults (25.5 per cent) were three times more likely to have experienced threats of physical violence than members of the youth sub-group (7.0 per cent). The adults were also much more likely to have felt that they were being avoided, with 53.2 per cent reporting this, compared with 28.2 per cent of the youth sub-group.

Table 2.1: Percentages of Minority Sample Who have Experienced Various Types of Abuse in Ireland

Type of Racial Abuse	Overall Sample	Minority Adult (n=47)	Minority Youth (n=71)
1. Outright Racist Insult	64.2%	70.2%	63.4%
2. Jokes or Snide Remarks	45.8%	57.4%	38.0%
3. Racist Phone Calls or Mail	5.8%	10.6%	2.8%
4. Deliberate Damage to Property	10.0%	21.3%	4.2%
5. Feelings of Being Avoided	37.5%	53.2%	28.2%
6. Feelings of Being Snubbed	20.8%	34.0%	12.7%
7. Persistent Verbal Harassment	17.5%	25.5%	14.1%
8. Threats of Physical Violence	13.3%	25.5%	7.0%
9. Actual Physical Attacks	16.7%	21.3 5	15.5%

The Experience of Racial Abuse: Settled versus Recent Immigrants

When comparing the recent immigrant and settled sub-groups, it was observed that 53.4 per cent of the recent immigrants had suffered outright racist insults compared with 89.3 per cent of the settled group. However, of the recent immigrant group, 35 per cent experienced feelings of being avoided while only 14.3 per cent of the settled group did; this difference was also found to be significant ($Z = -2.66$, $p < 0.01$).

The Perpetrators of Racist Abuse

The respondents were also asked to detail who had perpetrated the various types of racist abuse they had experienced. They were given a choice of "Strangers", "Class/Work Mates" and "Friends", as well as a "write-in" option and were allowed to select as many responses as they wanted. For the majority of items, the abuse was perpetrated by strangers or people unknown to the respondent. Of the 11 people who had been victims of deliberate damage to property, only one had any knowledge of the vandal. Similarly, of the 13 who had been threatened with physical violence, only one was acquainted with the person who threatened them. However, one in four of those who had been physically attacked knew their assailant. Most of the persistent verbal harassment (78.9 per cent) and racist insults (71.4 per cent) were also perpetrated by strangers. In the case of racist jokes or snide remarks, only 58.2 per cent were uttered by strangers and only 51.1 per cent of feelings of avoidance were the result of the actions of strangers. Feelings of being snubbed was the only item which reversed the trend, with 68.0 per cent of these feelings being the result of the actions of friends, colleagues or peers.

Group Differences in the Experience of Racial Abuse

The incidence of the different types of racial abuse was then examined in terms of its experience by the four minority sub-groups. These figures are presented in Tables 2.2 and 2.3. The Black sub-sample experienced more racial abuse than any of the other sub-groups with regard to every item on the checklist. The Oriental sub-group experienced the least racial abuse with respect to threats of physical attacks (0 per cent), deliberate damage to property (4.8 per cent) and actual physical attacks (4.8 per cent). The mixed race sub-group experienced least feelings of being avoided (17.4 per cent). The Asian sub-group experienced least abuse in terms of racist phone calls or mail (2.2 per cent), outright racist insults (45.7 per cent), racist jokes or snide remarks (39.1 per cent), feelings of being snubbed (10.9 per cent) or persistent verbal harassment (8.7 per cent).

Table 2.2: Percentages of Minority Sub-groups Who Experienced Different Types of Racial Abuse in the Emotional Sub-set

Type of Racial Abuse	Black Sample	Asian Sample	Oriental Sample	Mixed Race Sample
1. Outright Racist Insults	87.6%	45.7%	57.1%	78.3%
2. Jokes or Snide Remarks	53.3%	39.1%	52.4%	43.5%
5. Feelings of Being Avoided	70.0%	32.6%	23.8%	17.4%
6. Feelings of Being Snubbed	43.3%	10.9%	14.3%	17.4%
7. Persistent Verbal Harassment	26.7%	8.7%	23.8%	17.4%

Table 2.3: Percentages of Minority Sub-groups Who Experienced Different Types of Racial Abuse in the Criminal Sub-set

Type of Racial Abuse	Black Sample	Asian/Arabic Sample	Oriental Sample	Mixed Race Sample
3. Racist Phone Calls or Mail	10.0%	2.2%	4.8%	8.7%
4. Deliberate Damage to Property	13.3%	8.7%	4.8%	13.0%
8. Threats of Physical Attacks	30.0%	10.9%	0.0%	8.7%
9. Actual Physical Violence	26.7%	15.2%	4.8%	17.4%

The most frequent situations where minority group members reported ever experiencing discrimination (see Table 2.4) were finding accommodation or dealing with landlords (50.0 per cent), using public transport (39.0 per cent), gaining entry to pubs, clubs and restaurants (35.6 per cent) and dealing with banks (34.9 per cent). However, the experience of discrimination was consistently high on all the items, with dealing with the police (27.1 per cent) being the least frequent situation in which discrimination was experienced. A breakdown of the experience of discrimination of the various minority sub-groups is presented in Table 2.5.

Table 2.4: Percentages of Minority Group Who Felt that They Had Been Discriminated Against in Various Situations Due to Their Colour or Race

Situation	Ever	In the Last 6 Months
Gaining entry to pubs etc.	35.6%	16.1%
Shopping	33.1%	14.4%
Using public transport	39.0%	22.0%
Finding accommodation/ Dealing with landlords	50.0%	34.1%
Dealing with the Social Welfare	30.2%	11.6%
Dealing with doctors	27.9%	14.0%
Dealing with schools/ colleges	30.5%	10.2%
Dealing with banks	34.9%	16.3%
Dealing with the police	27.1%	7.6%
Finding a job	28.0%	12.7%

Table 2.5: Percentage of Each Minority Group Who Felt that They Had Been Discriminated Against in Various Situations Due to Their Colour or Race

Situation	Black	Asian	Oriental	Mixed Race
Gaining entry to pubs etc.	58.6%	43.5%	5.0%	17.4%
Shopping	37.9%	45.7%	15.0%	17.4%
Using public transport	58.6%	50.0%	5.0%	21.7%
Finding accommodation/ Dealing with landlords	60.9%	45.5%	33.3%	25.0%
Dealing with the Social Welfare	34.8%	30.0%	16.7%	25.0%
Dealing with doctors	21.7%	50.0%	16.7%	25.0%
Dealing with schools/colleges	48.3%	37.0%	5.0%	17.4%
Dealing with banks	39.1%	30.0%	16.7%	50.0%
Dealing with the police	41.4%	32.6%	15.0%	8.7%
Finding a job	55.2%	26.1%	15.0%	8.7%

Overall Experience of Racism Score: The Checklist Score

The checklist was broken down into two subsets of items for ease of further analysis. The first subset contained items 1 (outright racist insults), 2 (jokes or snide remarks), 5 and 6 (feelings of being avoided and snubbed), and item 7 (persistent verbal harassment). This is termed the "emotional and verbal racism" subset. The second subset contained item 3 (racist phone calls or mail), item 4 (deliberate damage to property), item 8 (threats of violence) and item 9 (actual physical attacks). This is termed the "criminal racism" subset. Each person was given a score of one for each type of abuse they had experienced, giving a potential score of five on the emotional and verbal racism subset and of four on the criminal racism subset. The discrimination items became the discrimination subset, on which there was a potential score of ten for adults and six for youths.

Using the three subsets, an overall "experience of racism" score was computed, which simply involved summing the scores on the three scales. The mean scores of the minority sub-groups on the checklist subscales are presented in Table 2.6.

Table 2.6: Mean Scores of Minority Sub-groups on Experience of Racism Sub-sets and Overall Checklist Score

Score Type	Black	Asian	Oriental	Mixed Race
Emotional Range (0–5)	2.80	1.41	1.71	1.79
Criminal Range (0–4)	0.80	0.39	0.14	0.58
Adult Discrimination Range (0–10)	4.12	3.40	2.29	2.20
Youth Discrimination Range (0–6)	3.40	2.62	0.08	0.79
Adult Checklist Range (0–100)	42.00	25.00	23.00	39.00
Youth Checklist Range (0–100)	37.33	30.39	12.82	16.14
Overall Checklist Range (0–100)	41.31	29.11	20.89	15.46

The general pattern in Table 2.6 is that black respondents suffered the most frequent and comprehensive expressions of racism, while the Oriental group were generally but not always the least abused group.

General Health Questionnaire

Psychological well-being (or lack of it) was assessed with the General Health Questionnaire (GHQ). The GHQ was scored using the commonly used format 0-0-1-1. However, Goldberg and Williams (1991) point out that there are advantages in using the Likert scoring method (format: 0-1-2-3) when the use of the subscales is required and this method was used to compute the subscales scores.

A threshold score of five was adopted for the present study since it is consistent with thresholds used in the previous research involving the GHQ-28 (Goldberg and Williams, 1991). The use of a threshold sub-divides the scores into those considered "cases" of psychological disorder and those who are not. As can be seen from Figure 2.1, 46.7 per cent of the sample scored above the threshold. Of the adult minority, 44.7 per cent scored above the threshold; this compares with 45.8 per cent of the youth minority and 40.7 per cent of the White Comparison group. These figures are displayed in Table 2.7.

Figure 2.1: Histogram Showing the Frequency Distribution of GHQ Scores among the Minority Sample

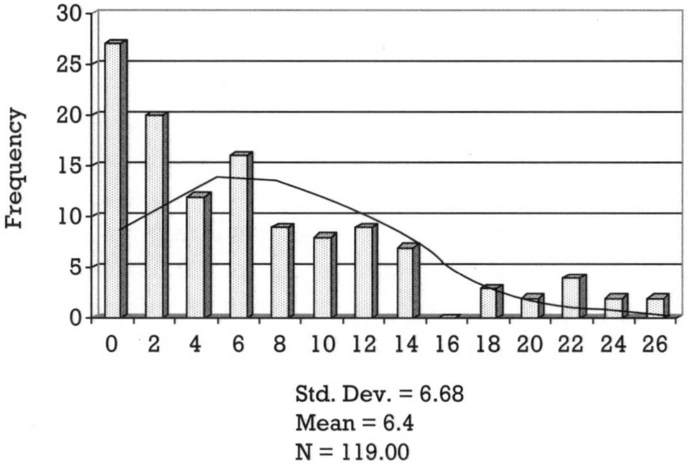

Table 2.7: Percentage of Adult, Youth and Control Groups Who Scored Above and Below the Threshold of Five on the GHQ

Group	% Below Threshold	% Above Threshold	Total
Adult Minority	55.3%	44.7%	47
Youth Minority	54.2%	45.8%	72
White Comparison	59.3%	40.7%	27

When the minority sample is further broken down into its constituent sub-groups, it can be seen that the Mixed Race and Oriental sub-groups have the best mental health levels, with only 30.4 per cent and 38.6 per cent respectively scoring above the threshold. However, the Asian and Black sub-groups have much higher incidences of "cases" with 58.7 per cent and 53.3 per cent presenting scores above the threshold established. This information is presented in full in Table 2.8 below.

Table 2.8: Percentage of Sub-groups Score Above and Below the Threshold of Five Applied to GHQ Scores

Group	% Below Threshold	% Above Threshold	Total
Black	46.7%	53.3%	30
South Asian	41.3%	58.7%	46
Oriental	61.4%	38.6%	21
Mixed Race	69.6%	30.4%	23

Statistical tests were performed on the overall GHQ scores and the subscale scores. This analysis showed no significant differences between the groups, except on the anxiety subscale. The Asian sub-group was found to have a significantly higher anxiety scale score than the Mixed Race sub-group ($p \leq 0.05$). The adult and youth groups were also compared but no significant differences were found.

Interaction between the Experience of Racism and Mental Health

An examination of the overall experience of racism and the GHQ scores revealed a direct correlation between the amount of racism experienced by the minority individual and their overall GHQ score. That is, generally speaking, the more racism a person had experienced, the higher their GHQ score (psychological distress). A correlation was highly significant ($r (119) = 0.42, p < 0.01$).

The correlations of the Checklist overall and subscale scores and the GHQ overall and subscale scores are presented in Table 2.9. All but one of the scale and subscale scores were shown to correlate. This demonstrates that there is a highly significant relationship between the experience of racism and general psychological distress. It would also indicate that the type of racism experienced is not particularly significant; rather it is the experience of racist events in general which correlated with psychological ill health.

Table 2.9: Correlation Matrix Detailing Pearson's r Correlation Coefficient between Checklist Overall and Subscale Scores and GHQ Overall and Subscale Scores

Checklist Scores	Somatic Subscale	Anxiety Subscale	Dysfunction Subscale	Depression Subscale	GHQ Score
Emotional	0.36 (119) p < 0.01	0.32 (119) p < 0.01	0.23 (119) p < 0.02	0.25 (119) p < 0.01	0.32 (119) p < 0.01
Criminal	0.32 (119) p < 0.01	0.25 (119) p < 0.01	0.20 (119) p < 0.03	0.25 (119) p < 0.01	0.29 (119) p < 0.01
Adult Discrimination	0.31 (47) p < 0.03	0.25 (47) p < 0.09	0.28 (47) p < 0.06	0.32 (47) p < 0.03	0.36 (47) p < 0.02
Youth Discrimination	0.25 (71) p < 0.04	0.17 (71) ns	0.30 (71) p < 0.01	0.24 (71) p < 0.05	0.25 (71) p < 0.03
Overall Checklist	0.42 (119) p < 0.01	0.34 (119) p < 0.01	0.36 (119) p < 0.01	0.35 (119) p < 0.01	0.41 (119) p < 0.01

Relationship between Item Checklist Scores and GHQ Scores

T-tests were performed to examine the differences in GHQ scores between those who experienced different types of racial abuse and those who did not. The mean GHQ scores of those who had experienced the various forms of racial abuse were consistently higher (except in the case of those who had experienced racist phone calls or mail) than those who had not experienced abuse. T-tests revealed that the differences in the means were significant for those who had experienced racist jokes or snide remarks, those who had felt avoided and those who had felt snubbed, as well as people who had experienced threats of violence or physical attacks than for the respondents who had not experienced these forms of racism. That is, in all of the above cases, people who had experienced the various forms of racism were (according to their GHQ scores) experiencing a great deal more psychological distress than those who had not. These results can be seen in Table 2.10.

Table 2.10: Mean GHQ Scores of Minority Group Members Who Had, and Had Not, Experienced Various Forms of Racial Abuse and Results of t-Tests Comparing These Means

Type of Abuse	Mean GHQ Score Group — Yes	Mean GHQ Score Group — No	t	df	p
Outright Racist Insults	6.90	5.31	1.29	92.3	ns
Jokes/Snide Remarks	7.83	5.09	2.27	117.0	$p < 0.03$
Racist Calls or Mail	5.33	6.42	0.43	6.82	ns
Damage to Property	8.09	6.14	–0.81	13.8	ns
Felt Avoided	8.69	4.93	3.08	117.0	$p < 0.01$
Felt Snubbed	10.08	5.36	–3.11	35.5	$p < 0.01$
Verbal Harassment	8.30	5.91	1.52	117.0	ns
Threats of Violence	11.13	5.56	3.32	117.0	$p < 0.01$
Physical Attacks	11.23	5.31	3.90	117.0	$p < 0.01$

DISCUSSION

The GHQ results revealed that a large proportion (47.6 per cent) of the minority group sample scored above the threshold of five that would therefore put them in the category of "cases", that is, in need of further psychological assessment. This result is a matter of concern, in terms of the levels of psychological distress which seem to be affecting the sample.

O'Regan (1998), who studied Bosnian and Vietnamese programme refugees in Ireland, found that 48.6 per cent of his Bosnian sample and 12 per cent of his Vietnamese sample scored above the threshold. This he compared with the Irish population; Whelan, Hannan and Creighton (1991) found that 17.2 per cent of their Irish sample (n = 6,095) scored above the threshold of 2/3 on the GHQ-12 (which is comparable to that adopted by O'Regan as well as by the current researchers).

All of the sub-groups in the current sample manifested a level above the threshold that was significantly higher than that of the Irish population. A high level of caseness was revealed in every sub-group; the Asian group had the largest proportion (58.7 per cent) above the threshold with the Mixed Race group having the lowest (30.4 per cent). It is obvious that these levels compare very unfavourably with the Irish population and indicate a far greater prevalence of psychological distress among minority groups here than among the host population.

The checklist results reveal the prevalence of racism in Ireland today. The unreconstructed viciousness which minority group members have been subjected to is quite alarming, as is the unprovoked aggression of some of the attacks. The Swann Report in the UK (1985) noted that "the essential difference between racist name-calling and other forms of name-calling is that whereas the latter may be related only to the individual characteristics of the child, the former is a reference not only to the child but also by extension to their family and indeed more broadly their ethnic community as a whole" (p. 35). Kelly and Cohn (1988) also suggest that ethnic labels are "labels of primary potency" and prevent alternative or cross-classification. They were also the ones rated most hurtful by school pupils. On a more positive note, the majority of the abuse encountered by minority group members has been from strangers, although this is not the case with respect to feelings of avoidance and being snubbed.

The results indicate that racial categorisation is highly salient among the Irish. Ethnic minority individuals in Ireland are discriminated against in personal and institutional settings and are sometimes even subjected to physical abuse. The results indicate that the Black group were the most frequent victims of racial abuse and discrimination. It seems that, in the Irish context, the darker one's skin, the more abuse one receives.

Another interesting aspect of the results is the lack of differentiation among the different subscales of the Checklist score. Every subscale of the Checklist correlated highly with the GHQ scores — this suggests that the type of racism experienced was not particularly significant. Rather, it seems to be the experience of racist events in general which correlates with psychological stress. Further analysis of the specific racist abuse items in the Checklist revealed that those who experienced threats of violence and actual physical attacks were scoring a great deal higher on the GHQ than those who had not. Instinctively, this would seem to be true. It makes a great deal of intuitive sense that those who had been attacked, threatened or abused due to their appearance would experience much higher stress levels and psychological problems than those who had not had such a potentially traumatic experience. Higher GHQ scores were also presented by those who had felt avoided and those who had felt snubbed in comparison to those who had not been subjected to this type of discrimination. The people who reported feelings of being avoided and snubbed presented much lower levels of psychological well-being than those who had not. This indicates that what might be perceived as the less damaging and traumatic experience can still generate a great deal more psychological stress than might commonly be expected. That is, social isolation and feelings of rejection can be just as psychologically damaging as aggressive and criminal forms of racism.

References

European Parliament Committee of Inquiry on Racism and Xenophobia (1991), *Report on the Findings of the Inquiry*, Luxembourg: Office for Official Publications of the European Communities.

Goldberg, D. and V.F. Hillier (1979), "A Scaled Version of the General Health Questionnaire", *Psychological Medicine*, No. 9, pp. 139–145.

Goldberg, D. and P. Williams (1991), *A User's Guide to the General Health Questionnaire*, Berkshire: NFER-Nelson Publishing Company Ltd.

Great Britain, Parliament, House of Commons (1985), *Education for All: The Report of the Committee of Inquiry into the Education of Children from Ethnic Minority Groups* (Swann Report), cmnd 9453, London: HMSO.

Harrison, G., D. Owens, A. Holton, D. Neilson and D. Boot (1988), "A Prospective Study of Severe Mental Disorder in Afro-Caribbean Patients", *Psychological Medicine*, No. 18, pp. 643–657.

Kelly, E. and T. Cohn (1988), *Racism in Schools: New Research Evidence*, Stoke-on-Trent: Trentham Books.

Landrine, H. and E.A. Klonoff (1996), "The Schedule of Racist Events: A Measure of Racial Discrimination and a Study of its Negative Physical and Mental Health Consequences", *Journal of Black Psychology*, No. 22, pp. 144–168.

Marriott, S. (1998), "Learning the Hard Way", *The Big Issues*, No. 100, pp. 22–23.

McVeigh, R. (1996), *The Racialization of Irishness: Racism and Antiracism in Ireland*, Belfast: Centre for Research and Development.

McVeigh, R. and A. Binchy (1998), *Travellers, Refugees and Racism in Tallaght*, Dublin: West Tallaght Resource Centre.

O'Regan, C. (1998), Report of a Survey of the Vietnamese and Bosnian Refugee Communities in Ireland, Dublin: Refugee Resettlement Research Project.

Whelan, C.T., D.S. Hannan and S. Creighton (1991), *Unemployment, Poverty and Psychological Distress*, Economic and Social Research Institute General Research Paper No. 150, Dublin: ESRI.

Appendix 1: GHQ-28

Please read this carefully:

We should like to know if you have had any medical complaints, and how your health has been in general, over the past few weeks. Please answer ALL the questions on the following pages simply by underlining the answer which you think most nearly applies to you. Remember that we want to know about present and recent complaints, not those you had in the past.

It is important that you try to answer ALL the questions.

Thank you very much for your co-operation.

1. Been feeling perfectly well and in good health?	Better than usual	Same as usual	Worse than usual	Much worse than usual
2. Been feeling in need of a good tonic?	Not at all	No more than usual	Rather more than usual	Much more than usual
3. Been feeling run down and out of sorts?	Not at all	No more than usual	Rather more than usual	Much more than usual
4. Felt that you were ill?	Not at all	No more than usual	Rather more than usual	Much more than usual
5. Been getting pains in your head?	Not at all	No more than usual	Rather more than usual	Much more than usual
6. Been getting a feeling of tightness or pressure in your head?	Not at all	No more than usual	Rather more than usual	Much more than usual
7. Been having hot or cold spells?	Not at all	No more than usual	Rather more than usual	Much more than usual
8. Lost much sleep over worry?	Not at all	No more than usual	Rather more than usual	Much more than usual
9. Had difficulty in staying asleep once you were off?	Not at all	No more than usual	Rather more than usual	Much more than usual
10. Been managing to keep yourself busy and occupied?	More so than usual	No more than usual	Rather more than usual	Much more than usual
11. Been taking longer over the things you do?	Quicker than usual	Same as usual	Longer than usual	Much longer than usual

12. Felt on the whole you were doing things well?	Better than usual	About the same	Less well than usual	Much less well
13. Been satisfied with the way you've carried out your task?	More satisfied	About same as usual	Less satisfied than usual	Much less satisfied
14. Felt you are playing a useful part in things?	More so than usual	Same as usual	Less useful than usual	Much less useful
15. Felt capable about making decisions?	More so than usual	Same as usual	Rather more than usual	Much less capable
16. Felt constantly under strain?	Not at all	No more than usual	Rather more than usual	Much more than usual
17. Been able to enjoy your normal day-to-day activities?	More so than usual	Same as usual	Rather less than usual	Much less than usual
18. Been getting edgy and bad-tempered?	Not at all	No more than usual	Rather more than usual	Much more than usual
19. Been getting scared or panicky for no good reason?	Not at all	No more than usual	Rather more than usual	Much more than usual
20. Found everything getting on top of you?	Not at all	No more than usual	Rather more than usual	Much more than usual
21. Been thinking of yourself as a worthless person?	Not at all	No more than usual	Rather more than usual	Much more than usual
22. Felt that life is entirely hopeless?	Not at all	No more than usual	Rather more than usual	Much more than usual
23. Been feeling nervous and strung-up all the time?	Not at all	No more than usual	Rather more than usual	Much more than usual
24. Felt that life isn't worth living?	Not at all	No more than usual	Rather more than usual	Much more than usual
25. Thought of the possibility that you might make away with yourself?	Definitely not	I don't think so	Has crossed my mind	Definitely have
26. Found at times that you couldn't do anything because your nerves were too bad?	Not at all	No more than usual	Rather more than usual	Much more than usual
27. Found yourself wishing you were dead and away from it all?	Not at all	No more than usual	Rather more than usual	Much more than usual
28. Found that the idea of taking your own life kept coming into your mind?	Definitely not	I don't think so	Has crossed my mind	Definitely have

Appendix 2: Checklist

1. Have you ever felt that you were the subject of jokes or snide remarks due to your colour or race?

YES ☐ *NO* ☐ *Go to Q.2.*

If YES:

(a) Does this occur:	*Rarely*	☐
	Sometimes	☐
	Often	☐
	All the time?	☐
(b) Who makes these jokes?	*Strangers*	☐
(Tick all that apply)	*Class/Work Mates*	☐
	Friends	☐
	Others (write in)	☐

....

(c) What is commonly said?

....

....

(d) Has this occurred in the last six months?

YES ☐ *NO* ☐ *Go to Q.2.*

If YES:

(e) What was said?

....

....

(f) By whom?

....

....

2. Have you ever experienced racist taunts or insults?

YES ☐ *NO* ☐ *Go to Q.3.*

If YES:

(a) Does this occur:	*Rarely*	☐
	Sometimes	☐
	Often	☐
	All the time?	☐
(b) Who insults you?	*Strangers*	☐
(Tick all that apply)	*Class/Work Mates*	☐
	Friends	☐
	Others (write in)	☐

....

(c) What is commonly said?

....

....

(d) Has this occurred in the last six months?

YES ☐ *NO* ☐ *Go to Q.3.*

If YES:

(e) What was said?

....

....

(f) By whom?

....

....

3. Have you or your household ever received racist phone calls or mail?

YES ☐ *NO* ☐ *Go to Q.4.*

If YES:

(a) What happened?

....

....

(b) When?

....

....

4. Has anyone ever deliberately damaged/vandalised any property belonging to you which you believe was due to your race or colour?

YES ☐ *NO* ☐ *Go to Q.5.*

If YES:

(a) Does this occur:	*Rarely*	☐
	Sometimes	☐
	Often	☐
	All the time?	☐
(b) Who was responsible?	*Strangers*	☐
(Tick all that apply)	*Class/Work Mates*	☐
	Friends	☐
	Others (write in)	☐

....

Thinking back to the most recent occasion this happened:

(c) What happened?

....

....

(d) When?

....

....

(e) Where?

....

....

(f) How did the situation end?

....

....

5. Have you ever felt that you were being avoided due to your colour or race?

YES ☐ *NO* ☐ *Go to Q.6.*

If YES: By whom?	*Strangers*	☐
(Tick all that apply)	*Class/Work Mates*	☐
	Friends	☐
	Others (write in)	☐

....

If you would like to tell us what happened, please do so here

....

....

6. Have you ever felt that you were socially isolated due to your colour or race?

YES ☐ *NO* ☐ *Go to Q.7.*

If YES: By whom?	*Strangers*	☐
(Tick all that apply)	*Class/Work Mates*	☐
	Friends	☐
	Others (write in)	☐

....

If you would like to tell us what happened, please do so here

....

....

7. Have you ever been persistently verbally harassed by a particular person/group of people due to your colour or race?

YES ☐ *NO* ☐ *Go to Q.8.*

If YES:

(a) Does this occur:	*Rarely*	☐
	Sometimes	☐
	Often	☐
	All the time?	☐

(b) Who was responsible?	*Strangers*	☐
(Tick all that apply)	*Class/Work Mates*	☐
	Friends	☐
	Others (write in)	☐

....

Thinking back to the most recent occasion this happened:

(c) What happened?

....

....

(d) When?

....

....

(e) Where?

....

....

(f) How did the situation end?

....

....

8. Has anyone ever threatened you with physical violence due to your race or the colour of your skin?

YES ☐ *NO* ☐ *Go to Q.9.*

If YES:

(a) Does this occur:	*Rarely*	☐
	Sometimes	☐
	Often	☐
	All the time?	☐
(b) Who was responsible?	*Strangers*	☐
(Tick all that apply)	*Class/Work Mates*	☐
	Friends	☐
	Others (write in)	☐

....

Thinking back to the most recent occasion this happened:

(c) What happened?

....

....

(d) When?

....

....

(e) Where?

....

....

(f) How did the situation end?

....

....

9. Have you experienced any physical attacks which you believe were racially motivated?

YES ☐ *NO* ☐ *Go to Q.10.*

If YES:

(a) Does this occur:	*Rarely*	☐
	Sometimes	☐
	Often	☐
	All the time?	☐
(b) Who was responsible?	*Strangers*	☐
(Tick all that apply)	*Class/Work Mates*	☐
	Friends	☐
	Others (write in)	☐

....

Thinking back to the most recent occasion this happened:

(c) What happened?

....

....

(d) When?

....

....

(e) Where?

....

....

(f) How did the situation end?

....

....

10. Do you believe that you have been discriminated against in any of the following areas due to your colour or race? (Tick all that apply)

(a) Gaining entry to pubs/clubs/restaurants ☐

(b) Shopping ☐

(c) Using public transport ☐

(d) Finding accommodation/dealing with landlords ☐

(e) Dealing with the Social Welfare, e.g. dole office/ rent allowance ☐

(f) Dealing with doctors ☐

(g) Dealing with schools/colleges ☐

(h) Dealing with banks ☐

(i) Dealing with the police ☐

(j) Finding a job ☐

CHAPTER THREE

SEEKING REFUGE IN IRELAND: ACCULTURATION STRESS AND PERCEIVED DISCRIMINATION

Olga Horgan

In recent years, Ireland has experienced dramatic increases in its number of resident refugees, asylum-seekers and international students. For example, the country's refugee population increased significantly with the government's admittance of up to 964 Bosnian "Programme Refugees" to the country between 1992 and 1997 (Irish Refugee Agency, 1998). In addition, recent figures indicate that, in 1999 alone, 7,724 individuals were seeking asylum in Ireland — an increase of over 3,000 individuals over the previous year's figures (Department of Justice, Equality and Law Reform Information Office, 2000). Moreover, one analysis of the Irish third-level student population reveals that the proportion of international students in Ireland has risen from the late 1980s figure of three to four per cent of all students to almost ten per cent of the total student body (Cox, 1997).

This growth in the number of refugees, asylum-seekers and international students in Ireland has been accompanied by increasing incidences of racial discrimination directed by Irish people against members of these groups (Gray et al., 1999; McVeigh and Binchy, 1998; Collins, 1995; Boucher, 1998). One recent study (Gray et al., 1999) of 157 asylum-seekers in Dublin found that 78 per cent had personally experienced racially motivated verbal or physical attacks. This study also reported that 20 per cent of the

African asylum-seekers, one quarter (or 25 per cent of the 20 per cent) of whom were women, had been physically attacked. Another study (Boucher, 1998) found that of 48 international students interviewed, 32 had reported experiencing a total of 82 incidences of everyday discrimination, 23 instances of university discrimination, and 23 instances of institutional racism since coming to stay in Ireland.

Although most studies on prejudice have focused on the prejudiced individual, rather than on the person targeted by the prejudice (Swim, 1998), several population studies have found positive associations between perceived discrimination and anxiety (Dion and Earn, 1975), lower levels of life satisfaction (Broman, 1997), high blood pressure (Krieger, 1990; Krieger and Sidney, 1996), lower levels of self-esteem (Pak, Dion, and Dion, 1991; Gil and Vega, 1996), and higher levels of psychological symptoms (Furnham and Shiekh, 1993). Studies particularly focusing on refugee and asylum-seeker populations have found similar negative effects of discrimination on psychological well-being (Sundquist and Johnson, 1996; Liebkind, 1996b; Gorst-Unworth and Goldenberg, 1998; Pernice and Brook, 1996b). One explanation of this observed relationship between perceived discrimination and poor psychological health is the sense of loss and helplessness that discrimination incurs in victims of racial discrimination (Fernando, 1984).

However, determining the effect of prejudice on the psychological well-being of refugees, asylum-seekers and international students in Ireland is confounded by the observation that members of these groups are significantly at-risk for developing psychological difficulties, regardless of perceived discrimination experiences. Studies examining the psychological well-being of international students have found that, regardless of nationality or host country, such individuals are prone to experiencing psychological difficulties (Furnham and Treize, 1983; Oei and Notowidjojo, 1990; Tanaka et al., 1994; Ying and Liese, 1991; Heiner et al., 1997). In addition, clinical and population studies with refugees and asylum-seekers have demonstrated a relationship between refugee and/or asylum-seeker status and depression (Bauer and Priebe, 1994; Kinzie et al., 1980; Beiser et al., 1989; Felsman et al., 1990; Hauff and Vaglum, 1995), post-traumatic stress disorder (Gorst-Unworth and Goldenberg, 1998; Lavik et al., 1996; Weine et al., 1999; Cheung, 1994; Silove et al., 1997), and anxiety disorders (Lavik et al., 1996; Pernice and Brook, 1996a, 1994).

Due to the reported high incidence of psychological difficulties among these groups, therefore, it is more appropriate to examine the relationship between perceived discrimination and psychological well-being within a context that recognises the multiplicity of factors that can impact on the health of these individuals. Berry's (1997, 1998) acculturation framework, in which the poor psychological health arising from exposure to a new culture is termed *acculturative stress*, provides such a context. Acculturative stress is said to occur if an individual adjusting to life in a new country is faced with stressors arising from this adjustment that overwhelm his or her coping resources (Berry and Sam, 1996). Within the acculturation framework, the level of acculturative stress experienced by any one person or group of persons can be affected by such factors as acculturation attitudes, migrant status, social support, employment status, age, gender and prior exposure to trauma (Ward, 1996; Berry, 1997, 1998).

In terms of factors relating to the acculturating individual, much research has focused on the relationship between the person's level of acculturation stress and acculturation attitude/behaviour, i.e. his or her manner of relating to and interacting with the new culture (Berry et al., 1986). There are four acculturation attitudes/behaviours: *Integrated*, *Assimilated*, *Separated* and *Marginalised* (Berry, 1997, 1998; see also the glossary in this volume). Each can be determined by the level at which the individual considers it to be of value to (a) maintain his/her own cultural identity and (b) maintain relationships with members of the new, dominant culture. For example, the *Integration* attitude/ behaviour occurs when the individual considers it to be of value to maintain his/her own cultural identity and relationships with members of the new culture. On the other hand, the *Marginalisation* attitude/behaviour occurs when an individual considers neither the maintenance of his/her own cultural identity nor the maintenance of relationships with members of the new culture to be of value (Berry et al., 1986; Berry, 1997, 1998).

In the research literature, an individual's level of acculturation stress is associated with each of these acculturation attitudes and their associated acculturation behaviours. According to Berry

(1997, 1998), the Integration and Marginalisation modes of acculturation are associated with the lowest and highest levels of acculturation stress, respectively, and the outcomes related to the Assimilation and Separation modes fall in between these two levels. Such relationships have been found among student populations (Ward and Kennedy, 1993; Zheng and Berry, 1991), immigrant populations (Rivera-Sinclair, 1997; Krishnan and Berry, 1992; Allen et al., 1996; Schwarzer et al., 1985; Gil and Vega, 1996; Scapocznik, Kurtines, and Fernandez, 1980) and refugee populations (Liebkind, 1996a, 1996b; Donà and Berry, 1994; Cheung, 1995; Berry et al., 1987).

The amount of social support that a person has in the new culture can also affect his or her level of acculturation stress. Among refugees and asylum-seekers, for example, social support has been found to be directly related to depressive symptoms (Gorst-Unworth and Goldenberg, 1998), anxiety symptoms (Silove et al., 1997) and other psychiatric symptoms (Hauff and Vaglum, 1995). In addition, social support has been found to moderate the risk of developing depressive symptoms (Beiser et al., 1989) and to buffer the effect of long-term unemployment on ill-health (Schwarzer et al., 1994). Similarly, among international students, increased social support has been associated with lower depressive symptoms (Ying and Liese, 1991), a reduction in depressive symptoms over a six-month period (Heiner et al., 1997), general adjustment in the new culture (Tanaka et al., 1994), and decreased mood disturbance (Ward and Searle, 1991). It has been suggested that social support, in this context, helps to alleviate acculturation stress by helping individuals to cope with the uncertainty of being in a strange culture and to achieve a sense of mastery and control over their lives (Adelman, 1988).

Unemployment has also been linked to acculturation stress in refugees and asylum-seekers (Schwarzer et al., 1994; Lavik et al., 1996; Young and Evans, 1997). For example, a survey of Vietnamese and Bosnian refugees in Ireland revealed that 27.6 per cent and 24.3 per cent, respectively, were unemployed and that these individuals were significantly more likely to score above the threshold for caseness on the General Health Questionnaire-28 (O'Regan, 1998). Since July 1999, asylum-seekers whose applications are more than one year old are permitted to seek paid employment in Ireland (Department of Justice, Equality and Law Reform, 2000). However, at the time the data were collected in the current study, no asylum-seekers were permitted to seek paid employment in Ireland. This ban has contributed, in part, to asylum-seekers' psychological deterioration (Irish Refugee Council, 1997) and marginalisation within the country (Nozinic, 1997). Indeed, it has been suggested that unemployment for refugees and asylum-seekers can mean a loss of the social status that was maintained in the home country (Hauff and Vaglum, 1993; Young and Evans, 1997) or to feelings of frustration (Fernando, 1984).

Finally, individual characteristics such as status as a forced or voluntary migrant (Berry et al., 1987; Sundquist, 1995), length of time in the host country (Church, 1982), age (Sundquist and Johnson, 1996; Weine et al., 1999), gender (Krishnan and Berry, 1992; Rohrlich and Martin, 1991; Hauff and Vaglum, 1995), and prior experiences of trauma (Sundquist and Johnson, 1996; Liebkind, 1996b; Cheung, 1994; Somasundaram, 1996) have each been found to affect an acculturating individual's level of acculturation stress.

In the light of all these factors that can impact on the mental health of refugees, asylum-seekers and international students, this study aims to examine the effect that prejudice has on members of these groups living in Ireland within the acculturation framework (Berry, 1997, 1998). In this respect, it will examine the effect of perceived discrimination on acculturation levels and the effect of both perceived discrimination and acculturation level on psychological well-being. In addition, it will examine whether such individual factors as employment, level of trauma experienced prior to arriving in Ireland, satisfaction with social support in Ireland, length of time in Ireland, age and gender also play a role in the occurrence of acculturation stress.

METHOD

Participants

Refugees and Asylum-seekers (Forced Migrants)

The forced migrant sample included 18 refugees and 15 asylum-seekers living in Ireland. Of these, 20 were male and 13 were female. The 18 refugees came from Bosnia (n = 11), Yugoslavia (n = 2), Nigeria (n = 3), Somalia (n = 1) and Zaire/Congo (n = 1). The 15 asylum-seekers came from the African countries of Nigeria (n = 5), Somalia (n = 2), Zaire/Congo (n = 2), Burundi (n = 2), Angola (n = 1) and Cameroon (n = 1). Two asylum-seekers reported only that they came from Africa and West Africa, respectively. Respondents ranged in age from 16 to 42 years (M = 30.27; SD = 6.81); length of residence in Ireland ranged from two months to 78 months (M = 24.51; SD = 16.10). Nine respondents were in full-time employment (all refugees), and 24 were unemployed. None spoke English as a first language.

Voluntary Migrants (International Students)

The voluntary migrant sample included 29 female and 10 male international students, all of whom were attending a full-time, third-level university course. These respondents came from Japan (n = 8), Spain (n = 7), Italy (n = 6), France (n = 2), Germany (n = 2), Switzerland (n = 2), Slovakia (n = 2), Mexico (n = 2), Somalia (n = 2), Austria (n = 1), Belgium (n = 1), Norway (n = 1), Sweden (n = 1), Argentina (n = 1), and Russia (n = 1). Respondents ranged in age from 18 to 41 years (M = 23.64; SD = 5.18); length of residence in Ireland ranged from one month to 40 months (M = 5.89; SD = 7.53). None spoke English as a first language.

Measures

Demographic Questionnaire

Respondents' gender, age, country of origin, nationality, length of time in Ireland, status as a forced migrant or voluntary migrant and employment status were assessed using a 7-item demographic questionnaire.

Perceived Discrimination

Perceived discrimination was measured using a modified version of the Recent Events Subscale (RES) of Landrine and Klonoff's (1996) Schedule of Racist Events. The RES is one of three subscales of the Schedule of Racist Events, and its internal consistency was found to be extremely high at .95 (Landrine and Klonoff, 1996). Modifications of this subscale included changing the wording of individual items to make them more appropriate for both black and white respondents in an Irish context. For example, the phrase "*. . . because you are black*" included in several of the questions was replaced by the phrase "*. . . because you are not Irish*". Individual items of the RES were answered by circling a number on a scale ranging from 1 to 6, with a score of 1 indicating that the event never happened and a score of 6 indicating that the event happens almost all of the time.

Acculturation Level

Acculturation Level (AL) was assessed using two self-report, bi-dimensional, 9-item subscales that were specifically designed for this study.

The Acculturation in Ireland Subscale (AIS) was designed to measure the extent to which respondents had acculturated to various aspects of Irish culture. Items on this scale assessed the level at which English was spoken in different situations; the level at which the Irish media was availed of; attitudes towards socialising with Irish people; and the extent to which it would be desirable to raise children in keeping with Irish culture and traditions.

The Home Country Subscale (HCS) was designed to measure the extent to which respondents maintained corresponding aspects of their own culture. Items on this scale consisted of questions equivalent to those of the AIS, but referring to the home country only. Responses to each question were scored on a Likert-style measurement ranging from *almost never*, *sometimes*, *often*, and *almost always*, with endorsement of the former resulting in a score of 1 and endorsement of the latter yielding a score of 4. The respondents' mean scores on each subscale were calculated to yield one score for each of the AIS and HCS subscales, and the median value of these scores were calculated. Individuals were then categorised as Integrated if their scores were above the median on both the AIS and HCS; Assimilated if their scores were above and below the median on the AIS and HCS, respectively; Separated if their scores were below and above the median on the AIS and HCS, respectively; and Marginalised if their scores were below the median on both subscales.

Acculturation Stress

Acculturation stress was assessed using Goldberg's (1992) General Health Questionnaire 12-Item (GHQ-12), which is designed to detect the possible presence of a clinical disorder. The GHQ-12 has been found to be reliable and valid in a variety of cross-cultural contexts (Pan and Goldberg, 1990; Mari and Williams, 1985). In addition, its psychometric properties compare well with those of its longer versions: its internal consistency, as assessed by Cronbach's alpha, has been found to range from 0.82 to 0.90 in a range of studies, and its validity (evaluated by determining its sensitivity in detecting cases of psychiatric disorder) was found to be 93.5 per cent (Goldberg and Williams, 1988). In the current study, responses from left to right of the scale were scored as 0, 0, 1 ,1, yielding scores that ranged from 0 to 12. A cut-off point of 3 was chosen to indicate "caseness", or the probability of a clinical disorder (Goldberg and Williams, 1988).

Social Support

Satisfaction with social support was measured using the Satisfaction with Social Support (SSQ6-S) subscale of Sarason et al.'s (1987a) self-report, 6-item Short form Social Support Questionnaire. The SSQ6-S has a high internal consistency of 0.93 (Sarason et al., 1987b). In this measure, respondents rate, on a 6-point scale, how satisfied they are with six types of social support.

Trauma Experience

The amount of trauma experienced by respondents was assessed using the following question: "In your home country, did you experience any traumatic incidents (for example, see someone being killed or injured, receive any injuries due to war, experience attacks of war)?". If respondents answered "Yes" to this question, they were then asked to rate on a five-point scale ranging from no effect to a very large effect, the effect that they perceived this trauma to have had on their lives. This method of assessing trauma experiences, which has been used in previous studies (e.g. Liebkind, 1996b), was preferred over the use of standard trauma questionnaires because, for the purposes of this study, brevity of information was considered to more important than were precise trauma details.

Procedure

Questionnaires were administered to international student members of the International Students' Society in Trinity College and international students learning English in three English-language schools in Dublin city centre. Before filling in questionnaires, all students were addressed by the researcher and asked to respond only if (a) English was not their first language and (b) they were attending a third-level university course. Questionnaires were administered to refugees and asylum-seekers by representatives of the African Refugee Network, the Bosnian Community Development Project, Interact Ireland, Access Ireland and the African Cultural Project. In addition, ten individuals were approached on O'Connell Street, Dublin 1 (in a manner similar to Gray et al.'s (1999) study) and asked if they were refugees, asylum-seekers, or international students. Nine individuals responded in the affirmative to one of the first two categories and six completed questionnaires.

Results

GHQ-12 Responses

The mean GHQ-12 scores for forced migrants and voluntary migrants were 3.27 (*SD* = 2.85) and 2.59 (*SD* = 2.77), respectively. The difference between these two groups was not significant (t = 1.03, df = 70, p = NS). Using a cut-off threshold of 3 and above to indicate "caseness" on the GHQ-12, 16 of the forced migrants (48.48 per cent) and 16 of the voluntary migrants (41 per cent) showed a possible clinical disorder.

RES Responses

The mean RES scores for forced migrants and voluntary migrants were 36.93 (*SD* = 16.78) and 21.35 (*SD* = 6.59), respectively. The difference between these two groups was significant (t = 5.02, df = 40.32, $p < .0001$). Africans had the highest mean RES of 37.72, and a one-way ANOVA indicated that these scores were significantly higher than were those of East Europeans (*M* = 30.31), Asians (*M* = 26.62), West Europeans (*M* = 20.30), and Middle/South Americans (*M* = 19.00) ($F = 5.62$, $df = 4$, $p < .001$). However, a 5 × 2 ANOVA with RES scores as the dependent variable and migrant status and country category as the independent variables revealed a main effect for migrant status ($F = 7.63$, $df = 1$, $p < .01$), and not for country category ($F = .52$, $df = 4$, *p* = NS). Respondents were subsequently classified into groups of high and low RES scores on the basis of whether they fell above or below the median RES score. As there was a significant difference between forced migrants' and voluntary migrants' RES scores, and a relatively large standard error of difference in RES means (3.10), each group's median score was calculated separately to avoid placing most of the voluntary migrants into a low RES category and most of the forced migrants into a high RES category (Runyon and Haber, 1991).

Acculturation Level

The mean AIS scores for forced migrants and voluntary migrants were 2.82 (*SD* = .539) and 2.76 (*SD* = .445), respectively. This difference was not significant ($t = .51$, $df = 70$, *p* = NS), and the median score of the total group (2.80) was used as a cut-off point for high and low AIS scores. The mean HCS scores for forced migrants and voluntary migrants were 2.65 (*SD* = .608) and 2.20 (*SD* = .566), respectively. This difference between the groups was significant ($t = 3.27$, $df = 70$, $p < .01$), such that voluntary migrants had a significantly lower maintenance of their home culture than did forced migrants. However, the median score of the total group (2.55) was used as a cut-off point for high and low HCS scores because the relatively small standard error of difference in HCS means (.139) meant that this would not bias the results by placing the majority of forced and voluntary migrants into high and low HCS categories, respectively (Runyon and Haber, 1991).

Table 3.1 shows the percentage and number of forced migrants and voluntary migrants who were placed, based on their AIS and HCS scores, within one of the four acculturation levels. A chi-square (χ^2) test of the relationship between migrant status and acculturation level almost reached significance ($\chi^2 = 7.44$, $df = 3$, $p =$

0.59), thus suggesting that forced migrants were more likely to have an integrated acculturation level and that voluntary migrants were more likely to have an assimilated acculturation level.

Table 3.1: Percentage and number of forced and voluntary migrants categorised, based on their AIS and HCS scores, as having an Integrated, Assimilated, Separated or Marginalised acculturation level

Acculturation Level Migrants (n = 39)	**Forced Migrants (n = 33)**	**Voluntary**
Integrated	12 (36.4%)	7 (17.9%)
Assimilated	7 (21.2%)	14 (35.9%)
Separated	11 (33.3%)	8 (20.5%)
Marginalised	3 (9.0%)	10 (25.6%)

Note: $\chi^2 = 7.44$, $df = 3$, $p = 0.59$.

Acculturation Level and Acculturation Stress

A 4 × 2 analysis of variance (ANOVA) with GHQ-12 scores as the dependent variable and acculturation level and migrant status as the independent variables revealed that neither acculturation level (F = 2.00, df = 3, p = NS) nor migrant status (F = 1.28, df = 3, p = NS) had a main effect or an interactive effect (F = .34, df = 3, p = NS) on GHQ-12 scores.

Perceived Discrimination and Acculturation Level

An ANOVA found no significant difference between the mean RES scores of forced migrants (F = 1.54, df = 3, p = NS) in the four different acculturation levels. Similarly, a one-way ANOVA found no significant difference between the mean RES scores of voluntary migrants (F = 2.11, df = 3, p = NS) in the four different acculturation levels. However, because there appeared to be a non-significant tendency for RES scores to increase as voluntary migrants became integrated, assimilated, separated and marginalised, the relationship between perceived discrimination and their scores on the AIS and HCS subscales of the AL were further examined. Two t-tests revealed that there was no significant difference between the RES scores of individuals with high and low HCS scores (t = .53, df= 37,

p = NS). However, voluntary migrants with low AIS scores had significantly higher RES scores than did voluntary migrants with high AIS scores ($t = 2.22$, $df = 22.11$, $p < .05$), thus indicating that international students with higher levels of perceived discrimination had significantly lower levels of acculturation to Irish culture than did those with lower levels of perceived discrimination.

Perceived Discrimination and Acculturation Stress

An ANOVA conducted with GHQ-12 scores as the dependent variable and forced migrants' RES category (high/low) as the independent variable revealed that the RES category was not significantly related to GHQ-12 scores ($F = .02$, $df = 1$, p = NS). However, an ANOVA using voluntary migrants' RES category as the independent variable revealed that their GHQ-12 scores were significantly associated with RES category ($F = 5.64$, $df = 1$, $p < .05$), thus indicating that international students with high levels of perceived discrimination had significantly higher levels of acculturation stress than did those with low levels of perceived discrimination. As a subsequent *t*-test revealed that there was no significant difference in the SSQ6-S scores of voluntary migrants with high and low RES categories ($t = -.81$, $df = 37$, p = NS), this indicates that satisfaction with social support is not likely to account for these results with voluntary migrants.

Social Support and Acculturation Stress

Pearson's *r* correlations revealed that SSQ6-S scores were significantly correlated with GHQ-12 scores ($r = -.35$, $p < .001$) and RES scores ($r = -.34$, $p < .05$).

Employment and Acculturation Stress

A *t*-test revealed that unemployed ($n = 24$) forced migrants had significantly higher GHQ-12 scores than did employed ($n = 9$) forced migrants ($t = -2.78$, $df = 28.20$, $p < .01$). As employed forced migrants also had significantly higher SSQ6-S scores than did unemployed forced migrants ($t = 2.70$, $df = 24.35$, $p < .01$), the effect of employment on acculturation stress may be related to the effect of social support on acculturation stress.

Individual Characteristics and Acculturation Stress

A 2 × 2 ANOVA with GHQ-12 scores as the dependent variable and gender and migrant status as the independent variable revealed that neither gender (F = .002, df = 1, p = NS) nor migrant status (F = .311, df = 1, p = NS) had a main effect or an interactive effect (F = .239, df = 1, p = NS) on GHQ-12 scores.

A Pearson's correlation analysis revealed that respondents' age was not linearly related to GHQ-12 scores (r = –.0208, p = NS). To assess whether individuals in a particular age range were particularly likely to experience acculturation stress, respondents' ages were placed into one of three categories ranging from 16–25 years (n = 37), 26–35 years (n = 25), and 36–42 years (n = 10). A 2 × 2 ANOVA with GHQ-12 scores as the dependent variable and migrant status and age category as the independent variables showed neither a main effect for migrant status (F = 1.87, df = 1, p = NS) nor for age category (F = .55, df = 2, p = NS) on GHQ-12 scores.

Pearson's r revealed that length of time in Ireland was not significantly related to GHQ-12 scores (r = .02, p = NS). To determine whether there was a U-shaped relationship between length of time in Ireland and acculturation stress, a 5 × 2 ANOVA with GHQ-12 scores as the dependent variable and time in Ireland categories (0–6 months, n = 12; 7 months–1 year, n = 19; 1–2 years, n = 15; 2–4 years, n = 20; over 4 years, n = 6) was conducted. Results revealed that neither migrant status (F = .77, df = 1, p = NS) nor time in Ireland category (F = 1.24, df = 4, p = NS) had a main effect or an interactive effect (F = .60, df = 4, p = NS) on GHQ-12 scores.

Pearson's r revealed that perceived effect of trauma experienced by respondents was not significantly correlated with GHQ-12 scores (r = .21, p = NS).

Discussion

The findings of this study revealed significant differences between forced migrants and voluntary migrants in terms of perceived discrimination experiences and acculturation level. The greater number of discriminatory attacks experienced by forced migrants may have been racially motivated. Supporting this view is Boucher's (1998) finding that, similar to the results of this study,

African respondents had significantly higher levels of perceived discrimination than did Western Europeans, Eastern Europeans, Asians, and Middle/South Americans. Further supporting this contention is that some African refugees have indicated that they are more likely than are Bosnians to be the targets of racial discrimination, as their colour makes them easier to identify (McVeigh and Binchy, 1998). However, the discriminatory attacks may be motivated more by migrant status and by individuals' false beliefs that refugees and asylum-seekers are taking advantage of the government social welfare system. In support of this view is the finding in this study that migrant status had a stronger relationship with perceived discrimination than did country category. In addition, Gray et al.'s (1999) telephone survey, which revealed that 71 per cent of Irish respondents believed that less than half of all asylum-seekers were genuine in seeking asylum, indicates that the discrimination may be based on attitudes towards all asylum-seekers and refugees, and not just those from African countries.

Status as a forced or voluntary migrant may explain why the forced migrants had higher levels of integration and lower levels of assimilation than did voluntary migrants. As forced migrants, refugees and asylum-seekers did not choose to come to Ireland and, therefore, they may have a continuing desire to maintain many aspects of their individual cultures. Support for this notion lies in the finding that the second highest acculturation mode within this group was the Separation mode. However, an awareness that they may have to remain in Ireland for an indefinite period of time may lead many refugees and asylum-seekers to the realisation that an Integrated mode of acculturation is one which affords the best social adjustment, a contention that is supported in the literature (Ward and Kennedy, 1994; Ward and Searle, 1991; Ward and Kennedy, 1993). On the other hand, international students may not feel a particularly strong desire to maintain aspects of their home culture because they are aware that their stay in Ireland is only temporary. Instead, they may wish to increase their experiences with and cultural awareness of Ireland by assimilating into its culture as much as possible.

Levels of acculturation stress in the sample were high, with 48 per cent of the forced migrants and 41 per cent of the voluntary migrants showing a possible clinical disorder. Although this level of "caseness" compares unfavourably with the 17.2 per cent level found among Irish adults (Whelan et al., 1991), these findings are consistent with the bulk of the literature that has found a relationship between psychological health and refugee, asylum-seeker and international student status (e.g. Lavik et al., 1996; Felsman et al., 1990; Furnham and Treize, 1983). In the current study, the observed relationship between RES scores and GHQ-12 scores suggests that voluntary migrants' acculturation stress may have been related to perceptions of discrimination in Ireland. In general, this finding is in line with previous research documenting a relationship between perceived discrimination and anxiety (Dion and Earn, 1975), low self-esteem (Pak et al., 1991) and psychological distress. On the other hand, the finding that RES scores were not related to the GHQ-12 scores of forced migrants may be due to more efficient coping resources that they had previously developed in response to previously experienced traumas. Indeed, studies that have found no relationship between experiences of trauma and psychological well-being (Gorst-Unworth and Goldenberg, 1998) or only a transient impact of pre-migration stresses on psychological well-being (Westermeyer et al., 1984; Beiser et al., 1989; Baker, 1992; McFarland, 1994) have attributed coping resources to these outcomes.

Perceived discrimination was also related to international students' level of acculturation to Ireland, as voluntary migrants with low AIS scores had significantly higher levels of perceived discrimination than did those with high AIS scores. This tendency to disengage from Irish culture with increasing levels of discrimination is in line with Berry's (1991) argument that prejudiced attitudes on the part of the host nation will result in the separation and marginalisation of ethnic minority groups in plural societies. Indeed, separation from the majority culture and disengagement from the minority culture are discrimination-avoidance strategies that have been discussed (Crocker et al., 1998) and demonstrated (Burke, 1984).

Satisfaction with social support was also related to forced and voluntary migrants' levels of acculturation stress and forced migrants' employment status. The observed relationship between social support and acculturation has been demonstrated previously in numerous studies involving both forced and voluntary migrants (Berry et al., 1987; Beiser et al., 1989; Tanaka et al., 1994; Heiner et al., 1997). One explanation for this relationship is that social support acts as a buffer against stressors in the environment (Cohen and Wills, 1985); another explanation is that perceived availability of social support helps the person to maintain a sense of control in the event that stressful situations occur in his or her environment (Schwarzer and Leppin, 1991). The most appropriate one in this context is Adelman's (1988) theory of social support and cross-cultural adjustment, which states that social support can prevent individuals from becoming overwhelmed by a strange environment, help them to understand the new culture, and subsequently enable them to feel a sense of mastery and control over their lives.

The negative relationship between social support and acculturation stress in the current study may also help to explain the finding that unemployment was positively related to acculturation stress among forced migrants. The finding that unemployment and GHQ-12 scores were related was not unexpected, as several studies had previously demonstrated similar relationships among immigrants, refugees and, indeed, Irish people (Lavik et al., 1996; Schwarzer et al., 1994; O'Regan, 1998; Whelan et al., 1991). However, as unemployed individuals in the current study had significantly lower levels of satisfaction with social support, it may be argued that social support may be the variable that mediates the relationship between employment and acculturation stress. In a previous study, social support has been found to buffer the effect of unemployment on ill health (Schwarzer et al., 1994). Moreover, lack of employment has been attributed to poor social support among female Indian immigrants in Britain (Furnham and Shiekh, 1993) and to social isolation from the wider community among Bosnian and Vietnamese refugees in Ireland (O'Regan, 1998). Therefore, the current finding that unemployment was positively associated with acculturation stress may be due to feelings of social isolation and poor social support.

One limitation of this study is the cultural heterogeneity of the respondents, which may explain the lack of relationships that were found between acculturation stress and acculturation level, gender, age, and length of time in Ireland. Indeed, studies that have found relationships between these variables and acculturation stress tend to be conducted on culturally homogeneous samples and have explained the development of psychological difficulties as the outcome of host culture and home culture conflicts. For example, the studies that have found a relationship between acculturation stress and gender have involved individuals from cultures in which the female role tends to be more traditional than that of the host culture, including Vietnamese (Hauff and Vaglum, 1995; Liebkind, 1996a, 1996b), Latin American (Sundquist and Johnson, 1996), Greek (Mavreas and Bebbington, 1990) and Indian (Furnham and Shiekh, 1993) cultures. In these cases, acculturation stress is argued to be a result of the stress women feel when their traditional lifestyle conflicts with that of their host culture. Similar conflict explanations have been invoked to explain the relationship between length of time in the host country and acculturation stress (Hauff and Vaglum, 1995; Kaplan and Marks, 1990) and between age and acculturation stress (Allen et al., 1996; Kaplan and Marks, 1990; Hauff and Vaglum, 1995).

Another limitation of the study is that the modest relationships among acculturation stress and perceived discrimination, unemployment and social support suggests that other unexamined factors may have played a role in the high GHQ-12 scores found among respondents. The lack of significant differences in GHQ-12 scores by country category suggests that, contrary to previous reports (Graham, 1983; Searle and Ward, 1990; Ward and Kennedy, 1993), perceived distance between the home culture and the host culture was not responsible for these high levels of acculturation stress. However, unexamined variables such as level of education (Krishnan and Berry, 1992; Cheung, 1995; Hauff and Vaglum, 1995) and individual personality factors (Ward and Searle, 1991; Ward and Kennedy, 1993) may have played a role in the development of acculturation stress.

Despite these limitations and the modest sample size, several implications arise from the findings of this study. The high levels of discrimination experienced by refugees, asylum-seekers and, to a lesser extent, international students in this study is consistent with previous research conducted in Ireland (Gray et al., 1999; McVeigh and Binchy, 1998; Collins, 1995; Boucher, 1998) and indicates that procedures are necessary to counteract this growing development in Irish society. At an institutional level, these could include the introduction of equal status and anti-discrimination legislation (McVeigh and Binchy, 1998). At a more local level, individuals with prejudicial attitudes towards refugees, asylum-seekers and international students could be made aware of the dangers of such prejudicial thinking through education and if possible, intergroup contact, which has been shown to reduce prejudicial thinking in some contexts (Pettigrew, 1997).

Many asylum-seekers in Ireland have reported the asylum-seeking process to be stressful (Collins, 1995; McVeigh and Binchy, 1998). The high levels of acculturation stress experienced by respondents in this study and its negative relationship with social support and unemployment are in keeping with these reports. Among recent asylum-seekers, these stressors are likely to persist, as they are still subject to the employment restrictions that no longer apply to those individuals who have been seeking asylum for more than one year. In this respect, emphasis could be placed on the development of awareness, among officials working in governmental and non-governmental support agencies, of the various stressors that could potentially lead to psychological difficulties for these individuals.

References

Adelman, M.B. (1988), "Cross-cultural Adjustment: A Theoretical Perspective on Social Support", *International Journal of Intercultural Relations*, Vol. 12, pp. 183–204.

Allen, L., J. Denner, Y. Hirokazu, E. Seidman and J.L. Aber (1996), "Acculturation and Depression among Latina Urban Girls", in B.J. Leadbeater and N. Way (eds.), *Urban Girls: Resisting Stereotypes, Creating Identities*, New York: New York University Press.

Baker, R. (1992), "Psychosocial Consequences for Tortured Refugees Seeking Asylum and Refugee Status in Europe", in M. Bašoglu (ed.), *Torture and its Consequences: Current Treatment Approaches*, Cambridge: Cambridge University Press.

Bauer, M. and S. Priebe (1994), "Psychopathology and Long-term Adjustment after Crises in Refugees from East Germany", *International Journal of Social Psychiatry*, Vol. 40, No. 3, pp. 165–176.

Beiser, M., R.J. Turner and S. Ganesan (1989), "Catastrophic Stress and Factors Affecting its Consequences among Southeast Asian Refugees", *Social Science and Medicine*, Vol. 28, No. 3, pp. 183–195.

Berry, J.W. (1998), "Acculturation and Health: Theory and Research", in S.S. Kazarian and D.R. Evans (eds.), *Cultural Clinical Psychology: Theory, Research and Practice*, Oxford: Oxford University Press.

Berry, J.W. (1997), "Immigration, Acculturation and Adaptation", *Applied Psychology: An International Review*, Vol. 46, No. 1, pp. 5–38.

Berry, J.W. (1991), "Understanding and Managing Multiculturalism", *Journal of Psychology and Developing Societies*, Vol. 3, pp. 17–49.

Berry, J.W. and D. Sam (1996), "Acculturation and Adaptation", in J.W. Berry, M.H. Segall and C. Kagitcibasi (eds.), *Handbook of Cross-cultural Psychology: Vol. 3, Social Behavior and Applications*, Boston: Allyn and Bacon.

Berry, J.W., J. Trimble and E. Olmeda (1986), "The Assessment of Acculturation", in W.J. Lonner and J.W. Berry (eds.), *Field Methods in Cross-cultural Research*, London: Sage Publications.

Berry, J.W., U. Kim, T. Minde and D. Mok (1987), "Comparative Studies of Acculturative Stress", *International Migration Review*, Vol. 21, pp. 491–511.

Boucher, G.W. (1998), *The Irish are Friendly, but . . . A Report on Racism and International Students in Ireland*, Dublin: Irish Council for International Students.

Broman, C. (1997), "Race-related Factors and Life Satisfaction among African Americans", *Journal of Black Psychology*, Vol. 23, pp. 36–49.

Burke, A.W. (1984), "Racism and Psychological Disturbance among West Indians in Britain", *International Journal of Social Psychiatry*, Vol. 30, No. 1–2, pp. 50–68.

Cheung, P. (1994), "Posttraumatic Stress Disorder among Cambodian Refugees in New Zealand", *International Journal of Social Psychiatry*, Vol. 40, No. 1, pp. 17–26.

Cheung, P. (1995), "Acculturation and Psychiatric Morbidity in Cambodian Refugees in New Zealand", *International Journal of Social Psychiatry*, Vol. 41, No. 2, pp. 108–119.

Church, A.T. (1982), "Sojourner Adjustment", *Psychological Bulletin*, Vol. 91, No. 3, pp. 540–572.

Cohen, S. and T.A. Wills (1985), "Stress, Social Support and the Buffering Hypothesis", *Psychological Bulletin*, Vol. 98, pp. 310–357.

Collins, A. (1995), *Racism and Intolerance in Ireland*, Dublin: National Youth Council of Ireland.

Cox, W. (1997), "ICOS and International Students", in O. Egan (ed.), *Minority Ethnic Groups in Higher Education*, Proceedings of a conference held on 27 November 1996 in St. Patrick's College, Maynooth. Cork: Higher Education Quality Unit.

Crocker, J., B. Major and C. Steele (1998), "Social Stigma", in D.T. Gilbert, S.T. Fiske and G. Lindzay (eds.), *Handbook of Social Psychology, Vol. 2*, 4th edition, Oxford: Oxford University Press.

Department of Justice, Equality and Law Reform (2000), 9 February, *http://www.irlgov.ie/justice*.

Department of Justice, Equality and Law Reform (2000), Information Office, 31 January.

Dion, K.L. and B.M. Earn (1975), The Phenomenology of being a Target of Prejudice, *Journal of Personality and Social Psychology*, Vol. 32, pp. 944–950.

Donà, G. and J.W. Berry (1994), "Acculturation Attitudes and Acculturative Stress of Central American Refugees", *International Journal of Psychology*, Vol. 29, No. 1, pp. 57–70.

Felsman, J.K., F.T.L. Leong, M.C. Johnson and F.I. Crabtree (1990), "Estimates of Psychological Distress among Vietnamese Refugees: Adolescents, Unaccompanied Minors and Young Adults", *Social Science and Medicine*, Vol. 31, No. 11, pp. 1251–1256.

Fernando, S. (1984), "Racism as a Cause of Depression", *International Journal of Social Psychiatry*, Vol. 30, No. 1–2, pp. 41–49.

Furnham, A. and L. Treize (1983), "The Mental Health of Foreign Students", *Social Science and Medicine*, Vol. 17, No. 6, pp. 365–370.

Furnham, A. and S. Shiekh (1993), "Gender, Generational and Social Support Correlates of Mental Health in Asian Immigrants", *International Journal of Social Psychiatry*, Vol. 39, No. 1, pp. 22–33.

Gil, A.G. and W.A. Vega (1996), "Two Different Worlds: Acculturation Stress and Adaption among Cuban and Nicaraguan Families", *Journal of Social and Personal Relationships*, Vol. 13, No. 3, pp. 435–456.

Goldberg, D. (1992), *General Health Questionnaire (GHQ-12)*, Windsor: NFER-NELSON.

Goldberg, D. and P. Williams (1988), *A User's Guide to the General Health Questionnaire*, Windsor: NFER-NELSON.

Gorst-Unworth, C. and E. Goldenberg (1998), "Psychological Sequelae of Torture and Organised Violence Suffered by Refugees from Iraq", *British Journal of Psychiatry*, Vol. 172, pp. 90–94.

Graham, M.A. (1983), "Acculturative Stress among Polynesian, Asian, and American Students on the Brigham Young University — Hawaii Campus", *International Journal of Intercultural Relations*, Vol. 7, No. 1, pp. 79–103.

Gray, E., H. Benedict, N. Leahy, B.A. Ryan, M. Smyth, D. O'Leary, M.F. Smyth, C. Carvajal, C. King, C. Finnegan, J. O'Leary, K. Quinn and A. Ogunloye (1999), *When I was a Stranger: Racism and Exclusion in Ireland*, Wexford: The Pilgrim Foundation.

Hauff, E. and P. Vaglum (1995), "Organised Violence and the Stress of Exile: Predictors of Mental Health in a Community Cohort of Vietnamese Refugees Three Years after Resettlement", *British Journal of Psychiatry*, Vol. 166, pp. 360–367.

Hauff, E. and P. Vaglum (1993), "Integration of Vietnamese Refugees into the Norwegian Labor Market: The Impact of War Trauma", *International Migration Review*, Vol. 27, No. 2, pp. 388–405.

Heiner, T., A. Weller and R. Shor (1997), "Stages of Acculturation as Reflected by Depression Reduction in Immigrant Nursing Students", *International Journal of Social Psychiatry*, Vol. 43, No. 4, pp. 247–256.

Irish Refugee Agency (1998), *Bosnian Programme Refugees in Ireland: Information Sheet*, Dublin: Irish Refugee Agency.

Irish Refugee Council (1997), *Annual General Meeting Report*, Dublin: Irish Refugee Council.

Johnston, M., S. Wright and J. Weinman (1996), *Measures in Health Psychology: A User's Portfolio*, Windsor: NFER-NELSON.

Kaplan, M.S. and G. Marks (1990), "Adverse Effects of Acculturation: Psychological Distress among Mexican American Young Adults", *Social Science and Medicine*, Vol. 31, No. 12, pp. 1313–1319.

Kinzie, J.D., K. Tran, A. Breckenridge and J. Bloom (1980), "An Indochinese Refugee Psychiatric Clinic: Culturally Accepted Treatment Approaches", *American Journal of Psychiatry*, Vol. 137, pp. 1429–1432.

Krieger, N. (1990), "Racial and Gender Discrimination: Risk Factors for High Blood Pressure", *Social Science and Medicine*, Vol. 30, pp. 1273–1281.

Krieger, N. and S. Sidney (1996), "Racial Discrimination and Blood Pressure: the CARDIA Study of Young Black Adults and White Adults", *American Journal of Public Health*, Vol. 86, No. 10, pp. 1370–1378.

Krishnan, A. and J.W. Berry (1992), "Acculturative Stress and Acculturation Attitudes among Indian Immigrants to the United States", *Psychology and Developing Societies*, Vol. 4, No. 2, pp. 187–212.

Landrine, H. and E. Klonoff (1996), "The Schedule of Racist Events: A Measure of Racial Discrimination and a Study of its Negative Physical and Mental Health Consequences", *Journal of Black Psychology*, Vol. 22, pp. 144–168.

Lavik, N., E. Hauff, A. Skrondal and O. Solberg (1996), "Mental Disorder among Refugees and the Impact of Persecution and Exile: Some Findings from an Outpatient Population", *British Journal of Psychiatry*, Vol. 169, pp. 726–732.

Liebkind, K. (1996a), "Vietnamese Refugees in Finland: Changing Cultural Identity", in G.M. Breakwell and E. Lyons (eds.), *Changing European Identities: Social Psychological Analyses of Social Change*, Oxford: Butterworth/Heinemann.

Liebkind, K. (1996b), "Acculturation and Stress: Vietnamese Refugees in Finland", *Journal of Cross-cultural Psychology*, Vol. 27, No. 2, pp. 161–180.

Mari, J. and P. Williams (1985), "A Comparison of the Validity of 2 Psychiatric Screening Questionnaires (GHQ-12 and SRQ-20) in Brazil, Using Relatively Operating Characteristics Analysis", *Psychological Medicine*, Vol. 15, pp. 411–415.

Mavreas, V. and P. Bebbington (1990), "Acculturation and Psychiatric Disorder: A Study of Greek Cypriot Immigrants", *Psychological Medicine*, Vol. 20, No. 941–951.

McFarland, E. (1994), *Bosnian Refugees in Glasgow*, Scottish Ethnic Minorities Research Unit, Research Paper, No. 1, Series 2.

McVeigh, R. and A. Binchy (1998), *Travellers, Refugees and Racism in Tallaght*, Dublin: West Tallaght Resource Centre.

Nozinic, D. (1997), "Educational Needs and Possibilities for Asylum-seekers and Refugees in Ireland", in O. Egan (ed.), *Minority Ethnic Groups in Higher Education*, Proceedings of a conference held on 27 November 1996 in St. Patrick's College, Maynooth. Cork: Higher Education Quality Unit.

Oei, T.P. and R. Notowidjojo (1990), "Depression and Loneliness in Overseas Students", *International Journal of Social Psychiatry*, Vol. 36, No. 2, pp. 121–130.

O'Regan, C. (1998), *Report of a Survey of the Vietnamese and Bosnian Refugee Communities in Ireland*, Dublin: Refugee Agency.

Pak, A.W.-P., K.L. Dion and K.K. Dion (1991), "Social-Psychological Correlates of Experienced Discrimination: Test of the Double Jeopardy Hypothesis", *International Journal of Intercultural Relations*, Vol. 15, No. 2, pp. 243–254.

Pan, P.-C. and D. Goldberg (1990), "A Comparison of the Validity of the GHQ-12 and CH-12 in Chinese Primary Care Patients in Manchester", *Psychological Medicine*, Vol. 20, pp. 941–951.

Pernice, R. and J. Brook (1996a), "The Mental Health Pattern of Migrants: Is There a Euphoric Period Followed by a Mental Health Crisis?" *International Journal of Social Psychiatry*, Vol. 42, No. 1, pp. 18–27.

Pernice, R. and J. Brook (1996b), "Refugees' and Immigrants' Mental Health: Association of Demographic and Post-Immigration Factors", *Journal of Social Psychology*, Vol. 136, pp. 511–519.

Pernice, R. and J. Brook (1994), "Relationship of Migrant Status (Refugee or Immigrant) to Mental Health", *International Journal of Social Psychiatry*, Vol. 40, No. 3, pp. 177–188.

Pettigrew, T.F. (1997), "Generalized Intergroup Contact Effects on Prejudice", *Personality and Social Psychology Bulletin*, Vol. 23, No. 2, pp. 173–185.

Rivera-Sinclair, E.A. (1997), "Acculturation/Biculturalism and its Relationship to Adjustment in Cuban-Americans", *International Journal of Intercultural Relations*, Vol. 21, pp. 379–391.

Rohrlich, B.F. and J.N. Martin (1991), "Host Country and Re-entry Adjustment of Student Sojourners", *International Journal of Intercultural Relations*, Vol. 15, No. 2, pp. 163–182.

Runyon, R.P. and A. Haber (1991), *Fundamentals of Behavioral Statistics*, 7th edition, New York: McGraw-Hill, Inc.

Sarason, I.G., B.R. Sarason, E.N. Shearin and G.R. Pierce (1987a), "A Brief Measure of Social Support: Practical and Theoretical Implications", *Journal of Personality and Social Psychology*, Vol. 44, pp. 127–139.

Sarason, B.R., E.N. Shearin, G.R. Pierce and I.G. Sarason (1987b), "Interrelationships of Social Support Measures: Theoretical and Practical Implications", *Journal of Personality and Social Psychology*, Vol. 52, pp. 813–32.

Scapocznik, J., W. Kurtines and T. Fernandez (1980), "Bicultural Involvement and Adjustment in Hispanic-American Youths", *International Journal of Intercultural Relations*, Vol. 4, No. 3–4, pp. 353–365.

Schwarzer, R., M. Jerusalem and A. Hahn (1994), "Unemployment, Social Support and Health Complaints: A Longitudinal Study of Stress in East German Refugees", *Journal of Community and Applied Social Psychology*, Vol. 4, pp. 31–45.

Schwarzer, R., R. Bowler and S. Rauch (1985), "Psychological Indicators of Acculturation: Self-esteem, Racial Tension and Inter-ethnic Contact", in L. Estrand (ed.), *Ethnic Minorities and Immigrants in a Cross-cultural Perspective*, Lisse, The Netherlands: Swets and Zeitlinger.

Schwarzer, R. and A. Leppin (1991), "Social Support and Health: A Theoretical and Empirical Overview", *Journal of Social and Personal Relationships*, Vol. 8, pp. 99–127.

Searle, W. and C. Ward (1990), "The Prediction of Psychological and Sociocultural Adjustment during Cross-cultural Transitions", *International Journal of Intercultural Relations*, Vol. 14, No. 4, pp. 449–464.

Silove, D., I. Sinnerbrink and A. Field (1997), "Anxiety, Depression, and PTSD in Asylum-seekers: Associations with Pre-migration Trauma and Post-migration Stressors", *British Journal of Psychiatry*, Vol. 170, pp. 351–357.

Somasundaram, D.J. (1996), "Post-traumatic Responses to Aerial Bombing", *Social Science and Medicine*, Vol. 42, pp. 1465–1471.

Sundquist, J. (1995), "Ethnicity, Social Class and Health: A Population-based Study on the Influence of Social Factors on Self-Reported Illness in 223 Latin American Refugees, 333 Finnish and 126 South European Labour Migrants and 841 Swedish Controls", *Social Science and Medicine*, Vol. 40, pp. 777–787.

Sundquist, J. and S.-E. Johnson (1996), "The Influence of Exile and Repatriation on Mental and Physical Health", *Social Psychiatry and Psychiatric Epidemiology*, Vol. 31, No. 1, pp. 21–28.

Swim, J. (1998), "Introduction", in J. Swim and C. Stangor (eds.), *Prejudice: The Target's Perspective*, London: Academic Press.

Tanaka, T., J. Takai, T. Kohyama and T. Fujihara (1994), "Adjustment Patterns of International Students in Japan", *International Journal of Intercultural Relations*, Vol. 18, No. 1, pp. 55–75.

Ward, C. (1996), "Acculturation", in D. Landis and R.S. Bhagat (eds.), *Handbook of Intercultural Training*, Thousand Oaks, CA: Sage Publications.

Ward, C. and W. Searle (1991), "The Impact of Value Discrepancies and Cultural Identity on Psychological and Sociocultural Adjustment of Sojourners", *International Journal of Intercultural Relations*, Vol. 15, No. 2, pp. 209–225.

Ward, C. and A. Kennedy (1993), "Where's the 'Culture' in Cross-cultural Transition?" *Journal of Cross-cultural Psychology*, Vol. 24, No. 2, pp. 221–249.

Ward, C. and A. Kennedy (1994), "Acculturation Strategies, Psychological Adjustment and Sociocultural Competence during Cross-cultural Transitions", *International Journal of Intercultural Relations*, Vol. 18, No. 3, pp. 329–343.

Weine, S.M., D. Vojvoda, D.F. Becker, T.H. McGlashan, E. Hodzic, D. Laub, L. Hyman, M. Sawyer and S. Lazrove (1999), "PTSD Symptoms in Bosnian Refugees One Year after Resettlement in the United States", *American Journal of Psychiatry*, Vol. 144, No. 4, pp. 562–564.

Westermeyer, J., J. Neider and F.-U. Tou (1984), "Acculturation and Mental Health: A Study of Hmong Refugees at 1.5 and 3.5 Years Post-migration", *Social Science and Medicine*, Vol. 18, No. 1, pp. 87–93.

Whelan, C.T., D.S. Hannan and S. Creighton (1991), *Unemployment, Poverty and Psychological Distress*, Economic and Social Research Institute, General Research Paper No. 150, Dublin: ESRI.

Ying, Y-W. and L.H. Liese (1991), "Emotional Well-being of Taiwan Students in the US: An Examination of Pre- to Post-arrival Differential", *International Journal of Intercultural Relations*, Vol. 15, No. 3, pp. 345–366.

Young, M. and D. Evans (1997), "The Well-being of Salvadoran Refugees", *International Journal of Psychology*, Vol. 32, pp. 289–300.

Zheng, X. and J.W. Berry (1991), "Psychological Adaptation of Chinese Sojourners in Canada", *International Journal of Psychology*, Vol. 26, No. 4, pp. 451–470.

CHAPTER FOUR

LOCAL AUTHORITY RESIDENTS: AN INVISIBLE MINORITY

Mary P. Corcoran

INTRODUCTION

There is considerable evidence that the benefits of Ireland's recent economic growth have not been evenly distributed across the population (O'Hearn, 1998). Socio-economic inequalities in Ireland have been deepening rather than attenuating. These deepening inequalities have been inscribed in the socio-cultural domain, creating what Zukin has termed landscapes of consumption and landscapes of devastation (1991: 5). Bauman has recently argued that it is one thing to be poor in a society of producers and universal employment but quite a different thing to be poor in a society of consumers, in which life projects are built around consumer choice rather than work (1998). This chapter will explore the social consequences of this change by drawing on the findings of a research study that explored the experiences of people living in the social rental sector in Ireland. Local authority housing in this country has become an increasingly residualised sector, reflecting the "emphasis on home ownership as the normal housing tenure" (Fahey, 1999: 5). Given the centrality of the principle of home ownership in Irish society, social housing is generally viewed, by home-owners and tenants alike, as an inferior option. If private ownership is for the upwardly mobile consumer, social housing tenancy is for those who are going nowhere. Social housing tenants, who are generally spatially segregated and socially stigmatised, occupy a minority status position within Irish society.

Agency, Structural Constraint and the Socially Excluded

Current theorising on the characteristics of modernity is predicated on the notion of the ever-increasing power of the social actor, or the triumph of agency over structure. The vision of the world presented is of a dynamic and interactive global space in which people and commodities circulate, transcending the constraints of time and space. In such a scenario, Lash and Urry among others argue, there is greater potential for individuals to act as reflexive agents, to take control of the shaping of their own lives: "The modernisation and post-modernisation of contemporary political economies produce, not just a flattening, but a deepening of the self" (1994: 31). Modernity is the harbinger of commodification, fragmentation and techno-scientific rationality. At the same time, modernity generates new opportunities for the individual through the provision of mass education, the growth of information technology, the rapid expansion of the specialist service sectors and increased flexibilisation in the labour market. Beck sees modernity as offering the individual greater opportunity "to reflect critically on those changes, and on their social conditions of existence, and potentially to change them" (Lash and Urry, 1994: 37). Giddens' conceptualisation of the reflexive individual is also infused with a sense of agency. In the era of modernity, we are not simply what we are, but what we make of ourselves (Giddens, 1991: 196). The apposite question we must pose at this point is: are we all equally empowered "to make something of ourselves"? Are all human agents as free, knowledgeable and skilled as Giddens seems to assume?

Lash argues that in modernity there are "reflexivity winners" and "reflexivity losers". The winners are the educated and skilled classes, who are hooked into the global information and communication structures, either through their work practices or through their leisure pursuits, or both. Their lives are defined by what Bauman describes as "the aesthetic of consumption" (1998: 23). It is the absence of routine and the state of constant choice that animates the consumer (1998: 25).

In contradistinction, reflexivity losers constitute an excluded underclass, victims of the increased class polarisation of post-industrial societies (1994: 130). Labour market erosion, the relocation of shopping facilities and the flight of families in employment out of social housing, creates a cycle of decline that eventually leads to a structural crisis. Young men of the underclass leave school early with no jobs and no prospects. The alternative to a job is gang bonding, the football terraces, racist violence or drugs. As Bauman points out, boredom is the psychological corollary of the stratification produced by a society structured around consumer choice. Money is the entry permit to places — shopping malls, restaurants and public houses, health and fitness centres — where boredom can be assuaged. But for those who have limited access to the consumer society, antisocial behaviour is often the only means of action (or expression of the self as agent) in the desperate attempt to escape boredom (Bauman, 1998: 39). As access to and participation in information and communication structures become increasingly integral to civil society, "exclusion from them becomes exclusion from citizenship, effectively both political and cultural exclusion from civil society" (Lash, 1994: 132–3). While urban space is functionally and economically shared, it is socially segregated and culturally differentiated (Robins, 1993: 313).

The Irish Social Housing Context and Methodology of the Study

According to the Combat Poverty Agency (1999: 31) more than half the population of Ireland live in urban areas which are spatially and socially structured according to the divisions in Irish society. Social segregation ensures that neighbourhoods are divided according to social class and status. Current research suggests that Dublin city is the most socially polarised of seven European cities being examined in comparative context (Betwixt Project, 1999). The effect of this pattern of segregation is to divide, isolate and exclude rather than integrate urban communities. One of the clearest demarcations occurs between private and local authority housing estates. According to Fahey (1998: 288), housing policy in

Ireland developed in urban areas only in the form of slum clearance programmes. Even at this early stage in the state's development, the practice of providing either direct or indirect subsidies to those purchasing houses had been established. The state support of private housing persists to the present, and has been a key factor in Ireland's internationally high (80 per cent) rate of home ownership. As was noted previously, the dominance of home ownership in Ireland means that social housing is perceived as the inferior option. Historically, local authority residents have availed of opportunities made available by local authorities to buy their own homes. Consequently, the social housing stock has been reducing over the years and the social profile of the tenant population has been worsening. Social housing in Ireland has become housing for the socially excluded.

In 1997, a research project funded jointly by the Combat Poverty Agency and the Katherine Howard Foundation was initiated to examine the quality of life on local authority housing estates in Ireland. The research team selected seven housing estates in all: three in the Greater Dublin area (Fatima Mansions, Fettercairn in Tallaght and South Finglas), one each in Limerick (Moyross), Cork (Deanrock), Dundalk (Muirhevnamor) and Sligo (Cranmore). In selecting the estates, we were careful to avoid atypical cases. We chose a variety of estates of different sizes, spatial configuration and locations. In terms of data collection, our guiding principle was to reflect in so far as possible the residents' views on the issue of quality of life in urban housing estates. To this end, the team engaged in several months of field investigation on each estate. This included detailed estate profiling, family interviewing and the conducting of focus groups. In addition, in-depth interviews were conducted with relevant service providers on each estate. An extensive data set, covering all seven estates, was compiled. (For details of methodology, see Corcoran and Fahey, 1999.) A key advantage of our methodological strategy was that the social world under investigation — everyday life on local authority housing estates — was studied in its "natural state". In conducting focus groups and interviews, we attempted to elicit naturalistic narratives rather than impose predetermined categories. The perspective of the local authority residents was taken as the empirical point of departure.

Spatial Segregation

The estates were selected in part because of their socio-spatial diversity. Some estates, such as South Finglas and Cranmore, cover a relatively large area and in fact constitute neighbourhoods. Others, such as Fatima Mansions, are relatively dense, forming distinct social units clearly delineated from the immediate neighbourhood (Rialto in the case of Fatima Mansions). In any event, all of the estates to a greater or lesser degree tend to be spatially differentiated from their immediate locales. This differentiation is historically conditioned by the original siting of the estates, and the perceived stigma that tends to attach to local authority housing. For example, in Togher, Cork City, most of the private housing is situated on the opposite side of the bridge to Deanrock, the local authority estate:

> The people of Deanrock interact with each other to the extent that they are a subculture within Togher and to an extent they have consciously isolated themselves from the rest of Togher. You hear them talking about those over the bridge. Togher has always been split in two because the track of the West Cork railway line forced a division in the area. This has been superseded by the South Link motorway built along the railway line.

In Fatima Mansions, residents said that relations with the adjacent Rialto community have been historically weak. Seventy per cent of residents questioned in the tenant survey undertaken by the research team in Fatima Mansions said that they did not feel part of the Rialto community. People recounted stories of how they had been snubbed by voluntary organisations and groups active in Rialto. For example, in the past, people in Fatima felt less welcome in the Rialto parish, and had been discouraged from becoming involved in the upkeep of the church. In West Tallaght, residents spoke of a perceived distinction between local authority estates and nearby private estates. Young people pointed out, for example, that:

> Fettercairn had been lobbying for speed ramps for seven years, yet Springfield (private estate) got ramps within a week, along with cobblestones, new street lamps and trees.

Furthermore, people in Fettercairn distinguished between people living to the east of the Tallaght Town Centre (the Square), who are considered to be more affluent and "on the pig's back", and those living to the west of the Square, in social housing estates such as Fettercairn. The comparisons do not stop there, however, but are also employed in order to distinguish between local authority estates within West Tallaght itself. In other words, people locate themselves along a continuum where they feel a sense of relative deprivation at different levels of intensity depending on the precise comparison group:

> Fettercairn is like the blacks of Tallaght. Everyone else seems to get everything, while we get nothing. Killinarden has four different summer projects for the children, each lasting a month. They get great help from the Gardaí and the council while we get overlooked. Maybe there is not enough of us or we don't shout loud enough.

Community workers are acutely aware of the challenge posed when operating in communities which are to a considerable extent segregated from adjacent neighbourhoods. By seeking more local services and creating networks at the local level, the community identity can be solidified. This militates, however, against building strategic networks with groups and potential employers outside of the immediate area. As the Manager of one community development project commented:

> In Togher we need services which will encourage people to come into the area . . . something like an ice rink or an Olympic-size pool. If you are too isolated you just die; community development shouldn't be all about your own area.

Recent research suggests that "network poverty" — the absence of a multiplicity of weak ties beyond the kin group — makes it extremely difficult to escape unemployment. On all of the estates studied, unemployment rates were far above the national average. This is partly the outcome of the decline of traditional working class employment. There are, however, weak linkages between the estates and local businesses and an absence of "network entrepreneurs" to create or match people with employment opportunities. Thus, the adult population on these estates are socially excluded in the sense that their labour market strategies are hampered by their inability to identify network entrepreneurs or persuade people to act as such in their interest (Perri 6, 1997: 6). Only the development of networks of weak ties beyond the estate will facilitate their inclusion into mainstream society.

Spatial and Social Divisions within Estates

Differentiation does not, however, begin and end along the perimeter of the estate. In fact, in all of the estates a complex intra-estate differentiation occurs, which has the effect of dividing the estates along social, spatial and even symbolic dimensions. Thus, as well as estates being clearly demarcated from their surrounding locales, as social units they themselves exhibit considerable internal stratification. As a consequence, the capacity of residents to coalesce around shared interest, or even to identify themselves as belonging to the same social category, may in fact vary not just between estates, but also within estates. It became evident that, on several estates, there were minority groups within minority groups.

In the Deanrock estate in Cork, for example, residents of the houses look down on those who live in flats, despite the fact that many people living in the flats have extended families living in the area. The snobbery between the houses and the flats on the estate is so acute that the Family Centre has been severely criticised for involving residents of the flats in their programmes. One interviewee remarked rather caustically that the FÁS courses are skewed in favour of the "rough element" and that "no parent worth their salt would send their children to train with that crowd". Indeed, in a number of other study estates there were complaints from residents that too much was being done for "the rough element" and not enough for the more law-abiding members of the community.

In Limerick, the Four Parks (formerly Glenagross) section of Moyross is spatially divided from the rest of the estate. This has resulted in a separate or even oppositional community identification developing there, as noted by Limerick Corporation officials:

> The physical location of Glenagross [Four Parks] is unfavourable, it's peripheral and down a hill. The railway line serves as a dividing line; people from either side won't mix, and they each want their own community facilities.

Field research suggested that the children in the Four Parks area of Moyross tended not to see themselves as part of the local community. They were reluctant, therefore, to avail of community facilities. Staff at the Bungalow project in the Four Parks suggested that children from that end of the estate were not welcome in the Community Centre. They believed that the youth clubs there "tended to favour a particular type of child, not the type of child who comes from the Four Parks". Indeed, Four Parks is seen within Moyross as a dreadful enclosure, physically and psychologically across the tracks and, therefore, different. This clearly demonstrates the local subtleties at work on large estates. These estates are heterogeneous and diverse, characterised by a level of complexity which is rarely alluded to in wider public commentary.

Internal divisions at the sub-estate level are most obvious in those estates where the overall quality of life is lowest. Often the most decrepit social space in the estate becomes the space most frequented by the "undesirables", contributing to the spiral of decline and exacerbating problems for adjacent residents. In Fatima Mansions, Block H is considered a no-go area by many residents, because it has been taken over by drug dealers and users. If a part of an estate becomes blighted, it prompts the other areas of the estate to distance themselves from the black spot. This sometimes has the effect of reinforcing or even exaggerating the latter's poor image. For example, young people in Cranmore said that while the estate as a whole had a bad name, it was Banks' Drive that was "the real black spot". Yet, a middle-aged resident who has lived on the estate for 24 years was adamant that quality of life in Cranmore was very good and that "even Banks' Drive is not as bad as it is made out to be". As a coping strategy, people in the least blighted or most respectable areas of the estates look down on their neighbours who occupy the undesirable areas. Seemingly small distinctions in status within the estates are an important aspect of everyday practice. Subtle social distinctions are drawn and barriers erected between the "superior" and "inferior" resident populations. These kinds of distinctions were less clear in some of the other estates than others but, nevertheless, were discernible.

Symbolic Representation

On all the estates, to a greater or lesser extent, residents spoke of being embattled. Quality of life is greatly affected by the problems of drug and alcohol abuse, vandalism, intimidation and harassment on the estates. As one lone parent in Muirhevnamor commented: "We have no space in our lives, every day is a battle".

The estate beset by the most severe problems in regard to social order is Fatima Mansions in Dublin. Here the most common motif employed by residents to characterise their daily lives is that of imprisonment. They think of themselves as "doing time", waiting for a release date from the estate. It is clear from the language that people use that they feel they have been sentenced to Fatima, and that this leads them to internalise a very negative self-image. This is expressed in terms of feelings of disengagement, alienation and dehumanisation:

> I feel as if I am in Mountjoy.
>
> It's like a life sentence here now, I have seen too much of it.
>
> We are like pigs in a pen here.
>
> Our children are like caged animals.
>
> We are like fish in a fishbowl.
>
> In Fatima you become a person you don't recognise.
>
> People shouldn't have to live like this.

The origin of this sense of "doing time" can be traced directly to the problems that pervade the estate. The key issue is that of the breakdown of social order in the estate and the seeming inability or unwillingness of Corporation officials and the gardaí to impact on the pervasive problems associated with a drug economy and drug culture. The residents of Fatima Mansions feel largely abandoned by the statutory agencies. As one resident remarked, "In Fatima there is law but no order". The feelings of alienation are clearly associated with the loss of control over the estate environment. Areas intended as communal space are simply empty spaces belonging to no one and ripe for colonisation by undesirable elements. Paradoxically, green spaces intended as an amenity have in fact become a liability for the estate. The resident population is contained within the complex as if it were a prison, while at the same time, the estate functions as a no-man's-land. Unable to either control or escape from the estate, they inhabit a gated compound. The drudgery of daily life is interrupted only by the spectacles created by brawling drug dealers and users, garda chases through the estates and joyriding.

On all the estates, people borrowed metaphors from cop shows, Hollywood movies and the evening news to characterise either the whole estate or parts therein. The estates' symbolic representation is independent of the status of the local authority residents. That is, regardless of whether or not a significant proportion of homes have actually been privately purchased — as is the case in South Finglas, Cranmore and Muirhevnamor— residents frequently resort to symbolic language to describe life on their estates:

> Castle Park [Moyross] was completely burnt out about ten years ago. It has a notorious reputation and became known as Beirut Alley.
>
> I had not been reared in an estate and when I moved into Muirhevanmor I immediately got, "oh, you're moving to the Bronx" . . . people outside the estate put the place down.
>
> It's like Beirut in here. [Fatima Mansions]

The use of metaphors, of course, has the effect of further stigmatising those on the estate who are already on the margins. But they also function to spectacularise life on the estate and young people, in particular, can find this spectacle addictive, as one young man from Fettercairn attests:

> In the summer its great to sit around all day and watch people punching the head off each other . . . junkies arguing over money and drugs. It's like the Bronx only much quieter in the winter. There is at least one riot a year sparked by confrontation. The police even call Fettercairn "Beirut".

The universal application of such metaphors demonstrates the extent to which local authority tenants have at one level internalised a view of themselves as war-torn, ghettoised and cut off from the mainstream society.

Residents of all the local authority estates in the study were acutely sensitive to how they are viewed from outside. The image of their estate which they most often see employed is that of a blight on the landscape. Focus group participants in Moyross recounted how a local politician had herself photographed outside a burnt-out house. The resulting photograph and her comments later appeared in the local press. She suggested that some of the housing in Four Parks be allocated to Institute of Technology students "to raise the tone" of the area. The residents were angry about this and demanded an apology. They were determined that this politician would not use their part of Moyross again as a political platform on "how to improve the standard of resident" in the area. Similarly, focus group participants in Muirhevnamor recalled that a local politician had asked incredulously at a public meeting: "Who would buy a house in Muirhevnamor?" Residents felt that this type of sensationalist comment amounted to a generalised condemnation of all local authority residents.

Although difficult to quantify, it is generally accepted that residents of areas with "bad reputations" suffer from "address effects" — an intangible but pervasive form of discrimination based on their place of residence (OECD, 1998: 57). This serves the dual effect of reinforcing their social exclusion and inhibiting the prospect of economic regeneration through inward economic investment (OECD, 1998: 51). Local authority residents across all the estates attested to the fact that they felt inhibited from using their address on job application forms. Furthermore, children on some estates felt that their address singled them out for discriminatory treatment in the schools they attended. Residents frequently expressed the belief that they are somehow all held to be collectively responsible for, or guilty of, antisocial behaviour. In other words, it is impossible to escape being labelled by virtue of being in residence. The labelling effect, which in some estates can be traced back for several decades, renders an estate "unable to escape the image which is reinforced by selective or sensational reporting in the media" (Page, 1993: 8).

Enduring Communities

The symbolic representation of the estates as blights on the landscape is tempered to some extent by the strong sense of social and communal solidarity that is anchored in residents' everyday social relations and practices. Alongside the simmering despair at the level of neglect and decline into which many of the estates in the study have fallen, there is a palpable sense of an enduring social fabric and strong social ties. Despite the problems, residents in general register high levels of satisfaction with their communities, if not with the physical environment in which the communities are housed. Daily life on some of the study estates is often a feat of endurance. Yet no estate has been totally abandoned by its residents. Even on an estate as blighted as Fatima Mansions, a majority (58 per cent) of those surveyed felt that there was some sense of a community spirit on the estate. These are communities that endure, both in the sense of suffering, but also in the more positive sense of continuing to sustain themselves. There is very real tension between the negatives of living in an area that is marked by dereliction and substance abuse problems, and the positives derived from being enmeshed in intense familial and neighbourhood networks. A key theme that emerges from the research is the importance of socio-familial bonds for maintaining a good quality of life. These estates exhibit a social network configuration that social analysts have suggested "is necessary to thrive in respect of health for children, adults and frail elderly people" (Perri 6, 1997: 22).

In most of the estates studied, people attested to the fact that members of their extended families lived on the estate, or nearby. The proximity of other family members acts as a bulwark against social isolation and contributes to quality of life. Baby-sitters are readily at hand and family gatherings occur relatively frequently: This comment from a Fettercairn resident was typical of many local authority housing residents:

> We are a close-knit family. My sister lives next door. We meet at my parents' house in Drimnagh every Christmas and Easter and on Mother's Day and Father's Day — religiously at 12 noon on the day. I phone my mother every day. Whenever

> the rest of the family go to visit my parents and they are not in, they land out to me.

In estates that are particularly badly affected by drugs problems, family networks become crucial in providing safe spaces and places for children who would otherwise be directly exposed to a drug economy and culture. One grandmother, who reared her own five children in Fatima Mansions, voiced her concern for her daughter's two children, also resident in a flat in the estate:

> I love me flat and I have good neighbours, but its like a life sentence being here now, I have seen too much of it. I see [daughter's name]'s kids growing up here and its terrible. They practically live in my place as it is. If I got a house tomorrow, I'd have them with me. It's terrible here for the likes of them.

On all the estates, people derive considerable happiness from the presence of good neighbours. In some cases, the worse things are in terms of social order and security, the more important the role of neighbours become in staving off feelings of despair and alienation.

> I have good neighbours [in Moyross]. I don't live in their houses, but I can approach them for help and they can approach me. People are great in times of funerals or accidents. They would do anything for you — looking after kids, providing food, taking people to the doctor and so on. It would not be half as good in a private estate.

> The neighbours [in Fettercairn] are grand, A1. People have been very helpful especially when our son had the problem [died from a brain haemorrhage]. We had back-up from absolutely everyone. The neighbours even organised a coach to bring them down to his funeral in Galway. They organised an anniversary mass for him on the green opposite the house. There is no estate like this in Dublin.

Neighbourliness is most effective when it empowers people to defend their immediate environment and provide deterrents against the misuse of that public space. It is notable that in all the estates, there are streets or blocks that are universally admired for their capacity to act effectively against the threat of vandalism, drug use and antisocial behaviour. So even on an estate like Fatima Mansions, which is generally considered ungovernable, there are blocks where neighbours acting in solidarity manage to maintain social order:

> There wouldn't be a problem outside my door. They wouldn't be allowed in the block. All the flats are occupied except one. There is a lot of nosy neighbours and nothing passes them. You'd be down at the shop and somebody would say, somebody is looking for you. Everybody does it and it's good, because everybody knows what is going on.

In the Moyross estate in Limerick and the Fettercairn estate in Tallaght, residents of particular streets engage in informal surveillance, which gives them a sense of control over their immediate environment:

> People watch out for each other in Delmedge [Moyross]. People what each other's back. People are happy here. I would know everyone on the road. If anything suspicious happened, they would report back to you.

> Surveillance is carried out by the residents, not the police [in Fettercairn]. People are very aware; if they see someone strange coming into the area, they will stop to see where they are going. It is not formalised like the neighbourhood watch kind of thing, nothing direct, people just keep on eye on the place.

Cut adrift from mainstream society, some of these communities have become denaturalised — deprived of the status and rights of citizenship. At the same time, residents on every estate take pride in their status as enduring communities — characterised by a high degree of sociability, supportive family networks and a norm of reciprocity — all features common to minority groups. Furthermore, residents on all the estates engage in acts of resistance to the deterioration of their living environment. Where community activism brings success, people's sense of themselves as agents, rather than as subjects that are acted upon, is enhanced. But community activism within the estates does not in and of itself provide a mechanism for integrating estate residents into mainstream society.

Are Local Authority Estates Socially Excluded?

In general, residents of local authority housing estates have a strong sense of community spirit, although their capacity to translate that spirit into community activism is affected by the nature and levels of social problems on the estate. People are generally comfortable in terms of their social relations with others on the estates. They respect each other and enjoy the camaraderie that derives from a shared life experience, particularly in the face of adversity. They are enormously concerned about their children's quality of life now and in the future. Their feelings, dreams and aspirations are culturally contiguous with other class groupings in Irish society. However, as communities, they are spatially segregated and socially stigmatised to the extent that many residents have internalised feelings of inferiority and low self-esteem. The problem for these communities is that Ireland's economic growth has been inherently unequal. The transformation into a high-technology, information-oriented and service-driven economy has militated against lower working class economic participation. The clearest evidence of this is in the presence of disaffected young boys and men on every estate who are not fully anchored in their communities. These young men tend to have low educational attainment, to be unemployed, and to abuse either alcohol or drugs. These are Lash's reflexivity losers, casualties of the economic transformation which has shifted society from an ethic of work to an aesthetic of consumption (Bauman, 1998). Their disaffection, expressed in antisocial behaviour, contributes to the degradation of quality of life on the estates.

The question of how the estates fit into the social structure of the wider urban environment, whether that is a city or a town, is crucial to the issue of quality of life. While social networks have been and continue to be the glue that holds these communities together, high levels of unemployment mean greatly reduced interactions with people beyond the estate. According to Wilson:

> . . . having a social network in which most kin, friends and neighbours are unemployed, in marginal or unstable employment or poor (which is the case for the majority of our respondents) — reinforces doubts about one's ability to exit. This can, over time, reinforce discouragement and a culture of fatalism (Wilson, quoted in Perri 6, 1997: 6).

Similarly, Bauman (1998: 37) points out that poverty is more than just material deprivation; it induces a particular social and psychological condition. "Poverty means being excluded from whatever passes for a normal life . . . and a happy life." Those who are thus excluded experience a fall in their self-esteem, feelings of shame and guilt. Furthermore, exclusion fosters resentment and aggravation, which can lead ultimately to violent acts. The remarkable feat of residents on local authority estates is that while they endure segregation, deprivation and stigmatisation, the majority reject antisocial behaviour and cling to the dream of a better life for their children.

References

Bauman, Z. (1998), *Work, Consumerism and the New Poor*, Buckingham: Open University Press.

Betwixt Project (1999), TSER funded study of "Precarity and Social Exclusion: A Comparative Study of Seven European Cities", Unpublished research in progress.

Combat Poverty Agency (1999), *Facts and Figures on Poverty*, Dublin: CPA.

Corcoran, M.P. and T. Fahey (1999), "Methodology and Overview of Estates" in T. Fahey (ed.), *Social Housing in Ireland: A Study of Success, Failure and Lessons Learned*, Dublin: Oak Tree Press.

Fahey, T. (ed.) (1999), *Social Housing in Ireland: A Study of Success, Failure and Lessons Learned*, Dublin: Oak Tree Press.

Fahey, T. (1998), "Housing and Social Exclusion" in S. Healy and B. Reynolds. (eds.) *Social Policy in Ireland: Principles, Practice and Problems*, Dublin: Oak Tree Press.

Giddens, A. (1991), *Modernity and Self Identity*, Cambridge: Polity Press.

Lash, S. and J. Urry (1994), *Economies of Signs and Space*, London: Sage.

Lash, S. (1994), "Reflexivity and its Doubles: Structure, Aesthetics and Community" in U. Beck, A. Giddens and S. Lash (eds.) *Reflexive Modernisation*, Cambridge: Polity Press.

OECD (1998), *Integrating Distressed Estates*, Paris: OECD.

O'Hearn, D. (1998), *Inside the Celtic Tiger*, London: Pluto Press.

Page, D. (1993), *Building for Communities*, London: Joseph Rowntree Foundation.

Perri 6 (1997), *Escaping Poverty*, London: Demos.

Robins, K. (1993), "Prisoners of the City" in E. Carter et al. (eds.) *Space and Place: Theories of Identity and Location*, London: Lawrence and Wishart.

Wilson, W.J. (1987), *The Truly Disadvantaged*, Chicago: Chicago University Press.

Zukin, S. (1991), *Landscapes of Power*, Los Angeles: UCLA Press.

This chapter draws on the findings of a national study on Quality of Life in Social Housing Estates supported by the Combat Poverty Agency and the Katherine Howard Foundation. See T. Fahey (ed.) (1999), *Social Housing in Ireland: A Study of Success, Failure and Lessons Learned*, Dublin: Oak Tree Press.

The research team was made up of Tony Fahey and Kathleen O'Higgins of the ESRI, Donal Guerin, Michelle Norris and Cathal O'Connell of the Department of Applied Social Studies, University College Cork, Seamus O'Cinnéide of the Centre for Applied Social Studies, NUI Maynooth, and Ruairi McAuliffe and the author of Department of Sociology, NUI Maynooth. The analysis presented in this chapter draws on the work of all the research team participants.

CHAPTER FIVE

THE PSYCHOSOCIAL HEALTH OF IRISH TRAVELLER MOTHERS

Sally Heron, Joseph Barry, Michael Fitzgerald and Malcolm MacLachlan

INTRODUCTION

The Travelling Community is an indigenous ethnic minority who live on the margins of Irish society (Ni Shuinear, 1994; Gmelch and Gmelch, 1976). Irish Travellers' ethnicity is embodied in their shared history, value systems, language, customs and traditions, which makes them a group that is recognised both by themselves and by others as being distinct (Pavee Point, 1998a). This distinctive lifestyle and culture, based on a nomadic tradition, sets them apart from the sedentary population or "settled people".

There are approximately 27,000 Travellers in Ireland today, about 0.05 per cent of the total Irish population (Pavee Point, 1998a). To date, there is no definitive historical account of Irish Travellers and consequently their origins have remained controversial. Crawford and Gmelch (1974), revising the ethnohistory and genetics of Irish Travellers, concluded that Irish Travellers differ genetically from their Romany and Gypsy counterparts, and are genetically more closely related to the Irish (settled) population than to any other nomadic people.

It is generally accepted that Irish Travellers are a disadvantaged group, although the particular reasons for this remain controversial. The Economic and Social Research Institute (Rottman, Tussing and Wiley, 1986) described Travellers as "impoverished, under-educated, often despised and ostracised" (p. 8). Quinlan (1998) suggested that Travellers are "a minority body of Irish people forced to live isolated, despised lives, compelled to trade their identity and heritage for every modicum of participation in our society, bestowed upon them through the condescension of the majority settled community" (p. 48).

The transient lifestyle engaged in by many Irish Travellers has long been perceived as a threat to the stability of the settled population. Settled people have found the conception of a nomadic psyche, or mentality, difficult to understand. This stance was reflected in Government reports which deemed Travellers to be "problems" which needed solving (The Report of the Commission on Itinerancy, 1963) and which advocated the assimilation of Travellers into "normal" settled society (Report of the Travelling People Review Body, 1983). This blatant denigration of the Traveller lifestyle has contributed to substandard accommodation provision for Travellers (Task Force on the Travelling Community, 1995; McKeowan and McGrath, 1996; Molloy, 1998; Noonan, 1994) leaving many Travellers living in squalor. Previous research has highlighted substandard living conditions as the primary cause of ill health in the Travelling Community (Brockbank, 1982; Lawrie, 1983; O Nuallain and Forde, 1992; Ginnety, 1993; Noonan, 1994; McCarthy, 1995).

TRAVELLER HEALTH

Every person has his/her own unique experience of health and illness. Nonetheless, the experience of health or illness is influenced by the set of standards, values, and traditions within a given community (Kleinman, 1980). An individual's ethnicity is also a relevant determinant of his/her health beliefs and illness behaviour (Chrisman and Kleinman, 1980). Lipton and Marbach (1984) proposed that

> . . . ethnic group membership influences how one perceives, labels, responds to and communicates various symptoms, as well as from whom one selects to obtain care, when it is sought, and the types of treatment received (p. 1279).

The health service model typically used in Great Britain and Ireland is based on Euro-centric biomedical explanations of health (Webb, 1996) and, as such, poses considerable problems for many ethnic minorities. Bhopal and White (1993) found considerable discrepancies between what health professionals thought were important health issues for ethnic minorities and what ethnic minorities thought themselves. Often, when a health professional interacts with a member of a different cultural group, "cross-cultural misattribution" occurs (Smith and Bond, 1993). Consequences of this may include people being

> . . . late for appointments, or early, or do not make appointments at all and simply arrive. People stand too close or too far away; talk too much, or too little, or too fast, or too slow, or about the wrong topics. They are too emotional, or too moderate, show too much or too little of a certain emotion, or show it at the wrong time, or fail to show it at the right time (p. 177).

Irish Travellers reported experiencing similar problems to the above while interacting with Irish health professionals (McCarthy, 1995; Pavee Point, 1995).

Research conducted on Travellers' health status in Ireland and Great Britain has concentrated on the individual's physical, rather than psychological, well-being (Brockbank, 1982; Lawrie, 1983; O Nuallain and Forde, 1992; Ginnety, 1993; Noonan, 1994; McCarthy, 1995). These studies have shown that Travellers' physical health status is very poor in comparison with their settled counterparts. The largest investigation of Travellers' health status in Ireland was conducted by Barry et al. (1989) and found that:

- Their infant mortality rate was 18.1 per 1,000 births compared to a national figure of 7.4;
- Travellers had more than twice the national rate of still births;
- The average life expectancy of a Traveller male was 10 years less than his settled counterpart's;
- Traveller women lived on average 12 years less than their settled peers;

- Travellers were only reaching the life expectancy that settled Irish people reached in the 1940s;
- Traveller males had over twice the risk of dying in a given year than settled males, whereas for female Travellers the risk was more than threefold;
- Travellers had higher death rates than their settled peers for all causes, particularly for accidents, metabolic disorders (0–14 age group), respiratory ailments and congenital problems.

There is little conclusive research on the psychological well-being of Irish Travellers, as previous studies have relied on anecdotal evidence. Collins (1989) described how rejection by the dominant (settled) society has led to feelings of low self-esteem and insecurity in Travellers due to the continuing pressure on Travellers to conform to the norm. Factors such as being female, living in poverty, having low self-esteem and poor self-efficacy have been identified as risk factors for the development of depression (MacLachlan, 1997) and are commonly found in the Travelling Community.

McLaughlin (1994) suggested that the oppression and demoralisation of Travellers throughout history has led to a gradual internalisation of feelings of social and racial inferiority. Leigeois (1987) proposed that the "settlement" ideologies imposed upon Travellers have meant less psychological, social and economic adaptability for Travellers. When Travellers can no longer travel, the consequences can be detrimental to the Traveller society — illness, break up of the family, aggression, and delinquency (Leigeois, 1987). Travellers' experience of racism and discrimination can lead to feelings of being a social outcast, having low self-esteem, having a lack of pride in one's ethnic identity coupled with anxiety about losing one's identity, and experiencing feelings of inferiority (Irish Traveller Movement, 1993; Helliner and Szuchewycz, 1994).

Aim of the Study

Women's health problems have typically been defined by experts, such as health care professionals, academics or policymakers

(Avotri, 1997). What has been generally absent in research is the voice of the Traveller women themselves, describing their health problems and showing how they are liked with the material and social circumstances of their lives. The Task Force on the Travelling Community (1995) examined the findings of Barry et al. (1989) and concluded that future research should examine Travellers' perceptions of health, as it would have much to contribute to improving their health status.

In the present study, we followed up a sample from Barry et al.'s (1989) investigation of Travellers' physical health status. This larger study was initiated in light of the fact that many Travellers were living in poor conditions that were perceived as negatively affecting their health status. Using a combination of both qualitative and quantitative methods, the present research aimed to "capture" Traveller women's own views of their health problems and how they explain them, and to provide data on their current psychological health. The research also aimed to assess any differences in the living status of the mothers since Barry et al.'s original study, conducted in 1987.

METHOD

Study Sample

The present study aimed to follow up 137 Traveller mothers, sampled from the Eastern Health Board's ten primary care areas, who gave birth in 1987 and took part in the study reported by Barry et al. (1989). In that study, it was believed that it was not possible to define a Traveller "objectively", as such a person was classified as a Traveller if two conditions were met: the social worker (or other public official) had to believe that a person was a Traveller, and the person had to agree with that assessment. The same definition was adopted in the present study.

The present study was conducted between March 1998 and January 1999. A large number of the mothers (84) were not living in Ireland at that time and as such the accessible sample size was reduced from 137 to 53. Due to the time constraints on the study, it was decided to stop interviewing at an agreed date (11 months after the initiation of the study); as such, 47 of the 53 mothers, who constituted the "accessible sample", were interviewed (response rate = 89 per cent). These mothers were aged 28–57 (mean = 37.5).

Measures

Information was gathered using a semi-structured interview schedule designed for the purpose of the study that included the General Health Questionnaire (GHQ-12) (Goldberg, 1978). The interview schedule was formulated using focus group results conducted for the purpose of the present study. Two focus groups were conducted with Irish Traveller women, aged 15–23 and 23–45 respectively. The groups were conducted on an official halting site in North Dublin, during July and August 1998. Twelve open-ended questions relating to Travellers' opinions on their own health status were used to prompt discussion. The sessions lasted for 75 and 85 minutes respectively. Each group was tape-recorded and a narrative report was produced. This report was carefully analysed using content analysis and formed a basis for the interview schedule (see Heron (2000) for more detail on the Focus Groups).

The socio-demographic section contained questions relating to the mother's accommodation status (based on the Economic and Social Research Institute Report, Rottman et al., 1986); the facilities available to the mother (on site/in housing estate); any maintenance problems in the mother's home; the mother's social linkage resources; and the mother's rating of her satisfaction with her neighbourhood (adopted from McGee and Fitzgerald, 1988). These answers were pre-coded and were usually scored on a Likert-type scale. For example, with a report mark ranging from "serious problem" (0) to "no problem" (5), mothers evaluated various aspects of their home, for instance, problems with draughts.

Many of the home characteristics were nominal variables, with two or more response categories, that we coded as "1" indicating "No" and "2" indicating "Yes". For example, household facilities were measured asking questions such as "Do you have electricity in the home?", "Do you have regular rubbish collection?" and "Do you have hot water in the home?". The total scores relating to the facilities, maintenance problems and satisfaction with the neighbourhood were used to create an *Environmental Index* (EI) score as a measure of exposure to environmental risk. Higher scores indicated better living conditions. The minimum score possible was 12 and the maximum score was 57.

The mother's social linkage resources were measured on a four-point scale ranging from "major problem" (0) to "no problem" (5). The total score was used to create the *Social Support Index* (SSI) score. The minimum score on the scale was 3 and the maximum was 25.

The mother's health behaviour was examined using closed questions that were pre-coded and scored on a nominal scale. For example, questions examining mothers' health behaviours included "Do you smoke?"; the answer "Yes" scored zero and the answer "No" scored one. The scores were used to create the *Good Health Index* (GHI). The minimum score was 0 and the maximum score was 7.

The *General Health Questionnaire* (GHQ-12) is a screening questionnaire used to detect forms of psychological distress. It has been standardised on a number of different populations across the world (Goldberg and Williams, 1991). The GHQ contains a checklist of statements and respondents were asked to compare their recent experience (during the past two to three weeks) to their usual state on a four-point scale of severity. The scoring scale consisted of Likert scores (0-1-2-3), or alternatively what has been referred to as the "GHQ score", coded 0-0-1-1. The threshold scores for detecting "caseness" adopted in the present study were 3–4 (on "GHQ score" method) based on Goldberg's (1986) recommendations.

The predictive validity of the GHQ in comparison with other well-known scaling tests of depression is good (Goldberg, 1986). There has been a large general factor found in previously reported analytic studies that support its construct validity (Goldberg, 1986). Six validity studies have been conducted of the GHQ-12 (the shorter version used in the present study). Sensitivity for the GHQ-12 ranges from 71 per cent to 91 per cent with a median value of 86 per cent (Goldberg, 1986). Split-half reliability on the GHQ-12 has been found to be 0.83 (Goldberg, 1986).

Procedure

The participation of each individual mother in the study took part in three phases: tracing the mothers; obtaining their participation; and conducting the interview. Initially the researcher was provided with a list of names, addresses, and dates of births of the mothers (n=137) who took part in the Travellers' Health Status Study (see Barry et al., 1989). The Mobile Clinic is a Traveller-specific service provided by the Eastern Health Board and services 41 Irish Traveller sites within the Eastern Health Board's ten Primary Care Areas. The Public Health Nurses working on the Mobile Clinic were contacted and the researcher accessed their database. A number of Traveller organisations, Travellers and people working with Travellers were contacted to ask for their help in the location of the sample.

To find out whether a current address was correct, the researcher contacted relevant bodies by telephone, meeting with the individual(s) or through "on site" visits, which involved going out on site (or to a housing estate) with a Public Health Nurse (from the Mobile Clinic or a specific Primary Care Area) or going out alone. When all the combined sources deemed a family to be residing out of Ireland, this was taken as fact. During 1998 and early 1999, 61 per cent of the original sample were found not to be living in Ireland.

Mothers who took part in the study were contacted in person by the researcher (who was usually accompanied by a Public Health Nurse). The purpose and method of the research were explained, and each mother was asked if she was willing to participate in the study. On indicating her willingness to take part, individual arrangements for interview were made. The interviews took place at a location and time to accommodate the different needs of each mother. Often it would take many visits to the site to establish trust with the Traveller family before the interview could be conducted. An average of 3.4 visits (median = 3, range 1–16) to the families were required to arrange and complete interviews.

The interviews were conducted between September 1998 and January 1999. At the beginning of each interview, the researcher asked the mother to sign a consent form. Given the high levels of illiteracy, the researcher carefully explained each question. A considerable amount of time was spent trying to gain the confidence of the mother prior to and during the interview. Interviews usually lasted between one and two hours. Generally those who were initially reluctant to voice their opinions became quite forthright as the interview progressed. Although none of the mothers refused to answer any particular questions, it is reasonable to assume that some mothers may have withheld some information.

During the interview, mothers were encouraged to respond in a conversational manner. The interviewer ensured that all questions were answered, but the sequence in which this was done followed the responses of the mother rather than being determined by the researcher. This was felt to be a more naturalistic and facilitative method of collecting data. Where required, the researcher intervened to encourage the mother to continue articulating her thoughts. The answers were entered by the researcher onto purpose-designed forms (similar to questionnaires). Thus, all the required information was collected from the mothers in the same manner, using the same answer coding.

Data Analysis

A number of analytic strategies were employed. First, we considered whether the GHQ was a psychometrically and culturally appropriate measure of psychological distress in the sample studied. Unrotated Factor Analysis revealed that all twelve items loaded onto the first factor, which explained 72.5 per cent of the variance, therefore supporting the construct validity of the instrument within this sample. All 12 items on the GHQ were retained and conventional scoring procedures were used. Mothers' GHQ scores were correlated with variables derived from the interview schedule (EI, SSI and GHI scores). For the purpose of statistical analysis, a Local Authority House, Other Standard House and Chalet were categorised as "Housed", and Trailer or Caravan and "Other" were categorised as "Unhoused". Chi-square analyses were used to examine differences between Housed and Unhoused mothers in comparison with all other variables.

RESULTS

Demographic Data

The majority of the women in 1987 (85.1 per cent) and in 1998 (91.5 per cent) were married. There was one single mother in 1987 (2.1 per cent) and four single mothers in 1998 (8.5 per cent). Since 1987, the average family size had increased from 3.7 (SD = 3.7, range 0–15) children in 1987 to 7.9 (SD = 3.7, range 3–19) children in the present study. The majority (91.5 per cent) of the children in the sample had a father figure, and for all of these children it was the biological father of the child. The characteristic family comprised a mother and father, with low occupational status, a high level of unemployment and a relatively large number of dependent children (see Heron, 2000).

Living Conditions

Fifty-eight per cent of mothers stated that they were unhappy with their accommodation status. The average EI score was 41 (SD = 11.3) on a scale where the minimum score possible was 12 and the maximum score was 57. Chi-square analysis revealed a significant difference between those mothers who were "Housed" and "Unhoused" [$x = 7.5$, $n = 47$, $p < 0.05$]; "Housed" mothers were happier with their accommodation status. Since 1987, there has been a 15 per cent increase in the number of families living in a house and a 17 per cent decrease in the number of families living in a trailer or caravan. However, 15 per cent of mothers had left previous Housed accommodation to return to Unhoused accommodation. Nineteen per cent of the Unhoused accommodations were located on unpaved ground.

At the time of the interview, 70 per cent of those not currently in "housing" had applied to be housed. In 1998, 13 per cent of the mothers lived in "settled" housing estates, the majority of the mothers lived on Official Halting Sites (29.8 per cent) or in Group Housing Schemes (23.4 per cent). There was a 31 per cent decrease in the number of families living in Unofficial Sites and a 6.1 per cent increase in the number of families living on the roadside.

Reasons why mothers were unhappy with their accommodation status included problems with sewage, closeness to electricity pylons and dangerous roadways; representative remarks included:

> "That outside river is a health hazard, I won't let my small kids out . . . look at the rubbish and sewage in the river."
>
> "Not with that canal . . . something needs to be sorted out, there's dirt of all descriptions there . . . bodies have been taken from that canal and no footways over it."
>
> "Not the way the site is . . . not with that open sewage and those pylons"
>
> "Farmers wouldn't have them [pylons] near their cattle, so what about humans?"

Half of the mothers reported having a problem with draughts, damp, structural defects, poor plumbing, bad smells and vermin in their dwellings. Noise and leaks were also highlighted as problems, although not as severe. Three-quarters of mothers had no access to hot water or to a shower or bath. Similarly, over half the mothers did not have a toilet inside their dwelling. Fifteen per cent of mothers had no access to a rubbish collection. Nearly half (49 per cent) of the mothers considered their dwelling to be in a dangerous or polluted area and did not consider their area as a healthy environment to live in; representative remarks included:

> "That tip is polluted [it's located behind the site] and all the rats come in . . . and the sewage and smells."
>
> "We have no running water, no facilities at all."
>
> "That river has germs, that water never runs clear . . . there's lots of rubbish from the site in it."
>
> "There are sixty families on top of one another . . . and that skip . . . the dirt from the dogs . . . we are too close to one another, when one person is sick the whole site is sick."
>
> "I would love to be out of it this minute. There's no running water, no toilets and loads of rats and dirt. This is a condemned area . . . a dog wouldn't live up here."
>
> "This site is not suitable for kids at all . . . not a proper site."

The vast majority of mothers (89.4 per cent) did not have access to play facilities for their children. Lack of adequate space was a problem for 34 per cent of the mothers. The lack of basic facilities, overcrowding and the location of electricity pylons were highlighted as three main problems which mothers believed contributed to ill-health:

Health Perceptions and Practices

Forty-seven per cent of mothers said they would consult a healer or curing person for a range of illness and concerns that we presented to them. The types of concerns discussed included depression, worries, kidney infections, arthritis, asthma, eczema, nerves, gastro-enteritis, diarrhoea, burns and heart problems. Of those who consulted "curers", 55.3 per cent found some benefit from their visit. The majority of mothers felt that a person who had energy and was capable of performing daily duties was someone who was healthy. Absence of illness and general mental well-being was also highlighted as important. Eating well and trying to get some form of exercise were the main ways in which the mothers kept themselves healthy. Scores from the GHI indicated that the average score for the mothers interviewed was 3.7 (SD = 1.2) on a scale of one to seven.

Twenty-nine per cent of mothers felt that being a Traveller negatively impacted upon their health; representative remarks included:

> "Wintertime is very hard for Travellers with the poor accommodation; it's all wet and muddy and causes a lot of problems."

> "The accommodation that Travellers lives in destroys their health. . . . Traveller women have the worst life, too dominated by men. . . . There should be someone to explain to women that they don't have to feel down . . . need someone to come around to Traveller women. . . . Traveller women have nowhere to turn. . . . when I go to mass or the shops other people don't see the effort I've made without facilities."

> "Yes, all the coldness and hardship . . . the crowds of kids in a two-bedroom caravan and if one gets sick they all do . . . you can't win with a caravan."

Those who did believe being a Traveller negatively affected their health strongly emphasised the lack of facilities and poor accommodation available to them. Twenty-eight per cent of mothers were unhappy with their health and this was generally due to their self-reported depression and general feelings of malaise; representative remarks included:

> "I don't go out. . . . I sit here all day. . . . I do be very depressed a lot and I can't talk to people. . . . I look after the childers before myself. . . . there wasn't as much sickness when I was growing up . . . now an awful lot of Travellers have sicknesses."

We also investigated the effect of type of accommodation quantitatively: a one-way ANOVA revealed that a difference in the type of accommodation (trailer, caravan, chalet, standard house) was associated with different scores on the Environmental Index [$F (4,42) = 6.93$, $p < 0.001$]. A post hoc Scheffe test revealed that the mean scores of mothers living in a trailer or caravan ($x = 35.1$) differed significantly from those mothers living in a local authority house ($x = 49.5$) or in any other type of standard house ($x = 54.3$). These results showed that those living in Unhoused accommodation were exposed to poorer environmental conditions than those living in Housed accommodation.

GHQ Analysis

A substantial percentage (46 per cent) of the Traveller women interviewed exceeded the cut-off for "psychiatric caseness" (Goldberg, 1986). In line with the qualitative data given above, we hypothesised that a high score on the environmental index (which indicates good environmental conditions) would correlate with a lower levels of psychological distress. This hypothesis was supported [$r = -0.36$, $n = 47$, $p < 0.05$].

Given many Travellers' poor living circumstances, it was hypothesised that mothers who had larger families (that is, have a higher mean number of children) were more likely to be psychologically distressed (that is, to score highly on the GHQ). This hypothesis was not supported [$r = 0.06$, $n = 47$, $p > 0.10$]. It was proposed that mothers who were experiencing psychological distress would not engage in good health practices (that is, who have lower scores on the Good Health Index). This hypothesis was supported [$r = -0.19$, $n = 46$, $p < 0.10$]. Mothers who have poorer social support have less opportunity to discuss any psychological distress. Levels of mothers' social support in the current study were measured using the SSI and results indicated that the average score mothers obtained was relatively high — 19 (SD = 3.2) on a scale that ranged from 3 to 25. Using this scale of measurement, it was postulated that those who had low SSI scores would be more psychologically distressed (score highly on the GHQ). This hypothesis was supported [$r = -0.36$, $n = 25$, $p < 0.05$].

Discussion

Demographic Data

It is traditional within the Traveller community to get married and, as such, a higher number of Travellers tend to be married than their settled counterparts. All the mothers in the present study were, or had previously been, married. This finding is consistently found in the literature. The Central Statistics Office (1998) conducted a national enumeration and found that marriage was more prevalent among the Travelling community that in the population in general. Fitzpatrick, Molloy and Johnson (1997) also found "significantly more Traveller mothers were married" (p. 301) than their settled counterparts.

Within the Traveller community, it is also very common for families to be larger than the national average. Similar to Rottman et al. (1986), the present study found an average of eight children per family that suggests that the average size of Irish Travelling families has not changed in the last decade. This is a somewhat surprising result, given that the Central Statistics Office (1996) conducted the most recent national enumeration of Travelling families and found that Traveller families had an average of 3.5 children. An average of eight children per family in the present study may have been skewed by a small number of very large families (ranging upwards to 19). Nonetheless, what is clear is that

Traveller family sizes are still larger than the national average of 1.8 children per settled family (Central Statistics Office, 1998).

The importance of family to the Travelling Community should not be underestimated. Historically, Travellers' survival has depended on the group's solidarity and cohesion, their acceptance of each other as similar, their sense of belonging and their unwillingness to conform to the lifestyle of the dominant society (McCann, O'Síocháin and Ruane, 1994). Theoretically, it is possible to surmise from the results in the present study, and from a perusal of the literature, that a type of "group psychology" has emerged in the Travelling Community, strengthened by marriage, in particular, endogamy. Endogamy has "profound implications for group membership: the one decisive factor in whether an individual is a Traveller or not is whether he has at least one Traveller parent" (Ní Shuinear, 1994: 55).

The Traveller group psychology provides Travellers with a protective shelter to deal with the negative psychological effects the continual pejorativisation and rejection of their culture causes. McDonagh (1988) notes that traditional ties of kinship in the Travelling Community are enhanced by arranged marriages and Travellers' isolation from the settled community. The value placed on marriage and family within the Traveller culture may also impact upon the individual Traveller. Anecdotal evidence suggests that getting married and having children is the "norm" and commands certain levels of respect and acceptance from the group as a whole.

Theoretically, the high level of dependence (by the families interviewed) on the government for survival may be attributable to the changes the Traveller economy has undergone in the last 30 years. Travellers have a history of being self-sufficient rather than being employees; however, with industrialisation, mechanisation and the exodus from the land, many of the traditional "Traveller trades and crafts" have become obsolete. A minority of Travellers have thriving businesses or are engaged in viable economic activities, but the majority live in relative poverty. Many Travellers are dependent on social welfare for survival and are unable to access the mainstream economy (Pavee Point, 1998).

Practically, the large number of families on social welfare only increases negative settled attitudes towards Travellers as "vagabonds" (Report of the Travelling People Review Body, 1983). Rottman et al. (1986) proposed that the lack of "work opportunities has caused widespread friction between the Travellers and the settled population" (p. 71).

Living Conditions

In theory, every Traveller family who needs appropriate accommodation (group housing, single housing, permanent sites and transient sites) should have received it by the year 2000 (The Task Force on the Travelling Community, 1995). The aspiration was that this accommodation will "acknowledge the distinct needs and identity of Travellers" (p. 17) allowing for safe fuel storage, with electricity, sewerage services, water supply, toilets, bathroom, washing and drying facilities. The living conditions found in the present study did not reflect these governmental aims.

The accommodation status of Travellers in Ireland and England has been extensively discussed and debated (e.g. see Report on the Commission on Itinerancy, 1963; Report of the Travelling People Review Body, 1983; Task Force on the Travelling Community, 1995; McKeowan and McGrath, 1996; Molloy, 1998). Theoretical discussion has often centred on whether Travellers should favour settlement or nomadism. Among Travellers, however, the debate has more often concerned the choice between living in a house or a trailer, rather than settlement versus nomadism.

Nomadism is understood as "more a state of mind than an actual situation. Its existence and importance is frequently more psychological than geographical" (Leigeois, 1987: 27). It is regarded as "the core value of Traveller culture" (Kenny, 1994: 180). For Travellers, living in a house "cannot be assumed to equate with a relinquishment of travelling. It may serve a purpose at a certain time of the year and at certain life stages, but that is all it is" (Ginnety, 1993: 19). In fact, while living in a house, many Travellers maintain a "nomadic mindset" (Kenny: 180), although they may no longer travel.

Our results suggest that the living conditions of many of the mothers interviewed were substandard and need to be immediately addressed. The homes of the mothers (housed and unhoused) interviewed varied considerably in the quality and condition of the facilities available to them. This is evident examining the large standard deviation found (11.3) on the EI index. Almost half of the mothers believed they lived in a polluted or dangerous environment. Homes were often located beside dumping grounds, electricity pylons or sewerage plants. Noonan (1994) found similar conditions on two sites in Northern Ireland. The Northside Travellers Support Group (1994) found that of the Travellers (N = 68) living in the Coolock area of Dublin, "37 per cent had no toilets, 50 per cent had only cold water supply, 60 per cent had no electricity, 62 per cent had no bath or shower facilities, 35 per cent had no rubbish collection . . . 87 per cent thought that they lived in a dangerous or polluted environment" (p. 2). McCarthy et al. (1995) conducted a study in Dublin and Galway (N = 200) and found that "20 per cent of the respondents had no toilet facilities, 27 per cent had only a shared cold water supply, 32 per cent had no electricity, 40 per cent had no bath or showers and 18 per cent had no refuse collection" (p. 22).

The present study's findings indicate a trend towards housed accommodation which included local authority housing, other standard housing, and chalet-style housing (found in Group Housing Schemes). Since 1987, there has been a 17 per cent reduction in the number of families living in trailers or caravans and a 15 per cent increase in the number of families living in housed accommodation. Similarly, Rottman et al. (1986) found that:

> ". . . almost two-thirds of families living on the roadside or on serviced sites said that they would prefer to live in standard housing . . . more than 75 per cent of those families that were previously housed but currently living on the roadside indicated a preference for some type of fixed housing" (p. 61).

Theoretically, living in a house does not serve the same psychological purpose for Travellers as it does for settled people. If settlement, as opposed to nomadism, was a priority for Travellers, one may expect a large majority of families to be living in "settled" housing estates. However, only 13 per cent of families interviewed lived in housing estates. Living in a house may even cause adverse psychological effects, including isolation, loneliness, loss of identity and feelings of being "closed in" (Ginnety, 1993). This may explain why seven of the families in the present study, who had been previously housed, had moved back onto the roads or sites.

Over 90 per cent of the families were living in the same accommodation one year before the interview. Anecdotal evidence suggested that many Travellers prefer to have a fixed location so that they may travel in the summer months. Mothers also remarked how difficult travelling has become with "nowhere to stop" with their trailer or caravan.

These results indicate that the accommodation status of Travellers is complex, with many extenuating factors. Receiving adequate accommodation (housed or unhoused) and access to basic facilities in environmentally healthy conditions, were the primary needs identified. To address this situation, we suggest that authorities should ensure the recommendations put forward by the Task Force on the Travelling Community (1995) are immediately implemented.

Health

Forty-six per cent of mothers were psychologically distressed at the time of the interview. Thirty-two per cent of these mothers were taking anti-depressant medication at the time of the interview. This high level of psychological distress is of great concern and is similar to previous research. In Great Britain, Pahl and Vaille (1986) found that 14 per cent of Traveller mothers interviewed had clinical levels of psychological distress such as depression and anxiety. Noonan (1994) found that 25 per cent of respondents surveyed said that someone in their family suffered from their "nerves" — a common Traveller term for anxiety.

Other minority cultural groups such as the Aborigines in Australia and the First Nation people in Canada have also had higher rates of mental health problems than their respective national populations (McCarthy, 1995). In Australia, the Aboriginal Medical Service Co-operative has found that mental health problems are the most common clinical problem presented to doctors in the specialist Aboriginal health service. Similarly, research has shown that First Nation people in Canada have high rates of depression with almost double the rate of suicide compared to the national population (Health and Welfare Canada, 1991).

A number of previous studies discussed the relationship between psychosocial health and the environment (e.g. see Pahl and Vaille, 1986; Noonan, 1994; Quinlan, 1998; Ginnety, 1993). An association between poor environmental conditions and high levels of psychological distress were found in the present study. Many of these women may be considered to be living in poverty. MacLachlan (1997) notes that "epidemiological studies have identified poverty as an important risk factor for the development of depression. This may be because it is related to other risk factors such as more frequently experiencing stressors, having low self-esteem, poor self efficacy and so on" (p. 272). Females are also more often identified as depressed (Shorter, 1994).

It may be expected that, given the emphasis Travellers place on group solidarity, a breakdown in the perceived social support available to a Traveller mother would have negative psychological effects. Results indicated that this was true for the women interviewed using the women's scores on the SSI and GHQ. The present study also found that mothers who did not engage in "good health" behaviours (as measured by the GHI) were more likely to experience feelings of psychological distress.

Limitations of the Study

The relatively small sample size (n = 47) limits the extent to which our findings may be representative of Traveller mothers in general, although it is noteworthy that similar sample sizes have been used in other Traveller studies (e.g. see Noonan, 1994; Northside Traveller Support Group, 1994; Pavee Point, 1995).

Achieving cultural appropriateness in the interview schedule was an aim of the present study. It is difficult to know how well this was achieved. Focus groups were used to try to ensure that the interview schedule was based on issues salient to Travellers rather than being determined by the researcher. Despite this, it is possible that certain questions may not have reflected the perspective of the Travellers interviewed. Pilot studies were conducted to address this issue. The women interviewed suggested that the phrasing of some questions needed to be changed. These recommendations were implemented as suggested.

The GHQ was factor analysed to ensure that it was "behaving" in the same way in the present sample as it has been reported to in a diverse range of much larger samples. Our factor analysis indicated that this was the case and this supports that likelihood that the excellent psychometric properties of the GHQ, extensively reported elsewhere (Goldberg, 1978), are also relevant to the sample reported here.

Interviewees may have told "untruths" to try to please the interviewer or because they were suspicious of her. It is possible that some of the women took part without perceiving any relevance to themselves. As many of the women interviewed lead very busy lives, the time the interview took to complete may have influenced the quality of the data. Nonetheless, all the mothers interviewed were very co-operative and did not appear hostile towards the researcher.

RECOMMENDATIONS

Poor living conditions appear to be significantly associated with poor psychological and physical health. The substandard conditions many unhoused Travellers currently live in must be remedied as soon as possible. Travellers, Traveller Organisations, Outreach workers, social workers, community nurses and others need to ensure that Traveller women have someone who can provide social support to them. This may be aided by primary health care initiatives and the Community Mothers Scheme. The importance of taking time to relax should be stressed. It is clear from the results of the present study that unless there are people (see above) who Traveller women feel they can trust and relate personal issues to, the high level of psychological distress is likely to increase. The present study found that almost 50 per cent of women interviewed were distressed at the time of interview; undoubtedly this figure could be reduced if the women felt that they had an opportunity to relieve themselves of some of the burdens of being the primary caretaker of often very large and demanding families.

Health promotion in the Travelling Community should be a priority in the health services. Travellers should be trained in all aspects of health care and health care issues. Funding should be provided to expand the current Primary Health Care projects that work with Travellers. These projects play a valuable role in the community and provide Travellers with an opportunity to become part of a health care system. Health promotion should continue with posters, videos and other applicable means of communication currently being used. The community and cultural identity of travellers should be embraced as conduits to health, rather than be seen as barriers to health promotion (MacLachlan, 1998). However, we believe that cultural identity should not be rooted to tradition, but be responsive to the contemporary social, economic and political contexts in which people live (MacLachlan, 2000). In particular, the high rates of psychological distress reported by women here suggest that, for whatever reason, many Traveller women suffer poor mental health. While this is not being, and should not be, construed as a consequence of Traveller culture per se, neither is it a phenomenon that Traveller culture can ignore.

Future research might examine the health professionals — those who do and do not work with Travellers — to elicit their views on problems of providing adequate health care. Such a study could incorporate an examination of current health care provision; the problems that health professionals believe they, and the Travellers, contend with in the health services; and what solutions the health professionals believe are noteworthy. Future research should also examine the health perceptions and behaviours, as well as the psychological well-being, of Traveller men.

References

Avotri, J.Y. (1997), "Thinking Too Much and Worrying Too Much: Ghanaian Women's Accounts of their Health Problems", PhD thesis, McMaster University, Hamilton, Canada.

Barry, J. (1996), "Maternal and Infant Health of Irish Travellers", Unpublished manuscript, Trinity College Dublin.

Barry, J., B. Herity and J. Solan (1989), *Vital Statistics of Travelling People, 1987*, Dublin: The Health Research Board.

Bhopal, R. and M. White (1993), "Health Promotion for Ethnic Minorities: Past, Present and Future", in W. Ahmad (ed.), *"Race" and Health in Contemporary Britain* (pp. 133–66), Buckingham: Open University Press.

Brockbank, J. (1982), *Gypsy Children and Their Health Needs*, London: Paediatric Project, Charing Cross Hospital.

Central Statistics Office (1998), *The Demographic Situation of the Traveller Community in April 1996*, Dublin: Central Statistics Office.

Chrisman, N. and A. Kleinman (1980), "Health Beliefs and Practices" in S. Thernstrom (ed.), *Harvard Encyclopaedia of American Ethnic Groups*, MA: Harvard University Press.

Collins, M. (1989), "Racism and Participation: The Case of the Irish Travellers", in *DTEDG File: Irish Travellers, Analysis and New Initiatives* (pp. 81–87), Dublin: Pavee Point Publications.

Crawford, M. and G. Gmelch (1974), "Human Biology of the Irish Tinkers: Demography, Ethnohistory and Genetics", *Journal of Social Biology*, Vol. 21, pp. 321–31.

Fitzpatrick, P., B. Molloy and Z. Johnson (1997), "Community Mothers' Programme: Extension to the Travelling Community in Ireland", *Journal of Epidemiology and Community Health*, Vol. 51, pp. 299–303.

Ginnety, P. (1993), *The Health of Travellers; Based on a Research Study with Travellers in Belfast*, Belfast: Eastern Health Social Services Board.

Gmelch, S. and G. Gmelch (1976), "The Emergence of an Ethnic Group: The Irish Tinkers", *Anthropological Quarterly*, Vol. 49, No. 4, pp. 225–38.

Goldberg, D. (1978), *Manual of General Health Questionnaire*, Windsor: NFER-Nelson.

Goldberg, D. (1986), "Use of GHQ in Clinical Work", *British Medical Journal*, Vol. 293, pp. 1188–89.

Goldberg, D. and Williams, P. (1991), *A User's Guide to the General Health Questionnaire*, Berkshire: NFER-Nelson.

Government of Ireland (1963), *Report of the Commission on Itinerancy*, Dublin: Government Publications.

Government of Ireland (1983), *Report of the Travelling People Review Body*, Dublin: Government Publications.

Government of Ireland (1995), *Report of the Task Force on the Travelling Community*, Dublin: Government Publications.

Health and Welfare Canada (1991), *Health Status of Canadian Indians and Inuit 1990*, Ottawa: Health and Welfare Canada.

Helliner, J. and B. Szuchewycz (1994), "Discourses of Exclusion: The Irish Press and the Travelling People", in *Others in Discourse: The Rhetoric and Politics of Exclusion*, Newbury Park: Sage.

Heron, S. (2000), "A Question of Health: An Investigation of Psycho-social Health in Irish Traveller Mothers and Children", MSc Thesis, Trinity College, Dublin.

Irish Traveller Movement (1993), *Anti-Racist Law and the Travellers*, Dublin: Irish Traveller Movement.

Kenny, M. (1994), "Final Thoughts: A Case for Celebration?" in M. McCann, S. O' Síochâin and J. Ruane (eds.), *Culture and Ethnicity* (pp. 170–179), Belfast: The Institute of Irish Studies, The Queen's University of Belfast.

Kleinman, A. (1980), "*Patients and Healers in the Context of Culture: an Exploration of the Borderland between Anthropology, Medicine and Psychiatry*", London: University of California Press.

Lawrie, B. (1983), "Travelling Families in East London: Adapting Health Visiting Methods to a Minority Group", *Health Visitor Magazine*, Vol. 56, No. 1, January.

Leigeois, J. (1987), *Gypsies and Travellers: Dossiers for the Intercultural Training of Teachers*, Strasbourg: Council of Europe.

Lipton, J. and J. Marbach (1984), "Ethnicity and the Pain Experience", *Social Science Medicine*, Vol. 19, No. 12, pp. 1279–1298.

MacLachlan, M. (1997), *Culture and Health*, Chichester: Wiley.

MacLachlan, M. (1998), "Promoting Health: Thinking Through Context", in E. McAuliffe and L. Joyce (eds.), *A Healthier Future? Managing Healthcare in Ireland*, Dublin: IPA.

MacLachlan, M. (2000), "Cultivating Health", in M. MacLachlan (ed.), *Cultivating Health: Cultural Perspectives on Health Promotion*, Chichester: Wiley.

McCann, S. O'Síochâin and J. Ruane (eds.) (1994), *Culture and Ethnicity*, Belfast: The Institute of Irish Studies, The Queen's University of Belfast.

McCarthy, P. and Associates and Centre for Health Promotion Studies, UCG (1995), *Health Service Provision for the Travelling Community in Ireland*, Dublin: Stationery Office.

McDonagh, M. (1988), *Pride and Prejudice: The Case of the Travellers*, Navan Travellers Committee.

McGee, H. and M. Fitzgerald (1988), *Pathways to Child Hospitalisation: Psychological, Social and Medical Factors associated with the Admission to Hospital of Children with Gastroenteritis: A Study of Mothers and Doctors*, Dublin: Health Promotion Unit, Eastern Health Board.

McKeowan, K. and B. McGrath (1996), *Accommodating Travelling People*, Ireland: Crosscare.

McLaughlin, J. (1994), *Travellers and Ireland: Whose Country, Whose History?* Cork: Cork University Press.

Molloy, S. (1998), *Accommodating Nomadism*, Northern Ireland: Traveller Movement Northern Ireland.

Ni Shuinear, S. (1994), "Irish Travellers, Ethnicity and the Origins Question", in M. McCann, S. O Síochâin and J. Ruane (eds.), *Culture and Ethnicity* (pp. 36–78), Belfast: The Institute of Irish Studies, The Queen's University of Belfast.

Noonan, P. (1994), *Travelling People in West Belfast*, London: Save the Children Fund.

Northside Travellers Support Group (1994), *A Case Study of Travellers' Health and Accommodation Status in the Coolock Area*, Dublin: Northside Travellers Support Group.

O'Nuallain, S. and M. Forde (1992), *Changing Needs of Irish Travellers: Health, Education and Social Issues*, Galway: Woodlands Centre.

Pahl, J. and M. Vaile (1986), *Health and Healthcare among Travellers*, University of Kent: Health Services Research Unit.

Pavee Point (1995). Primary Health Care for Travellers Project. Dublin: Pavee Point and Eastern Health Board.

Pavee Point (1998a), "Traveller Culture Factsheet" (Online), Available: http://ireland.iol.ie/~pavee/firish.htm

Pavee Point (1998b), "Traveller Economy Factsheet" (On-line), Available: http://ireland.iol.ie/~pavee/fsecon.htm

Quinlan, C. (1998), "Travellers in Blanchardstown: A Second Look", A Report Commissioned by the Blanchardstown Traveller Support Group.

Rottman, D., A. Tussing and M. Wiley (1986), *The Population Structure and Living Circumstances of Irish Travellers: Results form the 1981 Census of Traveller*, Dublin: The Economic and Social Research Institute.

Senior, P. and R. Bhopal (1994), "Ethnicity as a Variable in Epidemiological Research", *British Medical Journal*, Vol. 309, pp. 327–30.

Shorter, E. (1994), *From the Mind into the Body: The Cultural Origins of Psychosomatic Symptoms*, New York: The Free Press.

Smith, P. and M. Bond (1993), *Social Psychology across Cultures: Analysis and Perspective*, London: Harvester Wheatsheaf.

Webb, E. (1996), "Meeting the Needs of Minority Ethnic Communities", *Archives of Disease in Childhood*, Vol. 74, pp. 264–267.

Weber, A. (1992), *Social Psychology*, New York: Harper Perennial.

CHAPTER SIX

THE MINORITY EXPERIENCE: AN INTERNATIONAL COMMENTARY

Adrian Furnham

As a nation, are we like (a) All other nations; (b) Some other nations; (c) No other nations? Is the experience of minorities in Ireland fundamentally different from elsewhere or are the psychological processes much the same?

All countries are unique for different reasons, but Ireland is probably the only West European country to have a long and well-researched history of emigration and comparatively little immigration. Ireland became independent after the European and nineteenth-century fashion for empires and so never had the reverse flow of colonial peoples found over nearly every major European country. Further, Ireland's spectacular economic growth has also been recent.

Hence, there is, probably for the first time, migration of racially distinct people into the island of Ireland. This provides research scientists with an excellent and unique opportunity to study reactions to migrations on the part of both the migrants and natives.

There is now a rich literature on the psychology of intercultural contact, particularly on the outcomes of contact which include assimilation, segregation and integration. Psychologists have looked at issues such as culture learning as well as stress, coping and adjustment with the whole migration process. More recent work has looked at social identification and multicultural ideology. Perhaps more importantly, research has focused on training techniques for crossing cultures and the skills of multicultural living.

Culture shock (see glossary) has affective, behavioural and cognitive consequences. The emotional consequences are important, particularly for mental health, long-term coping and adaptation. Behaviourally, both migrants and host nations need to acquire specific skills to communicate with people of very different backgrounds. Cognitively, both host nationals and migrants have to develop cognitive processes involved in developing, changing and maintaining identity.

Casey and O'Connell, in Chapter Two, reported on a self-report study on over 100 ethnic minority Irish immigrants. Over half reported racist insults and a sixth threats of physical violence. Naturally, more recent immigrants reported a higher incidence of racial abuse. About a third felt discriminated against in social situations and dealing with professionals and there were noticeably different beliefs in different racial groups, the black sample reporting most abuse. The mental health of the black group was also the worst. Indeed, nearly 50 per cent of the group sampled put them in the category of "psychiatric cases". Also, as predicted, the more racism a person had experienced, the higher their psychological distress.

This study provides a starting point for assessing the consequences of culture shock. Hopefully, later studies can build on these findings by examining larger samples and dealing with other factors of interest such as demographic and health differences (education, social economic status, language), as these can have a considerable effect on coping with migration. The issue of causality also needs to be investigated further. Does mental illness lead to racial prejudice or result from it? A convincing case could be made for either argument.

In the third chapter, Horgan used Berry's acculturation model to examine perceived discrimination on acculturation levels and the effects of both on psychological well-being. She compared two groups — 33 refugees and asylum-seekers and 39 foreign students. She found that refugees experience more of the discriminatory attacks possibly because it is believed that they are deliberately taking advantage of the government social welfare system. Indeed, a third of the refugees' acculturation level was, in

Berry's terminology, the separation model. Many of the fairly straightforward hypotheses were confirmed. Horgan is appropriately self-critical: her very small groups were not very homogeneous and she did not (or could not) measure a whole range of other possibly salient variables that may have a direct impact on adjustment.

In Chapter Four, Corcoran looks not at migrants but at local authority residents, who she describes as an invisible minority. These are social housing tenants who are poor, spatially segregated and socially stigmatised. It was not an anthropological study, but using qualitative methodology, it attempted to understand the perceptions and problems of a particular group. The theme of social support and social inclusion is very strong. Certainly what this chapter illustrates is the extent to which the problems of refugees and migrants are almost identical to those of the urban poor. The feelings of exclusion and the processes that prevent it are almost exactly the same.

Chapter Five, with four co-authors, turns to examining Irish Travellers, a very small group but one which has suffered persecution in nearly every European country. Whilst Irish Travellers seem genetically different from their European cousins, their lifestyle seems the same. The study is unique in that it focused on health and particularly the health of Traveller mothers. The researchers mixed standard measures of minor psychiatric morbidity with other measures.

The "Traveller group psychology", like other social support networks, seems to be the key to health. What is particularly interesting is the way Traveller views or "mindset" has remained the same while their lifestyle has changed so drastically. Many live sedentary lives in social housing and their mental health and quality of life is poor.

There are both theoretical and methodology implications of the five chapters in this section. The first is that, despite the dramatic differences between asylum-seekers, migrants, refugees, foreign students, Travellers and local authority residents, they appeared to have much in common. Their mental and physical health suffered as a consequence of their economic and social circumstances. Their personal and collective self-esteem are continually threatened by the attitudes and behaviours of the majority community. Equally, the best predictors of their adjustment and health seemed to be the quality and quantity of their support network. These findings closely coincide with those in other countries and clearly have implications for social policy and practice in Ireland.

The five chapters in this section of the book relied heavily on self-report methodology. The limitations of interviews and questionnaires are well known but nevertheless important. There are good reasons why some groups may quite deliberately over- or under-report their problems. Further, it is not always certain the extent to which questionnaire measures validated in one culture are appropriate in another. Ideally, self-report data can be backed up by behavioural and observational data. More importantly, these studies were all cross-sectional rather than longitudinal. This makes it very difficult to understand causality. Future research should undertake large longitudinal studies, which, although very expensive, have the potential to address many of the complexities and questions identified in the above five chapters.

To conclude on an optimistic note, we should also remember that the experience of being an outsider can also have its benefits. One cannot be categorised and predicted as easily as members of the majority. One also has the option of being bicultural, being able to move between different cultures with greater ease.

Part Two

The Majority Experience

CHAPTER SEVEN

TALKING ABOUT THE OTHER: A VIEW OF HOW SECONDARY SCHOOL PUPILS CONSTRUCT OPINIONS ABOUT REFUGEES AND ASYLUM-SEEKERS

Anna Keogh

> Every version of an "other", wherever found, is also the construction of the "self" . . . (James Clifford, 1986)

This article is based on research conducted with transition year pupils (of about 16 years of age) in four secondary schools between April and May 1999.[1] The aim of this research was not only to locate what the pupils' attitudes to refugees and asylum-seekers are, but also to explore why they have these attitudes, what knowledge they use to construct these attitudes, and from what sources they get this knowledge. The research also attempted to locate the "Irishness" of these attitudes — that is, whether and in what ways the pupils' ideas are specifically Irish.

The pluralist ideal promotes a society in which everyone, regardless of race, ethnicity, nationality or religion, is able to choose their own way of living and for it to be respected. One of the most important factors involved in achieving a pluralist society is mutual tolerance and respect of the "other". However, this is easier said than done because it is not so easy to tolerate another person's

---

[1] A copy of this dissertation is available from the Department of Sociology, Trinity College Dublin. It provides a full analysis of the research data.

way of life when, as far as you are concerned, it interferes with your own lifestyle and habits. Something that is intrinsic to tolerance is understanding. Understanding another person's ethnicity, their way of life and culture, can often be very difficult because it seems so foreign to our own and in many cases it completely conflicts with our own. Before we can attempt to understand the "other" and thus tolerate difference, we must first understand how our own culture colours the way we perceive the world. We must understand our own ethnicity.

Joshua Fishman describes ethnicity as the "sense and the expression of collective, intergenerational cultural continuity" (1997: 330). It is the feeling of "belongingness". It is "being", "doing" and "knowing" (1996: 63). "Being" is the sense of feeling of physical continuation from generation to generation. "Doing" is the expressive obligations such as songs, sayings and jokes. "Knowing" is the feeling of "being in the know" — the understanding of something without having to explain it, the common sense. Refugees and members of other ethnicities living in Ireland "be", "do" and "know" differently to the Irish. In this way, I argue that they pose a challenge to "Irishness" and to Irish cultural continuity. We know that we are different to "others" and we can sometimes pinpoint these differences, but they will never be reconciled unless we can locate these differences and understand how we "be", "do" and "know". As Franz Boas once stated:

> . . . how do we understand the shackles that tradition has placed upon us? For if we can recognise them, we are also able to break them.[2]

Rather than trying to understand the "other", the research aimed to achieve an understanding of why we — the dominant majority — have certain attitudes about the "other". It aimed to locate the knowledge which is used to construct these (mis)understandings of the "other". At the roots of all opinions, there is a certain knowledge that is used to construct these opinions. What the pupils think about refugees and asylum-seekers is not just constructed by what they know, but also by representational experience. What the pu-

---

[2] As quoted by Norman Fairclough, 1989.

pils express is not just "fact"; it is "facts" and their own particular perspectives conditioned by their own realities. In other words, the pupils' attitudes are a reflection of their ideologies.[3]

The task is then to try and locate these ideologies. The method that was used in attempting to do this was discourse analysis. One of the most natural actions that people do is talk. Speech and language are physical functions and Fishman claims that they are related to the "being" dimension of ethnicity. Language is the prime form of communication. Therefore a detailed analysis of language use can provide key information about ethnic beliefs and ideology. An important thing to consider though is that language is neither passive nor transparent; it is active and creative. As Roger Fowler states: "Language is a reality-creating process" (1985: 62). Users of language are also active and creative. The pupils too were actively processing information and persuasively conveying their interpretations and representations to others. That is why discourse is so important. Norman Fairclough argues that discourse is based on common sense. Common sense itself is "naturalised ideology"; the shared knowledge that is accepted and taken for granted (1989: 107).

If we can locate these common-sense assumptions, we can get a much deeper insight into Irish ethnicity. It can also help us to understand why the Irish ethnic majority has certain attitudes about minority ethnic groups. If we can locate the roots of these assumptions, we can attempt to reconstruct them. In this way we can cultivate pluralism — we can develop and prune it.

Overview of Fieldwork

Attitudes to refugees and asylum-seekers, in particular, were chosen as a research topic, as refugees are often made the scapegoats for the "influx of foreigners into Ireland" — especially as they are here to seek asylum as opposed to "giving" to the community (this does not imply that they cannot give as well). Whereas tourists or sojourners are representatives of Ireland's new position in the global economy, refugees and asylum-seekers are representatives

---

[3] Fairclough (1989) gives a very good account of how knowledge and ideology intersect.

of our responsibilities of joining the global economy — responsibilities that we are not sure we want. It is also the refugee community that is thought to represent the most "different" kind of foreigner. In many cases they are more obviously ethnically and culturally different (considering most of the asylum-seekers in Ireland are from African nations).

Ideally, the best way to gather information on how people truly feel about something is by catching extracts of ordinary everyday conversation. However, this is very difficult because the very nature of research is constructed. Even being asked questions makes one think about the answer more carefully, and one is given time to formulate an acceptable answer. So to try and overcome some of these shortcomings, I constructed an environment to foster discussion, and discourse analysis as a methodology was chosen, which was mainly influenced by the work of Teun A. Van Dijk on discourse analysis, language and ethnicity (especially 1985; 1987; 1997a; 1997b).

Discourse analysis is a qualitative method that focuses on language itself, and especially the natural use of language (Van Dijk, 1997b). It is a way of getting to the root of a notion because it concentrates on extracts of natural action, which is basic communication. Throughout the research, attempts were made to dilute the subject/researcher dynamic, and the researcher actually participated and interacted in the research also, as an attempt to create a more natural balanced environment. In this sense, discourse analysis is especially suitable, as it attempts to meet the respondents where they are at, allowing them to articulate their genuine views, as opposed to limiting the boundaries of their discussion. This means that the whole process is based on listening and allowing the participants to say what they wish, putting the power back in their hands. Speech is something we do quite naturally, and our choice of words is often unconscious. By actually analysing the discourse surrounding an issue, a lot can be learned about people's attitudes to that issue. Interviews are constructed, surveys are limited, but discourse analysis is about simply listening to what people say and how they say it.

Doing research in schools had many advantages. It allowed a particular group in Irish society to be targeted — that is, secondary school pupils of about 16 years of age. It provided the researcher with a group of people who were comfortable with being in a group environment and therefore were, so to speak, as much of a "natural gang" as could be expected in a constructed environment. Also, all the pupils would be of similar age and social positioning. Doing the research in schools also allowed the monitoring of two very important factors: those of gender and class.

Schools in Dublin city centre were chosen, as it was felt that all the pupils would have had some contact with refugees. Two fee-paying and two non-fee-paying schools were picked, which loosely breaks the schools into class. There was one girls' school and one boys' school in each of the two class groups.

In each of the four schools, an 80-minute workshop was carried out. The aim of the workshop was to encourage the pupils to discuss particular issues as a group. It aimed to create a space for the pupils to express their views freely. This idea of creating a space was influenced by Cynthia Cockburn (1998). In her book *The Space Between Us: Negotiating Gender and National Identities in Conflict,* she talks about how women in three troubled areas in the world (Northern Ireland, Bosnia-Herzegovina and Israel/Palestine) set up groups to meet and to discuss national and women's issues. These groups are a safe space for the women to meet and express themselves. The workshop format, where the students do most of the talking and do it amongst themselves, aimed to create this kind of space. For the same reason, the researcher (who was a stranger but who also had not established any definite power relationships with the pupils) facilitated the workshops. This was done rather than observing a teacher, who the pupils already know and relate to in a distinctive way, initiate and facilitate a discussion. The presence of a teacher would have altered the space that the researcher intended to create because the pupils would be on their best behaviour and so possibly would not express what they really wanted to say. The main activity of the researcher in the workshop was to keep the pupils talking, to encourage them to feel that they could say what they wanted and to allow the conversation to go in its own direction. The point was made that the researcher was not there to lecture or to condemn the pupils' views, although their views would be challenged.

The workshop was divided into two main parts. The first part was designed to draw as much from the pupils as possible and to locate the issues that are most important to them, *without* having had any input from the researcher at all. Firstly, they were asked to write down three or more words that they associated with the word "refugee". Then the same was done with the word "asylum-seeker". Then the sheets were collected and the whole group did some brainstorming.

The second part was designed to encourage discussion. Controversial newspaper headlines were put on an overhead projector. The headlines were chosen for their relevance to the particular issue that was being discussed. For example, if someone mentioned social welfare, a headline that was concerned with social welfare was put up on the projector. There were a total of 22 headlines and quotes from newspaper articles. All the discussions were recorded on tapes and were then transcribed using basic transcription methods such as those described by Fairclough (1995) and Potter and Wetherell (1987).

KNOWLEDGE

The pupils base their knowledge on what they see on the television and from newspapers, but especially on radio. Pupils in all schools referred to Chris Barry and Adrian Kennedy's late-night radio talk shows, which often have public discussions on issues such as the refugee situation. Another source of knowledge is obviously the education system. Pupils in the fee-paying schools drew on historical facts to support their views. They said things like "we did this in class". Pupils in all schools also supported their views by "people say" and "people think". Of course, it is impossible to know who these "people" are that they are referring to — perhaps family and friends or media personalities.

Firstly, I would just like to summarise some of the specific beliefs associated with refugees and asylum-seekers, which the pupils use to construct their attitudes towards them. The first significant point is that there is a correlation between "asylum" and "insane". The only school that did not mention the words "insane", "crazy" or "mental" in their discussion or in their word-lists was the non-fee-paying girls' school. The first thing that occurred to me was that the pupils associated "asylum-seeker" with "seeking an asylum". However, only one boy volunteered why he wrote down "crazy" and this was because when refugees come to Ireland they don't have anything to do and they "freak out". This example shows how important the use of language is in constructing attitudes and opinions. "Asylum-seeker" itself, as a term, formulates a negative concept. Here is an example of how language itself can be a reality-creating process. The use of the term "asylum-seeker" brings to mind concepts of insanity.

An important factor that influences the pupils' attitudes is the fact that they find it hard to understand why people become refugees in the first place. There were constant questions about why somebody would become a refugee and also about what the difference is between refugees and asylum-seekers. One of the reasons why they find this hard to comprehend is because Ireland is relatively economically and politically stable. They cannot understand why someone would have to leave their country because of economic or political reasons. They also find it difficult to reconcile what they see on the television about refugees — for example, East Timor or the Kosovan crisis — with what they see on the streets of Dublin. They see Romanian gypsies begging and selling *The Big Issue*. They see many Africans who are well dressed and have mobile phones.

There is a belief that refugees somehow have a choice to leave their country. The pupils are more aware of the "pull" factors into Ireland than the "push" factors from their countries of origin. The pull factors include the welfare system, the labour shortage and the "Celtic Tiger". There is general consensus that refugees are poor, which supports the view that they "choose" to come to Ireland because of the "booming economy". As they find it difficult to understand why one would have to leave a country for political reasons, they assume that it must be due to deviant behaviour or crime. The boys in particular refer to refugees as being "kicked out", "on the run", in "exile" or that one becomes a refugee because of "something you did in the past". Deviance is confirmed by the fact that some refugees seem to be deviant when they are here. For example, some asylum-seekers have no identification, they seem to be working even though they were not permitted (at the time of the workshops, asylum-seekers were not permitted to work), and also that they are being "smuggled in". Also, because the pupils assume that refugees are poor, but then appear to be wealthy (because some are seen wearing labelled clothes and carrying mobile phones and pagers), they make an assumption that refugees must be abusing the welfare system or be involved in criminal activity here.

Beliefs about Multiculturalism and "Irishness"

The way one assumes a multicultural society to be has to do with how one perceives it to be. Boys in both schools talked about how America and England, as multicultural societies, don't have a "culture". More importantly that is what they fear will happen here — that Ireland will lose its culture. As one boy put it:[4]

> *P*: And that's like a good example of what will happen, like in America like, they don't really have a culture. . . . You're all gonna bring your identity with you, like there's too many of all different races in a country, you run the risk of losing it like.

This boy has a sense of feeling that if members of other ethnic groups come into the country, Ireland will run the risk of losing its identity. This suggests that he sees culture and identity as static and essential entities, which can be diluted, as opposed to adaptive and dynamic. He also seems to confuse culture and race, which highlights how conceptually inflated both these terms have become. Pupils in all the schools talked about "multiracial races", "racial cultures" and the "Irish race".

Another interesting discussion ensued when I commented to the fee-paying girls that some people argue that multiculturalism can be dangerous. To this they responded:

> *P1*: Yeah, it's anything that's not Irish
>
> *P2*: People think it's all American
>
> *P3*: Yeah, and gangs
>
> *P4*: Black

---

[4] "P" here stands for pupil.

Where did the girls get this idea from — that multiculturalism is "all American" and that it means "gangs"? One explanation could be from American television and cinema, particularly less recent productions, which often depict ethnic groups negatively through street gangs and ghettos.

One thing that all the pupils talked about was whether or not refugees will stay. At least one pupil in each school asked if the refugees would go back at some point. None of the pupils explained why they were antagonistic to the idea that refugees may actually stay. They seemed to fear a permanent change. However, clues as to why this should be came out through other sections of the discussion.

One of the newspaper headlines that was used was: "Now that we've finally got something to share with others we don't want to". Pupils from both the fee-paying girls' school and the non-fee-paying boys' school asked, "What do we have to share?" Another fee-paying girl felt that now because the Irish economy is so good, "everyone wants a bit". Also the non-fee-paying girls felt that Ireland was still not economically stable enough yet to support other groups. One pupil commented on how there are still many Irish people without jobs. All this implies that the pupils do not think that Ireland can actually afford to take in refugees, that we are still not economically stable enough.

Another interesting opinion that was displayed in all the workshops was the idea that refugees pose a threat to our space. The pupils queried where we would put refugees if a lot of them came to Ireland. There was discussion about "Dublin getting too packed" and that it would be a good idea to move refugees out into the countryside so as "not to spread the city". One of the fee-paying girls asked, "will we be able to handle it" when refugees start having babies and the population goes up. This also suggests a feeling of lack of control over minority ethnic groups perpetuating themselves.

Realistically, Ireland would need to have a huge increase in population before we would need to worry about over-population. In the workshops, a comparison was drawn with the Netherlands, which is much smaller than Ireland and has a population of 14 million, to see how the pupils would react. The Netherlands also takes in around 20,000–40,000 asylum-seekers a year. The pupils were generally really shocked, and one non-fee-paying boy asked, "Where do they put them?"

There was not very much discussion on cultural difference. A few pupils commented that refugees are dirty or that they shout. Interestingly, none of the pupils mentioned anything about religious difference. When I asked them about it, it did not seem to pose any threat at all. Perhaps this lack of awareness of cultural difference is because the only substantial minority ethnic group in Ireland, which poses a definite challenge to our own cultural habits, is the Traveller Community.

How the Irish Experienced the "Other" in the Past

Something that I found very helpful, in understanding why the pupils feel that refugees are posing a threat to our space and our resources, was the way in which they talked about our relationship with the "other" in the past. The Irish have dealt with outsiders mainly in three ways — as a colonised country, as emigrants or as benefactors (as a traditionally charitable country). It was evident by what the pupils said that these experiences influenced how they think.

There was not any discussion as such on Ireland as a colonised country, although the references to England were rather negative: "OK, don't get onto the English thing!"; "England robbed everyone! England robbed everyone!" Colonialism had taken our resources, our space (and land) and our independence. There is perhaps a fear that the "other" will do this again.

Ireland has also been a very charitable country. Traditionally, we have given money out to "others", mainly through missionary organisations which themselves played a major part in colonisation. This very action makes us active and the "other" passive. It gives the impression that the "others" are unable to provide for themselves. If these "others" are now coming into Ireland, they will continue to take from us. We are no longer the ones in control of how much we give *out*, rather the "other" is coming *in*. When charity is given to others far away, one is distanced from the injustices of poverty or war. The act of giving makes the donor feel some way superior, which assumes that the receiver is somehow inferior. When these others come into "our territory", they challenge the supposed superiority of the donors.

Ireland has traditionally been a country of emigration. The comparison is often drawn between refugees and the Irish during and after the Famine. The main objection that the pupils had to this was that when the Irish went to America, "we worked" and "we helped build that country"; "we were shipped over like slaves" but "we found a way". Even though we were not treated well, we provided for ourselves. Many asylum-seekers are not working (because they are not permitted), but are also receiving social welfare. There is very little awareness about the fact that immigrants may actually help build Ireland too. They are seen as only "here to abuse the system".

In one way, there is an image of the "other" as being passive, not self-sufficient. At the same time, the "other" is perceived as active, something that takes our resources and hinders our independent progression. It takes control of our territory, both geographically and socially. It threatens our identity.

PREJUDICE

All the pupils talked about prejudice, but they put the blame for it on other members of society. These other members are prejudiced because "they don't know better", or "they don't have that information". One of the fee-paying girls talked about how the pupils in her school were privileged because they receive a good education and that other people only know what their parents tell them. This in turn suggests that she blames the uneducated for prejudice. One of the non-fee-paying girls suggested that most people do not even realise they are being prejudiced. This transports the responsibility of prejudice to other members of society. Another of the girls in the fee-paying school also talked about how prejudice is "passed on from generation to generation".

Another girl commented on why she thinks that refugees are often treated badly.

> *P*: Very few people will want to be nice to them because they're afraid that they'll like it and want to stay.

Again, there is the fear that refugees might want to stay. It also occurred to me that by making refugees out to be deviant or threatening, prejudice towards them appears justified because it can be argued that they are hurting us.

It is also interesting to note that the non-fee-paying boys' school (the school that had done the most work on refugee issues before the research was carried out) showed the most negative attitudes. I suggest two possible reasons for this. One is that the pupils are rebelling against authority, or more specifically, authoritarianism — they are rebelling against what they are being told to accept. On the other hand, the boys perceive refugees to be predominantly male working class, and the working class boys thus perceive them to be a real economic threat.

Conclusion

James Clifford (1986) points out that "every version of an 'other' . . . is also the construction of a 'self'". Attitudes towards refugees say a lot about attitudes to the self. Through discussion of the "other', the self is mobilised and organised and the boundaries separating us from the other are relocated and maintained. Discussing the "other" makes us active and "them" passive. In this way, the workshops may have had more of a negative than positive effect. By offering the pupils the chance to discuss and debate the issues, they may have reaffirmed their negative beliefs as opposed to challenging them.

As Roger Fowler (1985) argues, language is not an innocent medium that reflects inequality, but a practice that may actually contribute to inequality. It is not enough to just discuss refugee and minority issues and prejudice. The way that we actually do it is very important, as we can do more damage than good. Discussing the "other" empowers us and disempowers "them", thus creating for them a certain reality. Those who are trying to combat negative attitudes have themselves to be tolerant of other cultures and to understand the complexity of the issues involved.

By becoming aware of how discourse determines and reproduces social structure, how it both contains and expresses ideology, we can attempt to identify and direct how language creates the reality of the "other".

RECOMMENDATIONS

Through this research I have tried to locate some of the roots to secondary school pupils' attitudes to refugees and asylum-seekers. However, I have been left with more questions than when I began. The roots of the knowledge, which the pupils use to construct their attitudes, lie deep in the way they have constructed Irish identity and ethnicity in their minds. The source of much of this knowledge is in the education system and in the media. Therefore, an in-depth review of the education curriculum and of how the media constructs Irish identity would also reveal a lot of information about the source of these attitudes and beliefs.

There is also a need for research on how anti-racism strategies in Ireland have worked over a long period of time, and there needs to be constant research on creating better anti-racist strategies, with special regard to the language that is used in the writing of these. Tolerance for cultural difference needs to be taught at a young age, while children are still discovering their own cultural identity. The state must also take responsibility for the changing society and not ignore it. Proper policies promoting equality and discouraging racism must be implemented.

Acknowledgements

I would like to express my thanks to Brian Torode, Tony Jarvis, Sarah Gahan and Clare MacCumhaill for their helpful comments and suggestions at various stages in the writing of this article.

References

Bhavnani, Kum-Kum (1991), "What's Power Got To Do With It? Empowerment and Social Research" in Ian Parker and John Shotter (eds.), *Deconstructing Social Psychology*, London: Routledge.

Clifford, James (1986), "Introduction: Partial Truths" in James Clifford and George Marcus (eds.) *Writing Culture: The Poetics and Politics of Ethnography*, Berkeley: University of California Press.

Cockburn, Cynthia (1998), *The Space between Us: Negotiating Gender and National Identities in Conflict*, London and New York: Zed Books.

Coupland, Nikolas and Adam Jaworski (eds.) (1997), *Sociolinguistics: A Reader and a Coursebook*, Oxford: Blackwell.

Fairclough, Norman (1995), *Critical Discourse Analysis: The Critical Study of Language*, New York and London: Longman.

Fairclough, Norman (1989), *Language and Power*, London and New York: Longman.

Fishman, Joshua (1996), "Ethnicity as Being, Doing and Knowing" in John Hutchinson and Anthony D. Smith (eds.), *Ethnicity*, Oxford University Press.

Fishman, Joshua (1997), "Language, Ethnicity and Racism" in Nikolas Coupland and Adam Jaworski (eds.) *Sociolinguistics: A Reader and Coursebook*, Oxford: Blackwell.

Fowler, Roger (1985), "Power" in Teun A. Van Dijk (ed.) *Handbook of Discourse Analysis, Vol. 4: Discourse Analysis in Society*, London: Academic Press.

Potter, Jonathan and Margaret Wetherell (1987), "How to Analyse Discourse" in *Discourse and Social Psychology: Beyond Attitudes and Behaviour*, London: Sage.

Tabouret-Keller, Andrée (1997), "Language and Identity" in Florian Coulmas (ed.), *The Handbook of Sociolinguistics*, Oxford: Blackwell.

Van Dijk, Teun A. (ed.) (1985), *Handbook of Discourse Analysis, Vol. 4: Discourse Analysis in Society*, London: Academic Press.

Van Dijk, Teun A. (1987), *Communicating Racism: Ethnic Prejudice in Thought and Talk*, Newbury Park, London: Sage.

Van Dijk, Teun A. (ed.) (1997a), *Discourse as Structures and Processes*, London: Sage.

Van Dijk, Teun A. (ed.) (1997b), *Discourse as Social Interaction*, London: Sage.

Van Dijk, Teun A., Stella Ting-Toomey, Geneva Smitherman and Denise Troutman (1997d), "Discourse, Ethnicity, Culture and Racism" in Teun A. Van Dijk (ed.), *Discourse as Structures and Processes*, London: Sage.

CHAPTER EIGHT

". . . SHE NEVER LET THEM IN": POPULAR REACTION TO REFUGEES ARRIVING IN DUBLIN

Philip Curry

"Mr Deasy halted, breathing hard and swallowing his breath.

— I just wanted to say, he said. Ireland, they say, has the honour of being the only country which never persecuted the Jews. Do you know that? No. And do you know why?

He frowned sternly on the bright air.

— Why, sir? Stephen asked, beginning to smile.

— Because she never let them in, Mr Deasy said solemnly."

— James Joyce, *Ulysses*

The mid-1990s witnessed a substantial increase in the number of people applying for asylum in the Republic of Ireland. Previous to this Ireland had been one of the most racially homogeneous countries in Europe. There had in the past been numbers of refugees allowed into the country but usually on a very limited basis and as part of an organised programme. However, 1994 saw a sharp increase in the number of people making their own way to Ireland and applying directly for refugee status. Figure 8.1 shows how this number continued to increase dramatically after 1994.

Figure 8.1: Applications for Asylum in the Republic of Ireland, 1991–1997

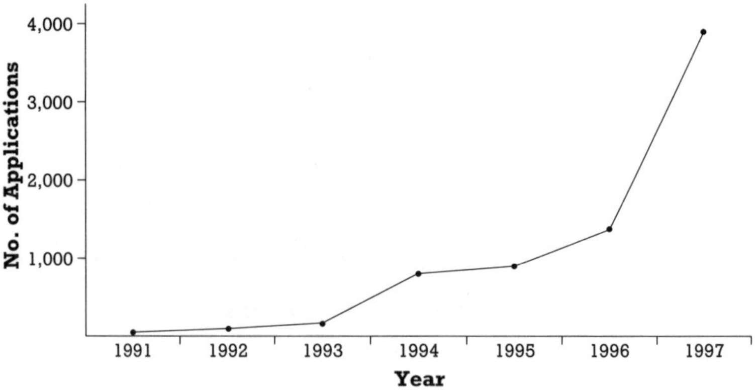

In 1995, the principal countries of origin of these asylum-seekers were Romania, Algeria, Somalia and Zaire (Irish Refugee Council, 1995).

Although overall the number of refugees in Ireland remained relatively small (0.1 per cent of the total population, representing only 0.4 per cent of the asylum-seekers in the EU) media reaction was intense. Philip Watt, co-ordinator of the European Year Against Racism in Ireland, claimed that the media misrepresented the refugee situation in three important ways:

1. By regularly suggesting that Ireland was experiencing a flood of refugees.
2. By associating refugees with begging, petty theft and crime.
3. By frequently repeating the claim that many asylum-seekers, especially the largest group, Romanians, were bogus, only coming to Ireland to exploit its social welfare system (Watt, 1997).

Such media coverage and a number of minor racist attacks raised fears in many sectors that prejudice toward newly arrived refugees could develop into a serious problem.

This chapter describes the results of a survey carried out in Dublin inner city to examine the extent and basis of hostility to recently arrived refugees. Two such groups were examined in particular, Bosnians and Romanians. In 1997, there were 761 Bosnians living in Ireland, most of whom came here as part of organised programmes during the war of 1992 to 1995. Romanians are the largest group that has come to Ireland in recent years without being part of any organised refugee programme. Although there are many reasons for their seeking asylum here, they have generally been represented in the media as being purely economic refugees (Keating, 1997). The reason for comparing these two particular groups was to determine if the local population was distinguishing between programme refugees and groups who had arrived here directly. The study also sought to determine which sections of the community are most hostile to refugees and how this hostility relates to holding negative stereotypical beliefs about asylum-seekers.

SURVEY OF ATTITUDES TO REFUGEES ARRIVING IN DUBLIN — SUMMER 1998

The Questionnaire

A postal questionnaire was administered to a large random sample of the Dublin population according to procedures developed by Dillman (1978) which improve response rates and sample representativeness. The questionnaire asked the subject to provide some basic demographic information, to complete a social distance scale and to indicate their level of agreement with various belief statements regarding refugees.

The demographic items elicited the person's gender, age group, present occupation, household weekly income, education and newspaper preference. The measure of hostility towards refugees used was based on the concept of social distance (Borgardus, 1933). This is a particularly useful conceptualisation of prejudice, which directly addresses the "action tendency" of hostile intergroup attitudes. Social distance is the degree of intimacy to which a person is willing to admit a member of any particular social group. MacGréil (1977, 1996) has used a version of the Borgardus social distance scale widely in Ireland. This is based on the following seven items:

1. Would marry or welcome into my family
2. Would have as a close friend
3. Would have as a next door neighbour
4. Would work in the same workplace
5. Would welcome as an Irish citizen
6. Would only allow as visitors to Ireland
7. Would deport or debar from Ireland.

The subject is asked if they would agree "yes" or "no" to each of these items if it was applied to a particular target group. This scale was formatted for postal use. Each social distance item was presented in a separate box with the list of target groups underneath and the subject was asked to tick those groups they would agree to apply the item to. The target groups used were Spaniards, Bosnians, Travellers, Arabs, Romanians and Africans. For the purpose of analysis, an aggregate social distance score could be calculated based on the first five social distance items.

Finally the subjects were asked to rate the extent to which they agreed or disagreed with seven positive and negative belief statements about refugees on a 5-point scale.

The Sample

Eight hundred people in all were asked to complete the questionnaire. These were drawn randomly from the 1997 electoral register for the Dublin area. Of these, 419 completed questionnaires were returned. Of the initial 800, 15 people were accounted for as unable to respond for non-study relevant reasons. This gave an overall return rate of 53.4 per cent. This group was made up of 196 women and 209 men. There was generally an even distribution of replies across age group except for a greater tendency for people between the ages of 26 and 35 to respond. As can be seen from Figure 8.2, there was a wide distribution of educational levels among the respondents, with the most common response being primary level. This is unusual, as low education groups are generally considered to be the least likely to respond to a postal questionnaire. Although this is a bias in the sample, low education and income groups are of special interest, as most refugees arriving in Ireland will most likely be housed in low-income communities.

Figure 8.2: Highest Level of Education Attained by Subjects

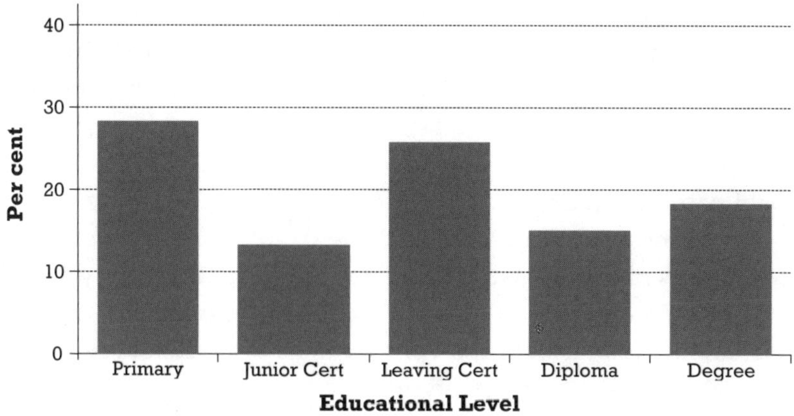

Many of the subjects reported their occupation as professional but there were also large numbers of housewives, retired and manual workers.

Results of Survey

On average, the group which was perceived to be the farthest from the individual was Travellers, with Spaniards being the closest. The mean scores for these groups on a scale of 0 to 5 are shown in Table 8.1.

Table 8.1: Average Social Distance Scores for the Six Social Groups

Spaniards	1.27
Africans	2.10
Bosnians	2.29
Romanians	2.39
Arabs	2.58
Travellers	2.75

For the least distant group, Spaniards, hostility was still quite high. Over 26.8 per cent said that they would not marry a Spaniard or have one marry into their family, while 9.3 per cent said that they should be deported. The results for Bosnians and Romanians are almost identical, with only a slight trend for people to express more distance towards Romanians. The social distance scores for the two groups were highly correlated ($r = .85$, $p < .0001$) suggesting that people respond to both groups similarly. Figures 8.3 and 8.4 present the social distance profiles for the two groups. On both of these graphs, higher levels of agreement indicate greater hostility on that item.

As can be seen from both of these graphs, granting citizenship to refugees is problematic, while people seem less likely to object to working alongside a refugee. Objections to marriage into family and having as a friend are very strong for both refugee groups, over 50 per cent of respondents refusing to both. From the two graphs, it appears that people respond to Bosnians and Romanians similarly.

Figure 8.3: Percentage Agreement with Social Distance Items for Bosnians

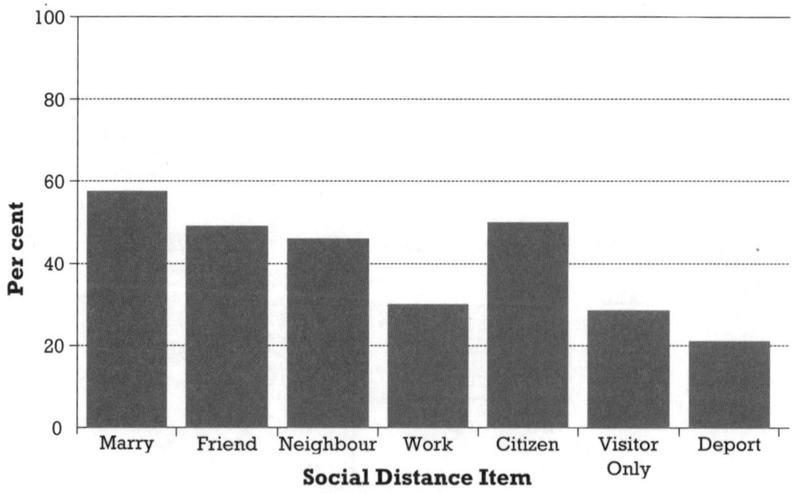

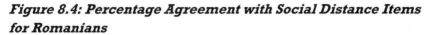

Figure 8.4: Percentage Agreement with Social Distance Items for Romanians

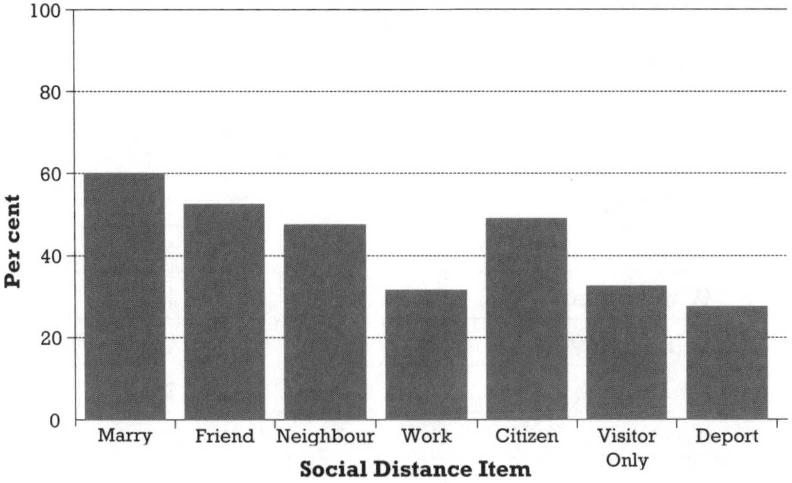

The survey allowed us to examine the way in which different social groups responded to refugees. There was a slight trend for women to show less social distance toward refugee groups than men, but the difference was not significant. There was however a consistent trend for social distance toward refugees to increase with increasing age (Romanians: $F = 5.37$, $df = 5$, $p < .0001$; Bosnians: $F = 6.82$, $df = 5$, $p < .0001$). The analysis presented a consistent picture of those over 55 being significantly more prejudiced than younger groups. The social distance scores for both refugee groups by occupation are presented in Table 8.2. These differences in social distance for different occupational groups were significant (Romanians: $F = 8.9$, $df = 8$, $p < .001$; Bosnians: $F = 9.2$, $df = 8$, $p < .001$). There was a linear decrease in social distance towards both refugee groups with increasing level of education, as can be seen from Figure 8.5.

Table 8.2: Social Distance to Romanians and Bosnians by Occupational Group

	Romanians	Bosnians
Housewife	3.6	3.4
Manual	2.5	2.5
Retired	3.2	3.1
Professional	1.1	1.0
Student	1.6	1.3
White Collar	1.9	1.8
Self Employed	1.9	1.8
Unemployed	2.7	2.6
Service	2.3	2.1

Figure 8.5: Increasing Education and Decreasing Social Distance to Refugees

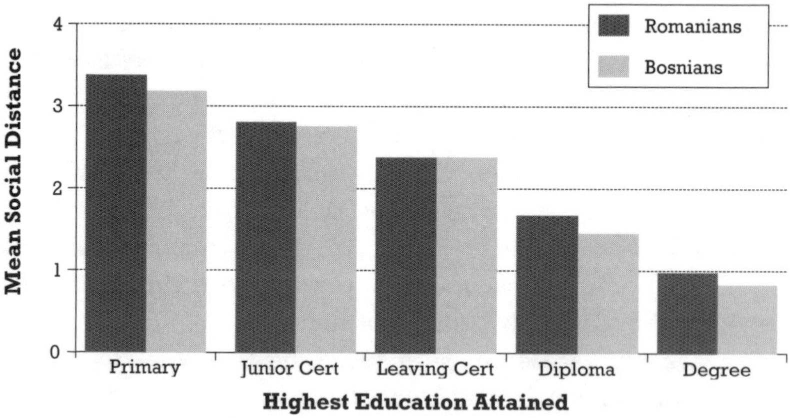

The effect of education was highly significant (Romanians: $F = 17.3$, $df = 4$, $p < .001$; Bosnians: $F = 18.9$, $df = 4$, $p < .001$). In general, social distance also decreased with increasing income, as can be seen from Figure 8.6. Again, these differences were significant (Romanians: $F = 3.6$, $df = 8$, $p < .001$; Bosnians: $F = 3.6$, $df = 8$, $p < .001$).

Figure 8.6: Increasing Income and Decreasing Social Distance to Refugees

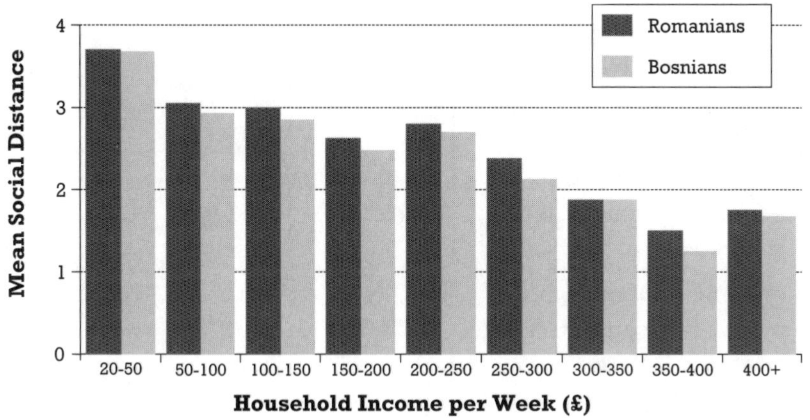

Overall, it can be said that the key differences predicting greater hostility to refugees were consistently between higher education and income groups and those of lower income, greater age and less education.

Finally, ANOVAs were performed to compare the effects of all these different demographic predictors on social distance to both refugee groups. When the demographic variables gender, age, education, occupation and income were used to predict social distance to Romanians, the key demographic predictor was education. What this means is that most of the variation observed for age, occupation and income was due to differing levels of education among those groups. Similar results emerged for social distance to Bosnians, again suggesting that level of education is the single most powerful demographic determinant of hostility toward newly arriving refugees.

Stereotypical Beliefs

Subjects were asked to indicate the extent to which they agreed or disagreed with seven different belief statements regarding refugees. These statements were both negative and positive. Table 8.3 shows the percentage of people who agreed (agree or agree strongly), neither agreed nor disagreed, and disagreed (disagreed and disagreed strongly) with negative beliefs about refugees.

Table 8.3: Agreement with Negative Beliefs about Refugees

	Agreed	Neither	Disagreed
a) Many foreigners are coming to Ireland to exploit its social welfare system.	57.3%	12.9%	29.8%
b) Ireland is currently experiencing a flood of refugees.	75.1%	7.6%	17.4%
c) Many refugees with money are begging in the streets of Dublin.	54.3%	18.3%	27.5%

As the results on the social distance scales would predict, large numbers of this sample appear to hold very negative beliefs about refugees. Although the numbers of refugees coming to Ireland are comparatively small, it seems that many people have accepted media representations, which have used the flood metaphor to describe the recent increase in refugee numbers. Furthermore, many people seem to believe that refugees coming to this country are acquiring income by illegitimate means: by exploiting the social welfare system and begging, even though they have independent resources. Popular support for such beliefs is also high-lighted by the results for the positive items regarding refugees, as can be seen from Table 8.4.

Again it appears from the item regarding political status that many people believe that most refugees coming to Ireland are bogus fortune hunters. The items regarding Ireland as a welcoming culture and responsible because of its own immigrants quite surprisingly had much support. This is interesting in that it appears to suggest that, under the right conditions, the subjects could be quite welcoming to foreign nationals. However, such potential for welcome appears to be countered by beliefs that suggest that most refugees are undeserving and counterfeit. Many people do however seem to be aware that the current methods of processing asylum-seeker applications are slow and ineffective.

Table 8.4: Agreement with Positive Beliefs about Refugees and Refugee Status

	Agreed	**Neither**	**Disagreed**
a) The current methods of processing asylum seekers looking for refugee status in this country are unfair	39.4%	28.7%	31.9%
b) Since Irish people have emigrated for so many years, it is only right that we welcome other nationalities to Ireland	67%	9.4%	23.7%
c) Ireland is traditionally a welcoming culture and should continue to be by welcoming foreigners seeking refuge here.	51.0%	13.9%	35.1%
d) The majority of immigrants coming to this country are genuine political refugees.	28.6%	16.0%	55.4%

In factor analysis of all seven items relating to positive and negative items about refugees, one factor emerged. This means that people holding one negative belief about refugees tend to hold others and to be low on positive beliefs. From this, it is possible to calculate an overall factor score that represents the person's overall agreement with negative beliefs about refugees. This score was highly correlated with social distance to Romanians ($r = .62$, $p < .0001$) and Bosnians ($r = .61$, $p < .0001$). Again it appears that people made little distinction between Romanian and Bosnian refugees, being hostile to both as a result of believing them to be fraudulent economic refugees.

Further Discussion of Survey Results

Some very interesting findings regarding the nature of the Dublin population's attitudes to foreign ethnic groups emerge from the above analysis. The first thing to notice is that the levels of social distance the local population perceive between themselves and minority out-groups are very high. Even for groups such as Spaniards, which are of West European origin, 9.3 per cent of respondents wish them deported. For foreign groups that are more exotic than Spaniards, levels of distance are at least twice as high. The social distance scale used was administered in such a way that people had to actively indicate their hostility. Put simply, if they left the social distance section blank, they were scored as indicating no distance between themselves and minority groups, whereas they had to respond in order to indicate the groups they felt distance towards. Given this, and the fact that minority prejudice questionnaires administered to the general public in the name of a prestigious university are likely to get a certain amount of "politically correct" responding, it appears that the levels of prejudice in the Dublin population were underestimated, if anything. It may be objected that the sample was over-representative of lower income, less educated groups. Although this is the case and probably did elevate the levels of distance observed, it is these groups with which most refugees will have principal contact.

Interestingly, Africans appear to be less distant than Bosnians, Romanians and Arabs, suggesting that simple skin colour is not as salient as other issues such as beliefs about the reasons for coming to Ireland. It may also reflect the influence of an "experimenter pleaser" effect. It is quite possible that in the current social climate, prejudice based on skin colour is perceived as politically incorrect while prejudice towards same skin colour groups is perceived as legitimate social judgement.

The respondents seemed to make little distinction between Bosnians and Romanians, suggesting that for the general public there is no perceived difference between programme refugees brought to Ireland to escape conflict in their home country and refugees who are not part of any organised programme and who have arrived here directly. This suggests that the Irish government, which has often been criticised for its sluggish processing of asylum-seeker applications, is also remiss in raising awareness about those groups that it has actually accepted. It may be objected that the respondents may be aware of the differences between the two groups but that they simply feel equally distant to both. It seems more plausible, however, that many people have confused accusations made in the media against newly arrived groups such as Romanians and all foreign ethnic groups residing in Ireland. Hence the factor which represents a cluster of beliefs which portray Ireland as currently experiencing a flood of bogus fortune-hunting refugees who are exploiting the social welfare system predicts equally well for both Bosnian and Romanian refugees. This also helps to explain why people should wish to keep Bosnians, a small group of well-established political refugees, at greater distance than other foreign groups such as Spaniards and Africans.

Although there have been only a few reports of serious hostility directed towards foreign nationals living in Ireland, it would seem that under certain conditions, serious ethnic tension could develop. The two factors which at present would seem to keep the expression of overt hostility in check are lack of organised structures for the expression of hostility and the current economic boom. As yet, there have been few organised social movements which are explicitly hostile to refugees, although some politicians have tried to manipulate the issue for electoral gain. This means that there is as yet no clear unambiguous way for most people to indicate their hostility toward refugees. The present research suggests that if the Dublin population were given a clear and economical way to express antagonism towards refugees (e.g. voting for an anti-immigration candidate), they would do so. The recent increase in the number of people seeking refugee status in Ireland has also coincided with a period of economic boom. The present research suggests that prejudice towards arriving refugees is maintained by common beliefs that such refugees are bogus, taking advantage of a social welfare system meant for Irish nationals. If this is the case, then it is likely that such beliefs will become ever more relevant and consequent prejudice ever more widespread and hostile if the present economic development should flounder.

When other factors, such as differences in income and age, were controlled for, education was the key demographic predictor of tolerance towards both refugee groups. Although the nature of educational influence on tolerance has been hotly debated (e.g. Jackman and Muha, 1984; Bobo and Licari, 1989) it appears that this may be a key way of reducing prejudice, at least in its more overt forms. It is quite possible that other forms of racism, such as symbolic (Kinder and Sears, 1981) or modern (McConahay, 1982) racism, which includes more covert socially acceptable forms of racial hostility, will be unaffected by education. However, although such forms of hostility may be distressing, they are the most immediate worry in the present situation, considering the extremely high levels of overt hostility among the Dublin population.

Newcomb (1943; Newcomb et al., 1967) argues persuasively that education leads to greater liberalism as a result of normative influence. Essentially, he argues that a person identifies with new in-groups when they enter higher education groups which act as reference groups from which the person learns more liberal attitudes. Thus, he would argue that the effect of education on more liberal values is not the result of greater knowledge or intellectual sophistication. This approach would suggest that the educated (most likely insofar as they constitute "informed opinion") are an important reference group for many people and identifying with that group tends to lead to reduced prejudice. As such, it is very important that this group is consistently perceived to be pro-refugee. If the effect of education is normative, the result of adopting what are believed to be educated values, then the effect of education on attitudes to minorities is not inevitably a positive one. In a society in which the dominant ideology is racist, normative influence (and more years in education) could also make a person more prejudiced e.g. pre-reform South Africa (Duckitt, 1994). This again highlights the importance of consistency in pro-refugee sentiment in education.

SUMMARY

A number of conclusions may be drawn from the present survey:

1. Levels of hostility toward refugees arriving in Dublin are very high.

2. From the stereotypical beliefs scores, it appears that Dubliners are hostile towards economic refugees who they believe have come to Ireland solely to exploit its social welfare system.
3. Furthermore, they believe that almost all refugees coming to this country are economic refugees, including well-established political refugee groups.
4. Among this sample, the more educated are less likely to be hostile towards refugees, suggesting the importance of highly educated groups being seen to be consistently pro-refugee in reducing prejudice towards these groups.

Acknowledgements

This research was conducted at Trinity College Dublin under the supervision of Dr Michael O'Connell. Ms Caroline Smyth and Ms Deirdre McLoughlin provided great assistance in entering data and following up leads in search of relevant material.

References

Bobo, L. and F.C. Licari (1989), "Education and Political Tolerance", *Public Opinion Quarterly*, Vol. 53, pp. 285–308.

Borgardus, E.S. (1933), "A Social Distance Scale", *Sociology and Social Research*, Vol. 17, pp. 265–271.

Dillman, D.A. (1978), *Mail and Telephone Surveys*, New York: John Wiley.

Duckitt, J. (1994), "Conformity to Social Pressure and Racial Prejudice among White South Africans", *Genetic Social and General Psychology Monographs*, Vol. 120, pp. 121–143.

Irish Refugee Council (1995), *Annual Report*, Dublin: Irish Refugee Council.

Jackman, M.R. and M. Muha (1984), "Education and Intergroup Attitudes: Moral Enlightenment, Superficial Democratic Commitment, or Ideological Refinement?", *American Sociological Review*, Vol. 49, pp. 751–769.

Keating, M. (1997), "Why Romania?", *Focus*, Issue No. 57/58 (Winter), pp. 42–43, Dublin: Comhlámh.

Kinder, D.R. and D.O. Sears (1981), "Prejudice and Politics: Symbolic Racism versus Racial Threats to the Good Life", *Journal of Personality and Social Psychology*, Vol. 40, pp. 414–431.

MacGréil, M. (1977), *Prejudice and Tolerance in Ireland*, Dublin: College of Industrial Relations.

MacGréil, M. (1996), *Prejudice in Ireland Revisited*, Dublin: Survey and Research Unit, St. Patrick's College.

McConahay, J.B. (1982), "Self-interest versus Racial Attitudes as Correlates of Anti-Bussing Attitudes in Louisville: Is it the Buses or the Blacks?", *Journal of Politics*, Vol. 44, pp. 692–720.

Newcomb, T.M. (1943), *Personality and Social Change*, New York: Dryden Press.

Newcomb, T.M., K.E. Koening, R. Flacks and D.P. Warwick (1967), *Persistence and Change: Bennington College and its Students after Twenty-five Years*, New York: Wiley.

Watt, P. (1997), "Reporting on Refugees", *Focus*, Issue No. 57/58 (Winter), pp. 29–30, Dublin: Comhlámh.

CHAPTER NINE

POLICING PLURALISM

David Walsh[1]

INTRODUCTION

In recent times, the arrival of refugees and asylum-seekers has acted as the catalyst for the opening of sociological debate around the issue of interculturalism (Lentin, 1999). Ireland's existing minority ethnic communities have remained mostly anonymous and hidden, preferring to lead their lives apart from controversies about racism. The most recent Irish census showed that over 250,000 people who are resident here recorded themselves as not having been born in the state (CSO, 1996). Not all are members of ethnic minority communities; most are probably the children of Irish people who had been living or working abroad or were born in the north of Ireland. However, in the absence of an ethnicity question in the census of population, this may be some indicator of a significant ethnic minority population in the state at present.

For Ireland as a host nation, the acceptance and understanding of ethnic and cultural diversity is one of the most important challenges faced by us in recent years. As a service provider, the Garda Síochána (Irish National Police Service) is at the forefront when it comes to interaction with ethnically and culturally diverse communities. This interaction provided the impetus for the research project which I undertook in 1998.

---

[1] This chapter has been written in a personal capacity and does not necessarily reflect the views of the Garda Síochána.

The project set out to examine the provision of a police service in a developing multiethnic and multicultural society and to examine the issues raised by the provision of such a service. The thesis, entitled "Policing Multiculturalism" (Walsh, 1998), examined the need for anti-racism and cultural diversity training in An Garda Síochána. I initially sought to examine the existing work undertaken in this area. What became evident was that very little work had been undertaken on Irish policing and interculturalism, with the exception of McVeigh in relation to Northern Ireland. It was therefore necessary to focus on work that had been carried out in other countries.

The research project consisted of:

- The distribution of questionnaires to almost 300 members of the Garda Síochána. The questionnaire sought information on attitudes and perceptions around the issues of racism and cultural diversity in the respondent's work.
- Interviews with members of ethnic minority communities in Ireland. This sample included ethnic, religious and national minorities and focused on their attitudes to, and perceptions of, An Garda Síochána.
- Interviews with members of the Irish Traveller community and with Traveller representatives.
- Interviews with a small number of individuals of minority ethnic origin who are members of the Garda Síochána.
- Interviews with individuals of minority ethnic origin who are the spouses/partners of members of the Garda Síochána.

In my research, I have employed both quantitative and qualitative methods (Denzin, 1970; see also Jary and Jary, 1995). By using questionnaires I hoped to investigate patterns and relationships, which I suspected did exist but about which, in the absence of other sources of relevant information, I could only generalise. I hoped to uncover as much personal experience as I could, both in the organisation and external to it.

An Garda Síochána

An Garda Síochána has just over 11,000 members, of which approximately ten per cent are female. The force is unique in comparison to other European police models in that it remains an unarmed service. In terms of policing ethnic minority communities, it is also unique, as evidenced in *The Framework Programme for European Year Against Racism* (1997), which states, "cultural diversity in the makeup of Irish society has, until recently, not been a feature of policy making and public debate" (Dept. of Justice, Equality and Law Reform, 1997: 5).

An Garda Síochána is a centrally controlled single force and all its members begin their policing careers at the lowest rung of the organisational structure and have the opportunity to progress right to Commissioner level. Membership of the organisation is open to all members of Irish society and, in general, is reflective of society across class and social boundaries. Micheál MacGréil, in *Prejudice in Ireland Revisited* (1996), contends that

> . . . the Gardaí are very highly thought of and would be classified as an "in-group" in the Irish Republic. It would be difficult to find a police force in any other country with such a high national standing. (MacGréil, 1996: 271)

An Garda Síochána has been involved in some radical restructuring over the past number of years. Recent structural change in An Garda Síochána includes:

- The introduction of the Walsh training system.
- The division of the state into operational policing regions.
- The establishment of the Criminal Assets Bureau to tackle organised crime.
- The establishment of a unit to implement the Government's Strategic Management Initiative.
- The establishment of a Garda Air Support Unit and Garda Mounted Unit.
- The establishment of units dealing with organisational development, research and equality.

- The implementation of Operation Dochas to deal with the drugs issue.
- The implementation of Operation Lifesaver to cut down on road accidents and deaths.

A significant amount of the criminal legislation which Gardaí presently use in their day-to-day operations has been enacted in the past ten years or so, again requiring structural change in order to meet the demands of such legislation. This restructuring continues into 2000 with the establishment of a new organised crime unit and a redrawing of operational boundaries.

A 1994 ESRI survey into public attitudes to An Garda Síochána indicated that 85 per cent of respondents found the Gardaí approachable with only three per cent saying they would not approach the Gardaí (Murphy and Whelan, 1994: 3). Some 90 per cent of the test sample group indicated that their experience of contacting Gardaí by phone was positive. Ninety-four per cent of the same sample found the attention given to them on visits to a Garda station was positive (Murphy and Whelan, 1994: 10). In the same survey, almost 90 per cent of respondents felt that they were satisfied with the service provided by the Gardaí (Murphy and Whelan, 1994: 13).

The Research

In *Policing Freedom*, Alderson looks at the issue of police power and contends that "police are related to power in two ways: by their very existence, they deny unconstitutional power to others, while at the same time they have the legal power to do their constitutional duty" (Alderson, 1979: 11). The exercise of power by police was central to my researching the effect a police service has on the diverse communities it serves.

The issue of police culture was another important focus of the research. In the Northern Ireland policing report, *Winning the Race: Policing Plural Communities*, the issue of internal policing culture was addressed when it states "there is a direct and vital link between internal culture and the way people are treated and external performance".

Lambert contends that:

> . . . meaningful levels of confidence between police and the public may be expected to play a positive part in race relations terms, for such a role will require some structure of communication and liaison between police and immigrant communities (Lambert, 1970: 177).

My study looked at the effect that people's perceptions of the police in their country of origin can have on the relationship they form with police in a host state. These perceptions can have very far-reaching consequences for the relationships formed between minorities. Lambert addressed this issue in his study in Birmingham, when he contended "the hostility which many West Indians feel towards police may be a result of experiences in the Caribbean rather than here" (Lambert, 1970: 177). He further contends that such perceptions, if left unchecked, can have a detrimental effect not only on police/community relations, but also on the recruitment of members of minority communities into the police.

My study also examined the implications of a culture shock for both host nation and immigrants (see Furnham and Bochner, 1986). This exposure to new cultures affects members of the Garda dealing with recently arrived immigrants and also the immigrants themselves adjusting to Irish society. An Garda Síochána has not had to alter their services in any dramatic way to take account of ethnic and cultural diversity. The implications for them in this new policing environment are wide ranging and it is vitally important to the development of future policing strategies that policing challenges are recognised and identified.

The study also looked at stereotyping and its implications for operational policing and on police training. Lambert contends that "when denied contact with the law-abiding majority, policemen are tempted to think of the whole immigrant community in derogatory terms" (Lambert, 1970: 185). I also examined the implications of the social construction of "race" and the intersection of this issue and stereotyping (Rex, 1986; Miles, 1989; Mason, 1994). I focused on the importance of including this area in police training programmes.

Gender: An Existing Minority

The study began by looking at an existing minority in the Garda organisation to examine its approach to such a minority. It focused on gender equality and looked at female membership to produce a comparative analytical framework. It is in relation to female membership that the greatest organisational change has occurred in recent times. The present female membership of the Garda Síochána is approximately ten per cent of the total membership. Originally, females in the organisation had been treated very differently to their male colleagues: they were required to resign on getting married; they were paid less; and the work they were required to do was different to men. The 1974 Anti-Discrimination (Pay) Act ensured that females were paid the same and fulfilled the same work functions. The 1977 Employment Equality Act exempted the Garda Síochána from its provisions and this remained the position until a 1985 EC directive altered this position in favour of females in the organisation. A 1991 working party set up to examine women's issues in the Garda organisation made 21 recommendations including:

- The need for an organisational policy statement on women's issues;
- Training on equal opportunities for all ranks;
- Guidelines on the health and safety of pregnant members;
- The establishment of a grievance procedure;
- Seminars to be conducted for female members only in order to examine issues relevant to their position in the organisation;
- The training and availability of female contact persons to offer help, assistance, support and understanding to female members needing such a service.

At the time of writing, the first female member has been appointed to the rank of Chief Superintendent and a number of others hold the rank of Superintendent.

I conducted interviews with a number of female members to examine the experiences of their membership in a largely male-dominated organisation and their attitudes to that situation. I discussed the issue of gender identity with respondents and asked if their position as women in the organisation affected them. Most indicated that it did not necessarily affect them but stressed that it depended very much on the individual herself. Some respondents indicated that they felt subordinated because of their gender and spoke of negative experiences, the sense of being in a minority, the sense of nobody understanding and of not being taken seriously. Interviewees suggested that some females could "buy into the macho thing in order to survive; it was their coping strategy" (Walsh, 1998: 32). Other respondents spoke of experiencing a sense of role expectation and that some male colleagues expected behaviour that conformed to their expectations of female Gardaí.

It was suggested that the organisation was not a caring organisation and did not provide services to members who are different and that "internally we do not treat ourselves well" (Walsh, 1998: 33). This finding is particularly relevant to the present research question and to the difficulties faced by existing and future Gardaí from minority ethnic groups. In response to a question about ethnic minority female members, it transpired that no awareness or training existed to cope with this small minority within a minority. This finding is relevant, as an EU-funded, "New Opportunities For Women" Programme has just been completed in the Garda Síochána and this programme did not focus on women of minority ethnic extraction in the organisation.

We discussed the position of members of the organisation who are married to partners from ethnic minorities and who were the parents of children of mixed origin and I asked what focus had been put on the position of these members of the organisation. The feedback was that very little attention had been paid to this group but it was suggested that this was an unsatisfactory position. It was stressed that organisational reaction to such diversity was slow and that "it's a big organisation and things move slowly" (Walsh, 1998: 34). Overall, respondents in this category indicated that things had changed in a positive sense for female members. It was stressed that women could be caught up in women's issues and fail to notice the minority in their own midst, not necessarily just ethnic minority membership, but also other minority groupings who are mostly silent and hidden.

The Internal Focus

The next stage of the research involved the distribution of a questionnaire to 300 members of the organisation. The questionnaire sought to establish the level and nature of contacts between Gardaí and members of minority ethnic communities and to identify the particular communities involved in such contacts. The second part of the questionnaire sought to examine the attitudes of respondents to the changing societal structure in order to examine what structural change would be necessary to meet the emerging demands on our police service. According to Oppenheim (1992), when commenting on the attitudes of police and inherent tendencies to prejudice, "most of an individual's attitudes are usually dormant and are expressed in speech or behaviour only when the subject of the attitude is perceived" (Oppenheim, 1992: 175). As previously stated, the Garda Síochána have not had to provide a police service to an ethnically diverse society until recently and, as such, individual members of the organisation have not had to examine their own attitudes to the challenges of multiethnic policing.

In all, 272 people responded anonymously to the questionnaire. The sample was representative in covering geographical distribution as well as gender and rank distribution. Respondents ranged from Garda rank up to and including Chief Superintendent. Respondents were asked if they had had any professional contact with a member of an ethnic minority community in the previous nine months. The purpose of this question was to establish whether society, which the Garda Síochána serves, had expanded in terms of its ethnic base and if so to what extent were Gardaí interacting with the resultant diversity. Of the population sampled, 143 respondents indicated that they had been in professional contact with a member of an ethnic minority in the previous nine months. In other words, over half of those who responded had as police staff been called upon to provide a police service to members of ethnic minority communities. When the ethnic profile of these contacts was examined, it was found that almost 30 different national groups were involved. Of the total number of interactions, just over half resulted in the Garda officer having to arrest the individual involved. An analysis of the responses showed that these arrests occurred across the criminal code, ranging from minor public order offences to more serious crime.

I also asked whether members of minority communities were the victims of crime. Twenty-three respondents (13 per cent) indicated that their contact had been as a result of the individual being a victim of crime. Respondents were asked for their opinion as to whether the victim of crime had been the victim of racially motivated crime. It is important to stress that this question was asked in the absence of any great degree of training in this area and respondents would be relying on their individual interpretations of what exactly was racist crime. A total of seven respondents indicated that they felt that the crime they were dealing with was racially motivated.

Respondents were asked what level of contact occurred as a result of members of ethnic minorities calling to Garda stations with social enquiries. There were 38 positive responses to this question. This aspect of the research indicates that as an organisation and service provider, the Garda Síochána are having daily contact with members of ethnic minorities and that greater challenges are being faced in the provision of this service. Let me stress that this research was undertaken in 1998 and this level of contact has increased since then in line with the expansion in ethnic minority communities in Irish society. The Irish police no longer police a "white" homogenous society and its members are being exposed to different cultures and nationalities to an extent previously unknown. This increase in contacts alone indicates the need for an education strategy.

The second part of the questionnaire focused on respondent attitudes to structural or cultural changes necessary to accommodate societal change. Respondents were asked if they had encountered racism in the course of their work and they were asked to interpret this question in the broadest possible sense. Over 51 per cent of respondents indicated that they had encountered what they considered to be incidents of racism in the course of their work. Over 85 per cent indicated that they felt there was a need for the development of training in this area. Over 72 per cent indicated that they felt that forms and information leaflets at Garda stations should be printed in various languages to accommodate minority ethnic communities. The provision of such information requires very little, if any structural change. Respondents were asked if they felt well enough trained to deal with issues of policing minority ethnic groups, understanding minority cultures and dealing with issues of racism. Almost 70 per cent indicated that they felt they did not have sufficient training and a further 15 per cent said they had "enough to get by". Asked if they felt that there was a need to develop training that deals with these areas, 85 per cent indicated that they felt there was such a need.

On a different level of structural changes, respondents were asked if they agreed that Garda height requirements should be lowered to accommodate ethnic minority membership of the organisation. The response to this question was that 83 per cent felt there should be no change. They were also asked if they agreed that uniform requirements (for example, in terms of headdress) should be changed to accommodate minority membership. Some 68 per cent did not agree with this structural change. It is important to stress that these responses were given in the absence of structured training in this area and emphasises the need for the provision of such training to facilitate acceptance of ethnic diversity. At the time of writing, the issue of abolishing the height requirement in respect of future membership is being actively addressed. It should also be pointed out that it is unlikely that the uniform change will become an issue for some time, as the numbers of potential candidates from minority communities such as the Sikh community is still relatively low (although in the absence of an ethnicity question, we cannot ascertain exact numbers).

Ethnic Minority Membership

There are very few members of the Garda who are of mixed ethnic origin and of those only two are "visible". As the only two black Gardaí in the force are of opposite gender, their experiences are obviously unique. I spoke to members of ethnic minority groups who are married to members of An Garda Síochána. The reason for including this group was to try and gain some insight as to how we treated ourselves as an organisation and whether or not there were issues that we needed to address. Again, the possible respondent base was small. By focusing on these people, I hoped to investigate feelings, attitudes and perceptions of the Garda organisation from an internal perspective. I expected that by adopting this approach, it would be possible to identify where change might be necessary.

Qualitative interviews are complex instruments from which to draw generalised conclusions. This is particularly true when the sample is numerically limited. However, as Schwartz and Jacobs (1979) argue, even the story of one life enables us to reach some understanding about society at large. For this project, I interviewed a small number of Gardaí who are members of ethnic minorities, plus a number of ethnic minority spouses/partners of members of the force and their Garda partners. Gardaí of ethnic minorities described their experiences in Irish society: "I just let people in so far, but I don't let them in any further." Another explained, "In the canteen, if there were people there that I didn't know, I would make a joke about me or my colour just to put them at ease." Some respondents spoke of being treated as exotic in their day-to-day lives and they described feelings of anger, embarrassment and isolation as a result:

> I felt ashamed at other people. . . . I would be ashamed of saying to myself that I come from the same culture as them, I would be ashamed of my Irishness then, because of the fact that these people claim to be Irish. (Walsh, 1998: 67)

One spoke of apprehension about joining the force:

> I felt apprehensive like everybody else . . . but I felt a little more apprehension that no matter how good I was that maybe they were not going to have me. (Walsh, 1998: 68).

They also felt that there would be extra pressure on them because of their difference "If I messed up, it wouldn't look good on me and it certainly wouldn't have looked good on the force" (Walsh, 1998: 68). While on balance they were happy about their membership of An Garda Síochána, respondents indicated the need for training around ethnic issues and for a definite code of practice covering organisational structures and policies in relation to Gardaí who belong to ethnic minority groups.

Minority ethnic spouses and partners of members of the force described their perceptions of the police in their countries of origin. Their impressions were varied. One respondent of Asian extraction commented of the police in her country: "The police are in a position of authority; they were there to help the public and had to be respected and obeyed" (Walsh, 1998: 74). Another respondent, who had been raised in an African state, spoke of the police in her country as being completely corrupt. She went on to say "only fools join the police; nobody has any respect for them" (Walsh, 1998: 78).

They then spoke about their present attitudes towards the Garda. All the respondents indicated that the recent changes in Ireland's ethnic composition has drawn greater attention to them than in the past; one remarked,

> I expect to be questioned in relation to my colour in the near future by a Garda or some other individual. I am very annoyed by the recent stereotyping of people by Gardaí and others. I now expect to be harassed because of my skin colour. (Walsh, 1998: 75)

This same respondent went on to say that in her opinion some Irish people feel that all blacks are poor and that she did very well to have married a Garda. Another respondent described her husband's work colleagues as being "ten out of ten, I treat them as friends, they are very sociable and I am very proud of them. They are gentlemen of the highest calibre" (Walsh, 1998: 76). Overall, these respondents spoke positively about their social interactions with Gardaí.

Gardaí married to members of ethnic minorities also spoke about the changing attitudes to minorities occasioned by the arrivals of asylum-seekers and the resultant racism:

> I have noticed recently and not just in the job, in the past few years things have started changing, we are becoming more racist, maybe we were always racist and just didn't see it, but it's a fear that I have now that I never had before. (Walsh, 1998: 77)

Respondents suggested that there are small minorities who they felt were prejudiced and that they would make their feelings known. A respondent commented: "The Gardaí are not trained for this job; sometimes I get fellas drifting into the canteen and telling racist jokes but I don't get annoyed, I just say nothing or laugh it off" (Walsh, 1998: 78). Another commented,

> What will happen when Turkey is admitted to the EU? There are a lot of coloured Turks and they will have the right to move around the EU. The Gardaí better get used to dealing with coloured people . . . if you are dealing with human beings then respect is an important issue. (Walsh, 1998: 79)

All respondents agreed that An Garda Síochána have to respond to these changes by including awareness of ethnic and cultural diversity in all future training programmes. It is from amongst the children of these families that some of the future membership of the Garda Síochána will be recruited.

The External Focus

My next research strategy was to ask the people most likely to be affected by racist attitudes for their feelings on the question. I spoke not only to recent arrivals such as refugees, asylum-seekers or students, but also sought the views of those who have been in Ireland for some time and who are well established here, as well as Irish people of mixed ethnic origin. The aim of this part of the research was to examine attitudes to and perceptions of the Garda Síochána and to examine attitudes to living in Irish society. I hoped to identify areas where the interviewees felt the Garda organisation could improve the service it offered to minority communities.

As a police service, the Garda Síochána is obliged to provide an immigration service at frontier posts throughout the State. This is a statutory obligation and the Garda have no discretion in the provision of this service. This function could, however, be contradictory, and to some extent damaging to the uniqueness of the Garda Síochána in its closeness to the communities as it moves towards policing a multicultural society. On the one hand, we must provide an unbiased police service to people, irrespective of national origin, creed or colour. On the other hand, we are required to act as immigration officers who have first contact with members of ethnic minorities who enter the state and it is usually to an immigration officer that an asylum application is first made. This apparent contradiction could have implications for the degree of trust between Gardaí and ethnic minorities.

Respondents were asked for their impressions of police in their countries of origin in an effort to establish what perceptions of police immigrants were carrying to Ireland. In general, respondents who were of African or Asian origin described their contacts with police in their countries of origin as very negative and described them as oppressive and untrustworthy. One respondent spoke of his contact with police in London: "I wouldn't have much personal contact, but as a black person in London I wouldn't have much trust in the police. I wouldn't trust the police at all" (Walsh, 1998: 85). A respondent from the former Yugoslavia said of police in his country: "I never had any problems with them, but they are extremely tough, I would be afraid to approach them because they had such a bad reputation" (Walsh, 1998: 86). A respondent of African origin said:

> The police in my country are set up to oppress people and that is what they do. They are poorly educated and perceived as oppressors. They are not fair in their dealings with people and I do not trust them. (Walsh, 1998: 86)

This negative perception towards the police has implications for the service provided by the Garda Síochána in this country. In some cases, respondents had in fact fled their countries because of mistreatment by police. The negative attitudes, particularly of refugees and asylum-seekers, to police could mean serious communication barriers when they have to deal with police in Ireland. Most respondents would admit that their reason for maintaining this distance was their previous experience with police elsewhere. They stressed that police corruption plays a significant role in creating environments where a lack of trust between police and local communities is an issue. The irony of this situation is that people involved in racist activities are often accused of stereotyping their victims and yet in a sense this is exactly what is happening here: police are being stereotyped. This stereotyping of Irish police could have damaging long-term consequences for Garda–community relations strategies if this issue is not recognised and steps taken to deal with it.

Respondents were asked for their impression of the Garda Síochána. Their responses indicate a general degree of acceptance of the organisation. That is not to suggest that there was no criticism of Irish police. However, most of the criticism that did exist was aimed at the actions of individuals and not the organisation itself. There was no suggestion of institutional racism. While the organisation has not come in for any great degree of negative comment, the possibility of a future charge of institutional racism is very real in the absence of a concerted and proactive policy around the issue of interculturalism and antiracism training. As was evidenced in the recent MacPherson report in the UK, organisational ambivalence, neglect or inaction can be as damning as overt or intentional acts of prejudice or discrimination. In this sense, comfort should not be taken from the fact that criticism has not yet come; the possibility of it in the future is there. Cashmore speaks of the need to examine "the unspoken assumptions on which organisations base their practices and the unquestioned principles they may use" (Cashmore, 1995: 169). She also speaks of the "need for organisations to engage in positive, continuous action in expunging racial discrimination rather than assuming it will fade" (Cashmore, 1995: 170).

Most respondents indicated that they felt the issue of education and training to meet the challenges of interculturalism was of particular importance. One respondent remarked, "policemen are people and they live in communities that might influence policemen's attitudes to refugees. So that is why I think it is very important that you train police" (Walsh, 1998: 98). Some respondents went on to say that the issue of police–community relations was of importance and that communication was central to any strategy. Respondents suggested that some members of ethnic minority communities would be reluctant to call police to their homes if they had problems because they would feel they might be drawing attention to themselves and their distinctiveness. The fact that the Irish police are an unarmed service was commented on in positive terms by respondents:

> It was so pleasant to come here and discover that the police weren't armed, it is very good. Instantaneously you feel

> comfortable and you are not afraid and have no problem going to a police station. (Walsh, 1998: 90)

The point was also made, however, that particular care was needed to ensure that people who were seeking refugee status or political asylum were treated properly and that the upholding of human rights was a primary responsibility of the Garda Síochána. Most respondents in this group were parents, most of whose children were Irish-born. Asked how they would feel if their children indicated a desire to join the Garda Síochána, the majority of the group indicated that, provided structures were adopted to accommodate ethnic minority membership, they would have no problem with their children becoming Irish policemen or women.

Irish Travelling Community

Members of the Travelling community were also asked for their perceptions of the Garda Síochána. A respondent commented,

> . . . there is a huge lack of trust between the Gardaí and members of the Traveller community. The Gardaí don't trust us and we don't trust them. Until these barriers are broken down we won't make progress. (Walsh, 1998: 92)

The Traveller representatives indicated that they felt that because of their nomadic lifestyle, they are treated differently and stressed that their distinct ethnic status was not recognised or respected and that this also caused tension. The need for acceptance as an ethnic minority was stressed by Traveller respondents (see Ní Shúinéir, 1994). They also indicated that stereotyping of Travellers was a major problem. They went on to say that they accept that the Traveller community had criminals in their midst, but that this was a minority, and yet every Traveller was regarded as a criminal. A respondent commented,

> . . . if anything happened in the town where I grew up, no matter who did it they'd come straight to us. We would be questioned about it and then they would discover that some local up the road did it (Walsh: 93, 1998).

Respondents were particularly angry about the treatment that Travellers received in the media.

The relationship between Travellers on a settled halting site in Ballymun, Dublin and the local Gardaí was highlighted as a model of good Traveller/Garda relationships. The genesis of this particular relationship involved high levels of communication in both directions and a degree of mutual trust, due in no small way to the efforts of a number of the local Gardaí at Ballymun station.

Respondents on this particular site suggested that the efforts of individual Gardaí had helped break down communication barriers and if problems arose this enabled dialogue to take place in an effort at resolution. It was suggested that the local Gardaí approached their jobs in a non-judgemental fashion and were fair in approach. What was particularly commented on was the fact that a number of the Gardaí had become involved in helping with football and other sports training with Traveller children.

> There's another Guard and he looks after my young fella on the football team . . . he calls and brings them training and drops them home later . . . I think it is good to have a relationship, to have that kind of relationship with the cops. (Walsh, 1998: 95)

Respondents pointed out that they understood that the Gardaí had a job to do. "The Gardaí in Ballymun tend to live and let live; if a new young Garda comes in here and starts throwing his weight around the older Guards tend to put him wide" (Walsh, 1998: 94). It was suggested that it was important that Travellers as a group should not be stereotyped. They indicated that, like any other community, they had a criminal population and suggested that they wanted criminals in the Traveller community dealt with by Gardaí the same as any other group. They suggested that Gardaí need to understand Traveller culture better and felt that more time should be spent with Traveller groups during training. It was suggested that community Gardaí were important to help bridge barriers.

The Future Policing Environment

Each of the groups involved in this research indicated that they felt the Garda Síochána needed to move to meet the challenges presented by our expanding society. Overall, the perception of people of the Garda Síochána reflects the contention of MacGréil. It is crucial that this level of organisational acceptance be used to best advantage in planning future strategies. A reading of the report produced in the wake of the Stephen Lawrence investigation (MacPherson, 1999) shows how absolutely critical is the need for the broadest police training in the area of interculturalism. The damage that can be inflicted on police/community relations because of a failure in this area will have long-term implications for an ambivalent police service. MacPherson contends that:

> it is incumbent upon every institution to examine their policies and the outcome of their policies to guard against disadvantaging any section of our communities (MacPherson, 1999: 46.27).

In the course of post-research work on training, what became apparent is that some individuals sometimes do not realise that their actions or words can be interpreted as being discriminatory or prejudiced. This sense of people feeling that they had to act in a definite or active way for racism to occur or that if their actions or thoughts were remote or in abstract from the subject of discrimination, then no harm was done, was evidenced in much of MacPherson's findings. The report used such terms as "insensitive, unwitting, thoughtless, collective actions, good intentions, patronising and failure to realise" to describe the actions or indeed inaction of some of the officers involved in this investigation and to define what "institutional racism" is.

What has also become apparent in post-research work is that, like other sections of Irish society, members of the Garda Síochána are having to come to terms with new language in their work. Terms such as ethnicity, ethnic group, race, racism and cultural diversity have all become part of our everyday language. I have found a degree of uncertainty amongst people as to exactly what these terms mean. That uncertainty has led to feelings of apprehension. I have interviewed Garda members who have been accused of racism in the course of their work and have found that such accusations can present them with new anxieties and concerns. Some of these concerns centre on the fact that they may not even be sure how they have come to be accused of racism. From this point of view, education on these issues as well as organisational support structures are important to Garda members.

My research shows a definite need for the introduction of antiracism and cultural diversity training in An Garda Síochána. This finding does not come only from members of ethnic minorities but also from the Gardaí themselves. As a colleague from a UK police force said to me recently:

> Ireland is now at a crossroads and the Gardaí are very lucky; you are only at the beginning of this process and you can learn from the experiences of other police forces all over Europe. Don't lose the opportunity.

In the same regard, MacPherson addresses the need for organisational development where it contends:

> . . . the need for training of police officers in addressing racism and valuing cultural diversity is plain. Improved understanding and attitudes will certainly help to prevent racism in the future, as will improved procedures in terms of recording and investigating racist incidents. (MacPherson, 1999: 46.35)

Training alone will not ensure racial harmony in the Irish context; there is a need for inclusiveness in our approach to interculturalism, and the development of an ethnic relations forum by the Gardaí is needed to ensure participation by ethnic minority groups in the future of Irish policing. In the same context, MacPherson contends,

> . . . the active involvement of people from diverse ethnic groups is essential. Otherwise there will be no acceptance of change, and policing by consent may be the victim. (MacPherson, 1999: 46.40)

Meeting the challenges presented by interculturalism will require organisational and structural change. Cohen suggests:

> The multicultural illusion is that the dominant and subordinate can somehow swap places and learn how the other half lives, whilst at the same time leaving the structures of power intact. As if power relations could be magically

> suspended through the direct exchange of experience and ideology dissolve into the thin air of face-to-face communication. (Cohen, 1988: 130)

The answers to some of the questions on the Garda questionnaire discussed above indicate that the issue of change should be addressed in future training strategies. They also suggest that the organisation should address the issue of change in its policies and strategies.

Earlier in this chapter, I highlighted the fact that the Gardaí were amenable to change and in this context they have already begun to meet the challenges presented by interculturalism. In November 1998, the findings of this research were presented at "The Expanding Nation Conference" in Trinity College, Dublin and in April 1999, the Gardaí held a conference entitled "Providing a Police Service in an Expanding Multiethnic and Multicultural Ireland". The Department of Justice, Equality and Law Reform and the European Union jointly funded this conference. As we enter this new millennium, the expansion in our ethnic base has presented new policing challenges. The Rotterdam Charter provides a conceptual framework for policing a multiethnic society, which would be of assistance to the Garda Síochána:

> The charter does not provide a standard formula for action, but it contains an agenda of themes requiring the attention of modern urbanised societies, if they do not wish to be surpassed by history. (Rotterdam Charter, 1996: 2)

The MacPherson report makes over 70 recommendations on policing and race relations and it is an invaluable source of guidance for the Garda Síochána in identifying future policing strategies.

While both of the above reports are undoubtedly important sources of information and suggestions as to the development of future policing strategies, *the* most important source of what is required for policing minority ethnic communities are those communities themselves. The issue is one of protection of human rights and the maintenance of a policing environment which ensures that respect for cultural, ethnic or religious diversity is the norm.

Postscript: Between 4 and 6 April 2000, the Garda Síochána, the Department of Justice, Equality and Law Reform and the European Union hosted a conference entitled "Intercultural Ireland, Identifying the Challenges for the Police Service" at Dublin Castle. A paper based on this research was presented at this conference. As part of his presentation to the conference, the Garda Commissioner Pat Byrne announced the establishment of an office at the Garda Community Relations section specifically to deal with the issues raised by Interculturalism. The Garda Racial and Intercultural Office now operates from Garda Headquarters, Harcourt Square, Dublin 2.

References

Alderson, J. (1979), *Policing Freedom*, Plymouth: Latimer Trend & Co Ltd.

Ben Tovim, Gabriel et al. (1986), *The Local Politics of Race*, London: Macmillan.

Cashmore, E. (1995), *Dictionary of Race and Ethnic Relations*, London: Routledge.

Cohen, P. (1988), *Multi-Racist Britain*, London: Macmillan.

Denzin, Norman (1970), *Sociological Methods: A Sourcebook*, London: Butterworths.

Department of Justice, Equality and Law Reform (1997), *Framework Programme for the European Year Against Racism*, Dublin: Stationery Office.

European Commission (1997), *The European Institutions in the Fight Against Racism: Selected Texts*, Luxembourg: Office for Official Publications of the European Communities.

Furnham, A. and S. Bochner (1986), *Culture Shock*, London: Methuen.

Jary, David and Julia Jary (eds.) (1995), *Collins Dictionary of Sociology*, 2nd edition, Glasgow: HarperCollins.

Lambert, J. (1970), *Crime, Police and Race Relations, A Study in Birmingham,* Oxford: Oxford University Press.

Lentin, R. (ed.) (1999), *The Expanding Nation: Towards a Multiethnic Ireland*, Dublin: Trinity College Dublin.

MacGréil, M. (1996), *Prejudice in Ireland Revisited,* Maynooth: St Patrick's College.

MacPherson, William (1999), *The Stephen Lawrence Inquiry: Report on an Inquiry by Sir William MacPherson of Cluny*, London: Stationery Office.

McVeigh, Robbie (1996), *The Racialization of Irishness: Racism and Anti-racism in Ireland,* CRD: Belfast.

Murphy, M. and B. Whelan (1994), "Public Attitudes to the Gardaí", *Communiqué: An Garda Síochána Management Journal*, No. 1, pp. 1–18.

Ni Shuinear, S. (1996), "Irish Travellers, Ethnicity and the Origins Question" in *Irish Travellers, Culture and Ethnicity,* Belfast: Institute of Irish Studies.

Oppenheim, A. (1992), *Questionnaire Design, Interviewing and Attitude Measurement*, new edition, New York: Pinter.

Rex and Mason (1998), *Theories of Race and Ethnic Relations,* Cambridge: Cambridge University Press.

The Rotterdam Charter (1996), *Policing for a Multi Ethnic Society.*

Schwartz and Jacobs (1979), *Qualitative Sociology, A Method to the Madness,* New York: Free Press.

Walsh, D. (1998), "Policing Multiculturalism: An Examination of the Need for Anti-Racism and Cultural Diversity Training in An Garda Síochána", MPhil Thesis, Trinity College Dublin.

CHAPTER TEN

IMMIGRATION AND RESETTLEMENT IN IRELAND: PLANNING SERVICES, SUPPORTING PEOPLE

Cathal O'Regan

OPPORTUNITIES AND CHALLENGES IN A NEW SOCIO-ECONOMIC CLIMATE

Irish society is looking towards its future with unprecedented confidence and optimism. The economy boasts the best rate of sustained growth in the EU, and unemployment is at its lowest point for more than two decades.[1] Increased investment in telecommunications and information technology has allowed Ireland develop rapidly as an "information-based" society, and our image as a rather hapless island perched on the periphery of Europe is fast becoming a fading memory. However, a fuller appreciation of Irish society at the dawn of the twenty-first century requires one to focus beyond the dynamic, exciting prowl of the Celtic Tiger to the wider spectrum of social and political change.

One important change on Ireland's socio-economic landscape has been the increased immigration rate. This increase is due to a number of factors, primary among these being the well-documented shortage of both skilled and unskilled workers in the

[1] According to the CSO, the seasonally adjusted standardised unemployment rate for July 2000 was 4.4 per cent and is predicted to fall below 4 per cent before the end of the year.

workforce. Ireland is fast approaching what some commentators call a "full-employment" economy. The IDA has recently announced an unprecedented strategic shift in policy, moving away from the priority of employment generation to one of employment maintenance. Forfás and FÁS are engaged in a strategy of encouraging the return home of some of the thousands of emigrants of the last quarter century. One of the country's most eminent economists estimates that as many as 23,000 immigrant workers will be required each year over the next seven years if the economic and social development outlined in the government's National Plan is to be implemented.[2]

Another change has been the increasing numbers of asylum-seekers in Ireland. While Ireland is now a natural destination for economic migrants, the absence of an immigration policy means that economic immigration may be happening through the mechanism of the asylum application process (although that is of course not to suggest that all those seeking to obtain refugee status are in reality economic migrants). While the numbers of asylum applications could be best described as having increased from negligible to minuscule, the short period between 1997 and 1999 saw the debate on immigration and asylum-seekers in Ireland move centre stage in the public consciousness. The debate reached a climactic stage in November 1999, as the Department of Justice and the Eastern Regional Health Authority struggled badly to provide adequate services to asylum-seekers, and the Dáil debated a motion of confidence in the Minister for Justice.[3]

Notwithstanding the ideological debate about Ireland's obligations and responsibilities towards asylum-seekers, one fact remains irrefutable: the immigration rate in Ireland will — indeed, needs to — continue to grow significantly over the coming years. Mindful that the economy cannot sustain its remarkable growth

---

[2] "Coalition to introduce work visa system", *The Irish Times*, Monday, 22 November 1999.

[3] There is now a considerable backlog of applications and appeals for asylum, many of which will not be heard for several years, while the resettlement functions of the State remain the remit of several Departments and agencies. The system for dealing with asylum-seekers was publicly described as a "shambles" by one Minister in the coalition Government.

without a substantial expansion of the workforce, in 1999 a high-profile ministerial committee set out to draft the first substantial immigration policy in the history of the state. Given the vista of a society with vastly enhanced ethnic diversity, how can the State prepare for and manage this change? What challenges face the Government, its Civil Service and its agencies, and which principles should guide policy development as this new society emerges?

The Genesis of a Policy on Immigration and Asylum

While views on immigration and asylum policy span the range of conservative and liberal ideologies, it is clear that future government policy will be based partly on the labour needs of the economy. Liz O'Donnell, Minister of State at the Department of Foreign Affairs, has called for an "inward non-EU migration policy linked to the needs of our economy".[4] Tom Kitt, Minister of State at the Department of Enterprise, Trade and Employment, has advocated a "positive and flexible" approach rather than the "reactive policy followed so far".[5] The Tánaiste, Mary Harney, outlined her views on the need for new policies:

> Fresh thinking will be needed in the area of immigration policy. . . . It is in our own economic self-interest that we adopt a more open attitude to immigration. . . . But this should not be merely about self-interest. . . . We should be prepared to show the same open door to others as was shown to us in times past. . . . we need to develop a reasonable and responsible immigration policy that will allow people to come here and make a real contribution to the life of this country.[6]

---

[4] "Government's refugee policy 'a shambles'", *The Sunday Business Post*, 14 November 1999.

[5] "Employing Immigrants", *Irish Times* Editorial, Monday, 15 November 1999.

[6] Remarks by Tánaiste Mary Harney at the Encounter Symposium "Managing Our Economies" in the Berkeley Court Hotel, Dublin, 29 October 1999.

Aside from the practical step of linking our immigration and asylum policy to the demands of the economy, significant challenges lie ahead for policy makers and service providers. The Government must transform a patently inadequate system for dealing with asylum applications into one that can cope properly and efficiently with the demands placed on it. Beyond that, a strategy must be developed by every relevant service provider for working with the many thousands of immigrants who will arrive in Ireland over the coming years. In this regard, empirical data can provide a rich vein of information upon which to develop policy and practice.

PRINCIPLES OF SUCCESSFUL RESETTLEMENT: THE EMPIRICAL VIEWPOINT

To date, research in Ireland into resettlement needs and patterns is quite limited in its scope. Elsewhere, however, extensive research has been carried out into the types of issues experienced both by economic migrants and by refugees as they attempt to rebuild their lives in new environments. The majority of the data pertains to refugees from war- and famine-torn nations resettling in Europe, Australia, Asia and the USA. Other data pertains to economic migrants settling in new countries, including studies focussing on immigrant Irish communities living in the United States and in Great Britain.

The data that follows is based on a major research project into the resettlement patterns of programme refugees in Ireland. While programme refugees come to Ireland under quite specific circumstances, the nature of the resettlement process they experience resembles closely that of other immigrants, including asylum-seekers, convention refugees and immigrant workers. The research, carried out during 1997, looked at the two largest programme refugee communities in Ireland — the Bosnian and Vietnamese communities.

The research was commissioned and overseen by five Government Departments[7] and two specialist agencies[8] primarily in-

---

[7] Departments of: Foreign Affairs; Health and Children; Social, Community and Family Affairs; Environment and Local Government; Education and Science.

volved in the resettlement of programme refugees. The primary aim was to investigate the resettlement patterns and needs of the Bosnian and Vietnamese programme refugee communities in Ireland. The research, based primarily on a structured interview schedule incorporating the General Health Questionnaire (GHQ-28),[9] was carried out by native-language fieldworkers over a three-month period in spring 1997. One hundred and two adults took part in the survey — 29 Vietnamese and 73 Bosnians, representing 13 per cent of the entire Bosnian and Vietnamese adult Programme refugee population in Ireland.

Several issues emerged during the research that could prove useful points of reference in the continuing development of a strategy for resettling immigrants and refugees in Ireland. The data is presented in such a way as to provide empirical support to particular points of view in the ongoing debate about supporting resettlement of refugees.

THE ACCULTURATION PROCESS

The development of a model of best practice to support refugees and other immigrants must be conceptualised in terms of the acculturation process. While it was previously considered that the longer a person spent in a new host country, the more characteristics of the host country he or she adopted, it is now accepted that acculturation is considerably more complex. In Berry's (1986) widely utilised model of acculturation, the process begins by the immigrant gradually adopting host cultural patterns in a given domain (for example, cognition, language acquisition, etc.), until a point of conflict is reached. It is at this stage that an adaptation is made in order to resolve the conflict. The adaptive process follows one of four directions:

- *Assimilation*: This is the continuous move towards the dominant culture, whereby one's original cultural identity is relin-

---

[8] The Refugee Agency and the Department of Psychology, Eastern Health Board.

[9] The GHQ-28 (D. Goldberg and P. Williams, 1991) measures the incidence of psychological distress among the target population.

quished. The concept of the "melting pot" can be used to illustrate the outcome of assimilation, whereby non-dominant groups are absorbed into established dominant groups, creating a new society.

- *Integration*: This is a balanced synthesis of the two cultures, whereby there is some adjustment to become part of a larger societal framework, while at the same time there is some maintenance of the cultural integrity of the original group. In this case, ethnic groups retain a distinguishable identity, while co-operating within a larger social system.
- *Rejection/Separation*: This is a process whereby the traditional culture is reaffirmed, at the expense of the host culture. Depending on which group has the power to determine the outcome, it can be the choice of maintaining a cultural independence by the non-dominant culture; or it can be the segregation of the non-dominant culture by the dominant.
- *Marginalisation*: In certain cases, the person or group can lose cultural and psychological contact with their traditional culture, and with the larger society within which they now live. This can be initiated by either side, and is characterised within the marginalised group by feelings of alienation, loss of identity, and a general acculturative stress.

Supporting Resettlement through Integration

The debate has evolved to the point where integration is seen as one of the key principles in successful resettlement. Successful integration means that the refugee is able to participate to the extent that he/she needs and wishes in all of the major components of the new society, without having to relinquish his or her own identity.[10] The host society facilitates this by identifying barriers to integration, and putting in place measures to overcome them. The experience in Ireland has shown that policies aimed at assimilating refugees into society do not work.

An interesting example is the housing policy adopted by the resettlement authorities during the period 1979 to 1980, when the

---

[10] O'Regan (1998).

initial group of Vietnamese arrived in Ireland. The policy of the authorities was to re-house this group in various locations throughout the country. Consequently, groups of Vietnamese were to be found in Portlaoise, Waterford, Tralee, Sligo and Dublin. There were several justifications for this policy at the time, prominent among them being the belief that this policy would prevent the Vietnamese community in Ireland becoming ghettoised. Using the model of acculturation outlined above, this policy would appear to be based largely on a wish to encourage assimilation of the Vietnamese community in Ireland.[11] However, over time a sizeable voluntary migration occurred, whereby Vietnamese families abandoned many of the original locations to relocate to Dublin (McGovern, 1990), where the majority of the Vietnamese community was to be found. Rather than leading to the formation of Vietnamese ghettos, this re-congregation appears to have served to provide a supportive environment whence Vietnamese families have developed self-sufficiency within small-sized social systems, centred mainly around family groups. The proximity and presence of family, friends, or merely those who have similar needs, and a shared language and culture allows the individual to develop a social support system, which is so vital in the resettlement process.

It is this same expatriate supportive environment which Irish emigrants tend to seek when they first go abroad. It is not simply for geographic and economic reasons that cities such as Liverpool, London, Boston and New York have such concentrated populations of expatriate Irish. Valtonen (1996) notes that for Vietnamese, it is generally the extended family rather than the wider expatriate community that remains the predominant and most important unit of reference and support.

Resettlement policy over the last decade has encouraged the development and maintenance of strong family and community-based links among refugee groups. Consequently, virtually the entire Bosnian community has been located in the Greater Dublin region. A further form of encouragement comes through the support provided for the establishment and funding of associations

---

[11] McGovern (1990) gives a detailed case study of how the resettlement approach (particularly in terms of education) impacted on the Vietnamese community in Ireland during their first decade here (1979–1989).

such as the Vietnamese-Irish Association and the Bosnian Community Development Project. The emphasis placed by the Irish Government in admitting a considerable proportion of programme refugees in family units, together with the operation of the Family Reunification Scheme, is further recognition of the importance for refugees of maintaining and fostering pre-existing support structures.

More recently, however, the government has asked local authorities around the country to take responsibility for resettling asylum-seekers. A number of reasons have been cited for adopting this strategy, including the Government's wish not to see the emergence of ghettos within Dublin, while at the same time not wanting to exacerbate the housing crisis in the capital. This strategy, similar to that used for Vietnamese arrivals in 1979, warrants close monitoring, as it begs the question of how dispersed individuals and families will be affected, particularly in terms of having weak social support networks. O'Regan (1998) and Sultan-Prnjavorac (1999) show that programme refugees, despite the relative proximity of their expatriate community, are still quite isolated, particularly women in the home, the elderly, and those with poor English language skills.

Understanding the Motives of Refugees

The first casualty in the often heated discussion about refugees, asylum-seekers and economic migrants tends to be an appreciation of the reasons why those concerned have come to Ireland in the first place. This lack of awareness is often the first point of misunderstanding that immigrants encounter as they arrive in the state. Public debate thus far has involved far too little informed comment, and has been fuelled to an unfortunate degree by political and media commentary rich in xenophobic undertones.

Of the programme refugees involved in this research, the majority had experienced significant personal loss. Many recounted their experiences of war, injury, the death of or separation from loved ones, loss of personal possessions, before their eventual flight to Ireland.

Asked to outline their reasons for leaving their country of origin, Bosnian refugees cited "ethnic cleansing", "concern for physical safety and survival", "to ensure the welfare of the family", and "fear" as the principal reasons for leaving. Among medical evacuees, the main reason was "to receive medical attention". Among the Vietnamese, the principal reasons cited include "because of the war", "ethnic cleansing", and "physical safety and survival". Among Vietnamese admitted under the Family Reunification Scheme, the predominant reasons cited for leaving Vietnam include "family reunification" and "because of the war". Many refugees were quite unprepared when they left their homes — often having very limited notice, and sometimes having only a few minutes to gather their belongings.

Participants felt overwhelmingly negative about having to leave home. The research participants spoke about emotions associated with widespread trauma, including feeling:

- Sad, depressed, grief-stricken, dejected, miserable
- Fearful, panic-stricken
- Lost, confused, concerned, insecure
- Distressed, upset, devastated, desperate.

In fact, the research provides a strong rebuttal to the perception by some that Bosnian and Vietnamese refugees are in Ireland primarily as economic migrants. Consider the statistic that only 17 per cent of Bosnian respondents stated that there had been an improvement in their living standards since coming to Ireland, while 40 per cent stated that there had been a noticeable drop in their standard of living. However, the extent of the experienced decline in standard of living is difficult to quantify — 43 per cent stated that it was impossible to compare the standard of living in Ireland to that which they enjoyed in their country of origin. In any case, it is crass to quantify loss or gain in purely financial terms, when the refugee's experience involves so much more, from the trauma and disruption of personal losses, to the challenges and opportunities of resettling in a new country.

SUPPORTING THE REFUGEE ON ARRIVAL IN IRELAND

For refugees who have left their homes, their culture, and perhaps their families, arriving in a new country can be a particularly disorienting experience. At this time, the refugee is generally dependent on the provisions made by others, and may feel that he or she has very little control over the situation. Nevertheless, there are many practical issues to be dealt with, including ensuring that there is food and shelter available. For many people, this business of survival must be carried out in a situation where they are dependent on interpreters in order to be heard. It is in these circumstances that a lot of refugees must begin the process of coming to terms with the events that have brought them to Ireland, and begin to look down the road at the implications of their circumstances.

For the immigrant, change happens at both group and individual levels. Berry (1986) has identified seven primary spheres within which change can be experienced at an individual level:

- *Physical changes*: including, for example, a new climate, a new living environment, exposure to new levels of urbanisation, often with greatly differing infrastructures and technologies from those with which the immigrant was previously familiar.
- *Biological changes*: these may occur due to new nutritional status, as a result of different basic foods; the encountering of new diseases; new medical technologies and drugs, etc.
- *Political changes*: these may involve exposure to new political ideologies, systems, and organisational structures, along with changes in one's legal status.
- *Economic changes*: consisting of people moving away from traditional pursuits towards new forms of employment, often necessitating further education, training or re-skilling. Upon arrival in the host country there can often be substantial changes (in either direction) in standard of living for the refugee.
- *Cultural changes*: whereby social norms, taboos and lifestyles change, along with the diminishment or replacement of original linguistic, religious, educational, and technical institutions.
- *Social relationships* are altered, involving changing inter-group and interpersonal relationships.

- *Psychological changes*, at the individual level, almost inevitably take place, including changes of identity, changes in values and attitudes, abilities, motives, and goals.

It is clear that a wide range of services are required to facilitate the resettlement of immigrants. One much-debated policy issue relating to programme refugees is the merit of providing reception centre facilities upon their arrival in Ireland, as opposed to resettling people directly into the community as soon as possible. This research shows that the vast majority of programme refugees hosted initially in a reception centre or hospital appear to have enjoyed very positive experiences. The benefits outlined included:

- Being able to have one's family together;
- Having the opportunity to learn English;
- Having the opportunity to get used to a new way of life, and to become familiar with the local area, and how to get around;
- Being able to meet with fellow Bosnians and develop friendships;
- Being provided with security, food and accommodation;
- Being given practical assistance, and having health needs attended to.

A small minority of those questioned also outlined some negative aspects to their experience of staying in reception centres or hospitals on initial arrival. These included

- A lack of privacy and quiet;
- Difficulties getting used to Irish food;
- A desire to be resettled in the community more quickly.

The vast majority of those admitted under the Family Reunification Scheme went directly to their family on arriving in Ireland, and found and reported this process to be helpful. Some 88 per cent of Bosnian and 92 per cent of Vietnamese participants identified particularly helpful aspects, which included:

- The overwhelmingly positive emotional benefits of being reunited with family members;
- The substantial practical and emotional support that family members were able to provide to help in resettlement.

Asked whether there were any particular disadvantages to having joined other family members immediately, only two Bosnians and one Vietnamese person had any negative comments to make. These included two cases where the accommodation was overcrowded, and one person who felt that it would have been better to be resettled independently immediately.

Participants were also asked about the supports they had on arriving in Ireland. Among Bosnian participants (n = 74), the main sources of support after arriving in Ireland included the Refugee Agency (57 per cent), the Irish Red Cross (23 per cent); Cappagh Hospital staff (23 per cent), Irish friends; family and relatives in Ireland; and the Cherry Orchard Reception Centre.[12] Among Vietnamese participants, the main sources of support included the Refugee Agency (41 per cent of participants); family and relatives (37 per cent); the Red Cross (22 per cent); Sr Phil Sinnot[13] (19 per cent); and the local parish (19 per cent). Asked how satisfied they were overall with the practical assistance they received when they first arrived in Ireland, participants expressed a significant degree of satisfaction.

It is clear, therefore, that there has been a wide range of supports for refugees arriving in the country, each with something to offer. These supports have been available in a structured fashion in reception centres, while the type of support available to those being reunited with their families includes the vital elements of emotional support and caring offered within the family structures. The important issue, of course, is not where refugees spend their

---

[12] The Irish Red Cross was responsible for running Cherry Orchard Reception Centre during the initial intake of Bosnian programme refugees. This responsibility eventually moved to a Management Committee chaired by the Department of Foreign Affairs.

[13] Sr Phil is a member of the Sisters of Mercy order, and has been involved in providing support to the Vietnamese community in Ireland since the first arrivals in 1979.

initial time in the country, but whether they are likely to be in a position to benefit to the maximum extent from the range of services that are available.

In this context, the survey has identified that refugees who stayed initially in a reception centre or hospital clearly benefited from the ease of access to various services, particularly English language classes (see below). One of the primary functions of reception centres is to facilitate access to various services, including health, education, social welfare, housing and psychological services. It appears that the reception centres have functioned very effectively as a point of arrival for refugees. At the same time, there have been, and will continue to be, many cases where it is much more desirable that the refugee joins his or her family unit on arriving in Ireland. The challenge for service providers, therefore, is to develop innovative service delivery strategies to those refugees who have minimal contact with the relevant authorities and agencies at the outset, to ensure they receive supports comparable to those received by those whose initial stay is in a reception centre.

Delivery of English Language Training

A useful case example relates to the delivery of English Language Training to refugees. As one of the foremost predictors of social, psychological and economic adjustment, promoting the development of proficiency in English is a vital consideration in any strategy for supporting refugee resettlement in Ireland. Figure 10.1 shows that those who spent longer than two months in ELT had significantly better proficiency in English than those who spent less than two months in ELT.

Figure 10.1: Relationship between Length of Time in ELT and Number of Skills Acquired

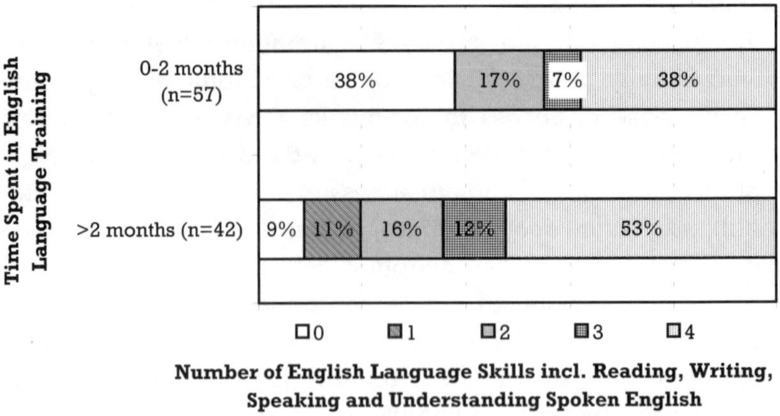

Figure 10.2 shows that participants who accessed English language training for two months or longer were more likely to have stayed initially in a reception centre, while those with very low levels of attendance at English Language Training were more likely to have been admitted under the Family Reunification Scheme — and therefore to have gone directly to stay with their family upon arrival in Ireland.

Figure 10.2: Relationship between Initial Destination in Ireland and Take-up of ELT

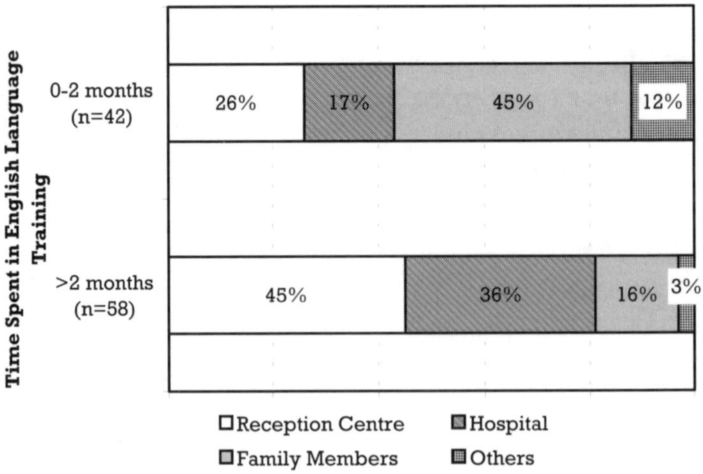

This data indicates that while accommodating programme refugees in reception centres for a period affords an opportunity for effective service delivery, a challenge exists for service providers to deliver effective levels of ELT to refugees who are not so easily accessed. If tracking and outreach mechanisms are not developed for such refugees, then their resettlement and integration will be hampered by inadequate English language skills. The same lessons regarding accessing can be drawn by services offering social, vocational, medical, psychological, legal or other supports.

SUPPORTING RESETTLEMENT THROUGH EFFECTIVE LEGISLATION AND POLICY

The feelings of uncertainty and insecurity associated with resettling in a new country have been documented among immigrants everywhere. For refugees, who have left their country of origin under duress or stress, the resettlement process involves a high degree of stress and uncertainty. The research highlights several elements of the legislation in relation to programme refugees that are of particular value in promoting successful resettlement.

Prior to their arrival in Ireland, both Bosnian and Vietnamese programme refugees were given rights that essentially guarantee them the same treatment as Irish nationals in terms of access to education, health, social welfare, housing, employment and training opportunities. In addition, both Bosnian and Vietnamese programme refugees enjoy the right to remain in Ireland for as long as they wish, and the right to apply for Irish citizenship after three years of residency here. The Government also has the right to admit into Ireland family members of programme refugees, under the Family Reunification Scheme.

NATURALISATION, CITIZENSHIP AND PLANS TO REMAIN IN IRELAND

At the time of the survey, there was a high naturalisation rate among the Vietnamese sample. While no Bosnian participants had yet received citizenship, interest was shown to be very high (86 per cent of the sample had either already applied, or intended to apply in the future).

The Vietnamese participants indicated a strong level of commitment to remaining in Ireland. There was less certainty among a section of the Bosnian sample, 20 per cent of whom stated that they planned to return to where they came from. Another 37 per cent were undecided about their future, stating that it depended on a number of factors, including the wishes of their children, and practical issues like the resolution of the war. Nevertheless, 40 per cent of the Bosnian sample intended to remain in Ireland for the foreseeable future.

This decision to remain or repatriate seems to bear heavily on the person's ability to resettle here in Ireland. There was a strong correlation between the intention to remain in Ireland and the extent to which refugees felt part of the community in which they lived. Of those who intended to remain living in Ireland, only 32 per cent said they did not feel part of the community in which they lived. This compares with 62 per cent of those who planned to repatriate to their country of origin, and 71 per cent of those who remained undecided about their future.

There was also a highly significant relationship between participants' plans for the future and their psychological well-being. Of the 48 people who planned to remain in Ireland for the foreseeable future, 40 (83 per cent) scored below the GHQ threshold, and 8 above. Of the 28 people who indicated that they hadn't made up their minds yet, 15 scored below, and 13 above, the threshold mark. In contrast, of the 19 participants who planned not to stay in Ireland (wanting to return home or to emigrate elsewhere), 16 (84 per cent) scored above the threshold, and the remaining 3 people (16 per cent) scored below. This finding, outlined below in Figure 10.3, illustrates the relationship between having a secure vision of the future and one's present psychological well-being.

Figure 10.3: Relationship between Future Plans and Psychological Distress

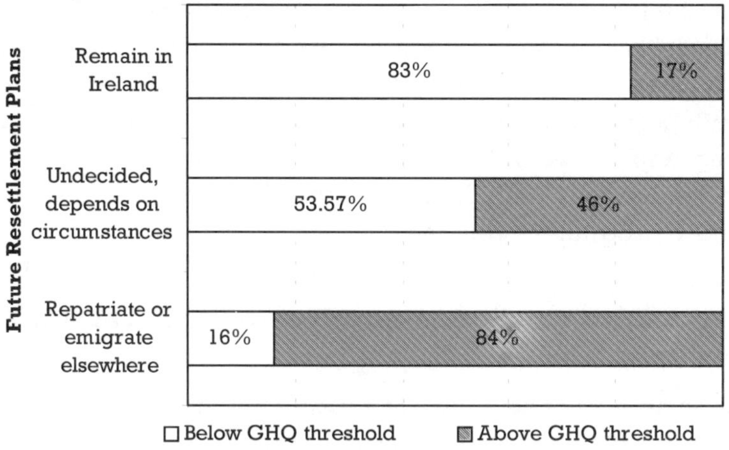

n = 95; LR chi-square = 28.52; df = 2; p < .001

THE FAMILY REUNIFICATION SCHEME

The Family Reunification Scheme (FRS) for programme refugees allows for certain family members to join their relatives in Ireland. The FRS was demonstrated throughout the research to be an important element of resettlement for the refugee. The anxiety of refugees to have other family members admitted into Ireland was clear from the research. Among Bosnian participants, less than 20 per cent thought the present FRS was adequate, while 41 per cent felt that it was "inadequate" or "very inadequate". The remaining 40 per cent responded that they were "unsure". Among Vietnamese participants, 32 per cent felt that the FRS was "adequate" or "very adequate". Only 2 people (10 per cent) stated that they felt the FRS was "quite inadequate", while the majority (58 per cent) stated that they were "unsure".

Generally, those who did not understand the criteria or implementation of the FRS felt that it was unfairly implemented. While there was considerable use of the "not sure" category by both Bosnian (44 per cent) and Vietnamese (47 per cent) participants, 22 per cent of Bosnian and 37 per cent of Vietnamese participants felt that the FRS was being operated either "fairly" or "very fairly", while 33 per cent of Bosnian and 16 per cent of Vietnamese participants felt that the FRS was being operated "quite unfairly" or "very unfairly".

In the period since the research was conducted, a Government decision has allowed for the admission of 350 Bosnians and 200 Vietnamese under the Family Reunification Scheme during the 12-month period from March 1999. This decision is well on the way to being implemented. This quota will complete the intake of relatives under the Family Reunification Scheme for Bosnian and Vietnamese programme refugees.

Supporting the Socio-economic Resettlement of Refugees

The socio-economic status of programme refugees emerged as one of the key indicators of successful resettlement.

Promoting Employment and Tackling Unemployment

The survey highlighted significant levels of unemployment and underemployment among refugees. Twenty-one Bosnian participants were in receipt of unemployment assistance, with a further three receiving unemployment benefit, amounting to 32.4 per cent of the sample being unemployed. All were long-term unemployed (out of paid employment for longer than 12 months). There were clear divisions of role along gender lines — women were more likely to be on home duties, with men more likely to be in paid employment. The majority (77 per cent) of those out of work had never been employed in this country.

Those who were unemployed were quite pessimistic about their prospects over the next 12 months. Asked how good or bad they thought their chances were of finding the kind of job they were looking for over the next 12 months, 8 out of 11 participants rated their chances as "bad" or "very bad"'. The remaining 3 had "moderate" hopes of gaining employment. Five Vietnamese participants reported that they were in receipt of unemployment assistance, with a further two in receipt of unemployment benefit, amounting to 24 per cent of the sample being unemployed.

Survey participants made several suggestions for improving employment prospects, including obtaining better qualifications, being assisted with translation and accreditation of qualifications obtained abroad, being given assistance in approaching employers, and improving English language ability. These findings have been replicated by Sultan-Prnjavorac (1999), who identified fluency in English, childcare provision and accreditation of existing qualifications as some of the supports required by Bosnian women.

Those who were unemployed were significantly more likely to be experiencing financial difficulties, and were more likely to be experiencing high levels of psychological distress (Figure 10.4).

Figure 10.4: Relationship between Employment Status and Psychological Distress

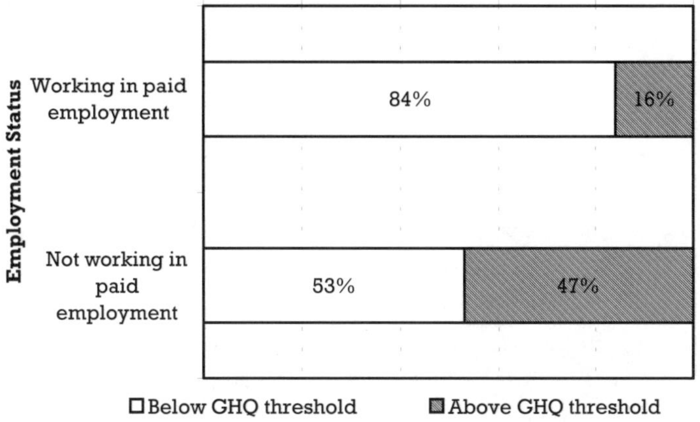

Participants experiencing "great difficulty" in coping with their household income had higher levels of psychological distress than those coping "very easily" or "quite easily" with their household income level, the vast majority of whom enjoyed good mental health (Figure 10.5).

Figure 10.5: Relationship between Perceived Economic Strain and Psychological Distress

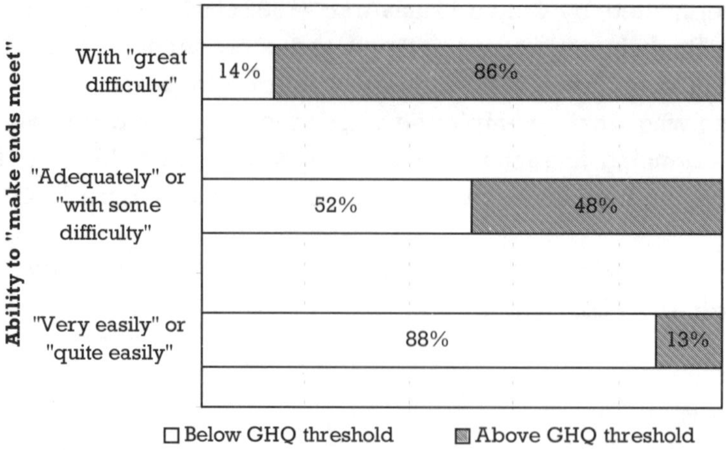

n = 95; LR chi-square = 19.60; df = 2; $p < .001$

These data correspond with the findings of the ESRI study (Whelan et al., 1991) on the effects of unemployment on psychological distress. Researching a large sample of the adult Irish population, they found that 34 per cent of unemployed people in their sample were above the GHQ threshold, while only 7 per cent of employees were above the mark (experiencing psychological distress).

Supporting the Social Integration of Refugees

Identifying Vulnerable Refugees

The research identified several vulnerable groups that warrant particular attention by service providers. Older refugees, women in the home, unemployed refugees and refugees who are retired are more likely to have poor English language skills, feel isolated, have a sense of not belonging to the community in which they live, and have higher levels of mental health difficulties.

Figure 10.6 shows that those who have poor English language skills are statistically more likely to experience mental health difficulties (i.e. score above the GHQ threshold). The significant role that English language acquisition plays in supporting the adjustment of refugees to living in this country, and particularly in buffering the refugee against psychological distress, cannot be emphasised enough.

Figure 10.6: Relationship between English Language Skills and Psychological Distress

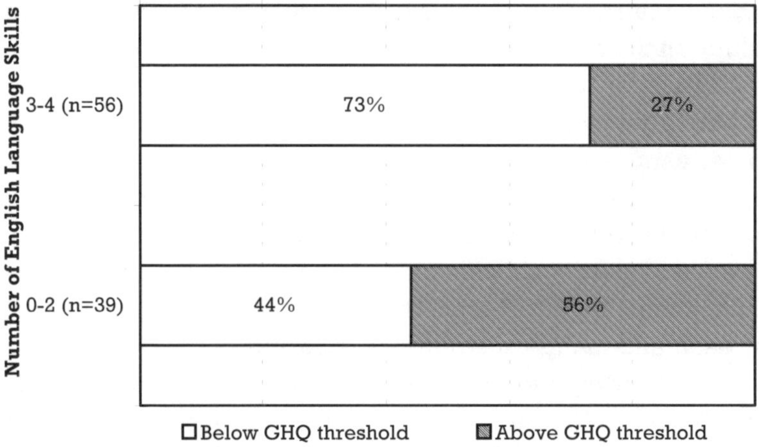

Lack of social interaction, both with the wider community and even among the expatriate community to which they also belong, was also identified as an issue for the more vulnerable refugee groups. All of those who reported having no English language skills stated they did not interact on a daily basis with members of the wider community, with 42 per cent never interacting with the wider community. By contrast, of those who reported being able to read, write, speak and understand English (to at least a basic functional level), 56 per cent interacted daily, a further 30 per cent once or twice a week, and only 7 per cent report never interacting with the wider community.

CONCLUSIONS

While the data presented here is a brief summary of the survey data, it sheds useful light on the experiences of programme refugees as they strive to resettle in Ireland. While programme refugees represent a particular type of immigrant, the resettlement issues they face may be related readily to the wider body of immigrants that will arrive in Ireland over the coming years. Integration and empowerment are seen as two of the key principles involved in successful resettlement.

It is clear that service provision, even to programme refugees with full legal status and rights, and with the expert resettlement support available to them from the Refugee Agency, is no easy task. It requires focused outreach, particularly to more vulnerable groups such as women in the home, the unemployed and the elderly. However, this outreach should not be left entirely to refugee support agencies and charities, but must be incorporated into mainstream service provision. Health, social welfare, housing, education, training and employment support services must recognise that in Ireland, as elsewhere, refugees and other immigrants experience particular difficulties in accessing services. These difficulties must be addressed by service providers through explicit outreach and inclusion strategies, bearing in mind the vulnerability of such groups to isolation, unemployment, poverty and poor mental health. Without appropriate service delivery strategies, the enormous potential of immigrants to contribute socially and economically to Irish society will not be realised, and they will instead become marginalised and dependent members of society. Furthermore, it is apparent that the role played by the Refugee Agency in co-ordinating and supporting the resettlement of programme refugees should be replicated for all those granted full refugee status. A similar agency with executive function will be required to co-ordinate the State's support for the resettlement of immigrants with residency status in Ireland.

Primary among the strategies of any resettlement policy should be the provision of training, including English language training. This has been shown to be essential for accessing employment, support services, and for social participation and integration. Such training must be innovative and integrated, given the fact that refugees and immigrants are anxious not to have their lives in Ireland put on hold. Many wish to commence training, education or employment as soon as possible, but may have childminding responsibilities and other needs.

Finally, the short- and long-term social integration of immigrants must take place on the basis that integration is a two-way process. Immigrants must receive support in developing social support networks and participating in Irish society, while we as a society must become educated and informed about the rights, needs, talents and dreams of the newest members of our society.

References

Berry, J.W. (1986). "The Acculturation Process and Refugee Behavior" in C.L. Williams and J. Westermeyer (eds.), *Refugee Mental Health in Resettlement Countries*, pp. 25–7. Washington, DC: Hemisphere.

Central Statistics Office (2000), Principal Statistics, http://www.cso.ie/principalstats/pristatlab.html

Goldberg, D. and P. Williams (1991), *A User's Guide to the General Health Questionnaire*, Berkshire: NFER-Nelson Publishing Company Ltd.

McGovern, F. (1990), "Vietnamese Refugees in Ireland, 1979–1989: A Case Study in Education and Resettlement" Unpublished M.Ed. Thesis, Trinity College, Dublin.

O'Regan, C. (1998), "Report of a Survey of the Vietnamese and Bosnian Refugee Communities Living in Ireland, Dublin: The Refugee Agency.

Sultan-Prnjavorac (1999), *Barriers and Needs of Bosnian Refugee Women with Regard to Education, Employment and Social Inclusion*, Dublin: The Zena Project.

Valtonen, K. (1996), "East Meets North: The Finnish-Vietnamese Community", *Asian and Pacific Migration Journal*, Vol. 5, pp. 471–498.

Whelan, C.T., D.S. Hannan, and S. Creighton (1991), *Unemployment, Poverty and Psychological Distress*, Economic and Social Research Institute General Research Paper No. 150, Dublin: ESRI.

CHAPTER ELEVEN

REFUGEE STATUS IN EXILE: THE CASE OF AFRICAN ASYLUM-SEEKERS IN IRELAND

Treasa Galvin[1]

INTRODUCTION

This chapter is concerned with processes of transition and change in the meaning attached to refugee status for asylum-seekers in the Republic of Ireland. It focuses on the link between asylum and refugee status and the construction of the refugee's social world as reflected in adaptation and incorporation processes. For asylum-seekers, the transition to their host society has meant changes in status and identity and ambivalent incorporation and adaptation processes. This chapter considers how, for these asylum-seekers, their social world is altered, redefined and remains incomplete in their new environment.

BACKGROUND

The period since 1994 marks a significant re-definition in Ireland's role as a refugee host society. Prior to 1994, that role had largely been limited to programme refugees (Table 11.1) and very small numbers of asylum-seekers. Over the past five years, the arrival of an increasing number of asylum-seekers marks, for Ireland, a

---

[1] This chapter is based on the situation that pertained to asylum-seekers in Ireland prior to the Government's introduction of a dispersal policy and direct provision in April 2000.

transition to a more permanent and extensive role as a refugee host society (Table 11.2).

Table 11.1: Programme Refugees Admitted to Ireland 1956–1999*

Year	Place of Origin	Number
1956	Hungary	530
1973-74	Chile	120
1979	Vietnam**	212
1985	Iran (B'hai)	26
1992	Bosnia***	178
1993	Bosnia	13
1994	Bosnia	9
1995	Bosnia	80
1996	Bosnia	83
1997	Bosnia	89
1998	Bosnia	3
1999	Kosovo****	1,032

Notes: * Figures are for each "new intake" and do not include those who were admitted under the family reunification programme. ** 1979–1998: a total of 382 relatives have been admitted under the family reunification programme. *** 1993–1999: a total of 833 relatives have been admitted under the family re-unification programme. This includes 276 in 1999. **** 1999: a total of 21 relatives were admitted under the family reunification programme.

Source: Refugee Agency, 1998, 1999.

Table 11.2: Number of Asylum-seekers' Applications in Ireland 1988–1999

Year	Number of asylum applicants	Year	Number of asylum applicants
1988	49	1994	362
1989	36	1995	424
1990	60	1996	1,179
1991	31	1997	3,883
1992	39	1998	4,626
1993	91	1999	7,724

Source: Department of Justice, 2000.

Given the past emphasis on emigration and the arrival of a relatively small number of refugees and asylum-seekers prior to 1994, it is perhaps not surprising that Ireland has found itself poorly equipped for its more extensive role as a "refugee host society". Though a signatory to the 1951 Geneva Convention, prior to 1996 Ireland had no specific legislation governing refugees and asylum-seekers and only a very rudimentary administrative machinery for dealing with the them.[2]

Given then the need to establish adequate legal, administrative and procedural mechanisms to deal with asylum applications, the Government's emphasis since 1994 has centred on determining the individual's legal status as refugee. The enactment of the Irish Refugee Act (1996), the employment of additional staff, the creation of a one-stop-shop,[3] and the establishment of an appeals process have been the main features of the Government's attempts to establish adequate mechanisms for dealing with applications for asylum.

On arrival in Ireland, asylum-seekers are defined as homeless and are provided with temporary emergency accommodation in designated hostels or guesthouses.

The Refugee Act (1996) stipulates that in the period between arrival and acquiring their refugee status, asylum-seekers are prohibited from taking up paid employment. As a result and irrespective of their educational background and skills, asylum-seekers "are entirely dependent on state subvention for their housing and income needs" (O'Sullivan, 1997: 5). They are entitled to claim a weekly supplementary welfare allowance (SWA), a rent supplement, a clothing allowance on arrival and a fuel allowance during the winter months. As recipients of the SWA, they are entitled to free health care. Families with children are entitled to claim children's allowance. The children of refugees and asylum-

---

[2] The 1935 Nationality and Citizenship Act, the 1935 Aliens Act, Amendments to the Aliens Act in 1946 and 1975, together with a letter from the Irish Minister for Justice to the UNHCR in 1985 setting out the procedure for establishing refugee status and granting asylum, provided the legal framework for state policy until 1996 (Shipsey, 1994).

[3] Opened in 1998, the one-stop-shop houses staff from all relevant Government Departments to which asylum-seekers require access when they arrive.

seekers are allowed to attend school. In essence, asylum-seekers are entitled to the same social welfare benefits as Irish nationals who claim SWA. When individuals are granted refugee status they retain their entitlements to the above benefits and have the same rights to education, employment, etc. as Irish nationals.

The Research Group

This chapter arises from research work among African asylum-seekers in Ireland, which began in 1996 and is ongoing. It is specifically based on one research group of 28 asylum-seekers from different African countries (Table 11.3) who have acquired their refugee status during the course of the research. The 28 respondents included 21 men, four couples, and three other women asylum-seekers. African asylum-seekers in Ireland are a heterogeneous group whose diversity lies, among other things, in their ethnic background, age, education, and the causes of flight. While for the majority (20) Ireland was their first country of refuge, five had prior experience of exile. They arrived alone (18), with their spouses (4) or in small groups of two or three (6) and had left family members behind in their countries of origin. Ireland was not necessarily chosen as a country of final destination, as individuals left their countries of origin unaware of which country would be their host society.

Table 11.3: Asylum-seekers' Countries of Origin (N=28)

Country of origin	Number
Angola	2
Burundi	2
Cameroon	1
Democratic People's Republic of Congo	11
Nigeria	4
Rwanda	2
Somalia	1
Sudan	5
Total	28

Respondents were drawn from the social networks of specific asylum-seekers. The manner of generating the research group precluded the possibility of having an equal number of asylum-seekers from different countries of origin or of having an equal number of male and female respondents. Data was collected through the use of unstructured but focused in-depth interviews using an open-ended interview guide, rather than a set questionnaire.

REFUGEE POPULATIONS

The creation of refugee populations and ensuing patterns of migration is inherently linked to events, frequently outside individual control, which precede and accompany displacement. Not infrequently, forced migration involves the movement of people between different countries and continents. Uncertainty surrounding the place of final destination is part of the context in which the decision to seek refuge is made. Why individuals become refugees depends on a host of factors, but "Above all they included wars, especially civil wars" (Roberts, 1998: 378).

Throughout the 1990s, both within and between African states, long-standing conflicts continued while new ones emerged. In post-colonial Africa, the 1994 genocide in Rwanda was unprecedented in scale. While Sudan's civil war has continued, internal conflicts in Somalia and Sierra Leone together with the war between Ethiopia and Eritrea (which emerged during the 1990s) seem set to become protracted in nature. The post-Mobutu era conflict in the Democratic People's Republic of the Congo has involved the neighbouring states of Rwanda and Uganda together with the West African State of Chad and the Southern African states of Angola, Zimbabwe and Namibia.[4] At the same time, the failure of the Angolan cease-fire has led to the continuation of a conflict whose roots lie in part in the cold war era.

While the causes of such conflicts are complex and varied, the consequences are similar. Large numbers of people are forced to

---

[4] Chad, Angola, Zimbabwe and Namibia intervened to support the Government of President L. Kabila, while Rwanda and Uganda support various rebel groups opposed to the current Government.

migrate either internally, to neighbouring states, or further afield. While small numbers of refugees from Africa arrive in Europe even smaller numbers seek refuge in Ireland.[5]

In dealing with the causes of forced migration, Fuglerud (1997: 446–447) notes that:

> Due to changes in patterns of conflict, most refugees today are not individually persecuted but civilians fleeing from other people's violence.

The research group on whom this paper is based may be divided into three groups, namely: individuals who fled generally dangerous situations; those who had been imprisoned and/or tortured for political and other activities; and those individuals who anticipated being persecuted if they remained within their own societies.

EXILE RECONCEPTUALISED

That the category *refugee* is conceptually problematic has been demonstrated by a number of authors (Waldron, 1988; Zetter, 1988; Marx, 1990). Harrell-Bond (1986) notes that a wide discrepancy may exist between the host society's definition of refugee and the individual's own definition of their status. Individuals make the decision to seek refuge within the confines of situations and societies where the meaning attached to refuge and exile are wholly different from that found in exile.

Prior to arrival in Ireland, individuals had conceptualised exile within the context of push factors (the causes of flight), and the right to protection from persecution (outside one's own society) enshrined in international legal instruments.[6] When individuals arrive in Ireland, they encounter a society in which the meanings attached to migration, exile and refuge are vastly different to those they had previously experienced or conceptualised. While prior knowledge of Ireland does not provide the necessary details about

---

[5] Presently Ireland is host to asylum-seekers from a number of African countries, including Algeria, Angola, Burundi, Cameroon, Democratic People's Republic of the Congo, Ethiopia, Libya, Nigeria, Rwanda, Somalia and Sudan.

[6] The 1951 Geneva Convention, the 1967 Protocol and the OAU Charter on Refugees.

Ireland as a place of refuge, past experiences of exile cannot be readily transferred to Ireland as a host society.

Though they had conceptualised their host society as a country totally different to their own, individuals had not associated such difference with long-term changes in their socio-economic status or their status as refugee. In many cases, not having lived outside their own society or previously been in exile, it was difficult to envisage how aspects of a new environment could drastically change individual status and identity.

In host societies, asylum-seekers are confronted with new meanings and interpretations as a consequence of which exile and asylum are reconstructed (Al-Rasheed, 1993). For individuals, adjusting to their new environment most importantly meant adjusting to the meaning of refugee status within a new normative order.

In Ireland, migration is conceptualised within the confines of "emigration" as a historically dominant feature of Irish society. Inmigration by non-Irish nationals seeking refuge is a relatively new feature of Irish society. As in other countries, refugee status in Ireland is determined within the context of the 1951 Geneva Convention. In this host society, individuals seeking refuge confront a bureaucratic state machinery (the Irish Department of Justice) that determines the individual's right to refugee status.

> Asylum-seekers not fulfilling these legal requirements tend to be perceived, and portrayed, as attempting to deceive the system, thereby exploiting the generosity of the host country (Fuglerud, 1997: 459).

At the same time, individuals are confronted with legislative provisions in the Irish Refugee Act (1996) that govern their rights and entitlements within their host society. For those seeking refuge, the trauma of flight and of the journey into exile is replaced by the trauma of acquiring the right to a place of refuge. Exile is transformed into a host society wherein others determine one's right to refuge. For individuals, adjusting to this new environment means adjusting to exile but most importantly to a process of transition to their status as asylum-seekers and refugees.

ASYLUM AND REFUGEE STATUS

The Irish Government's response to those seeking refuge has been characterised by: an emphasis on pull factors to the exclusion of push factors; a slow and ambivalent response at legislative and policy levels; the portrayal of asylum-seekers and refugees as a temporary bureaucratic problem; and an inability to conceptualise the permanent transformation taking place in the nature and composition of Irish society.

During the period since 1994, government statements and media coverage are two of the most significant factors that have influenced the meaning attached by the public to refugee and asylum-seeker in Ireland. In the Irish context, as generous social welfare payments are portrayed as pull factors, the label *asylum-seeker* has acquired a "selective and materialistic meaning" (Zetter, 1991: 39). Additionally, the indiscriminate use of the terms *refugee*, *asylum-seeker* and *illegal immigrant* categorises those seeking refuge as a homogeneous group. As such categorisation de-emphasises push factors and the heterogeneity of the refugee population, it serves to obscure the uniqueness of the individual's past, most especially the individual causes of flight and exile.

It cannot be assumed that host society populations are familiar with the multiple and complex causes of forced migration. Public education campaigns play a significant role in counteracting inaccurate information and "myths" surrounding the asylum process e.g. that asylum-seekers receive higher social welfare payments or that all asylum-seekers receive mobile phones. To date, no attempt has been made by successive Irish Governments to provide, through a public education campaign, essential information on what is a new phenomenon in Irish society.

The continued weak bureaucratic machinery for processing asylum claims combined with an increasing number of applicants has meant long delays in processing cases. The constant reference by Government to the need to "clear the backlog" portrays the asylum issue as a temporary bureaucratic and legal problem, which fails to deal with the broader policy issues of refugee resettlement.

On arrival, an individual may have defined himself or herself as a refugee but finds no automatic entitlement to that status in their host society. Within the host society, they are initially conferred the status of asylum-seeker, which they retain throughout the lengthy application process. Adjusting to their new environment primarily means adjusting to the new temporary and insecure status of asylum-seeker.

In essence, the process of applying for refugee status marks a transition to the status of asylum-seeker and a subsequent change in the meaning attached to refugee status. The process of seeking refuge devalues and transforms the status of refugee from a respected and dignified position to one that is questioned and requires proof. While to recount the past is frequently traumatic for individuals, providing evidence of that past is especially problematic. By its very nature, forced migration precludes the individual from having in their possession those very documents required as proof of the need for refuge. At the individual level, the status of refugee should imply a degree of dignity and respect wherein the trauma of the past gives way to hope for the future. On the contrary, individuals find that their identity is no longer derived from the cause of flight but from the status of asylum-seeker as legally and socially defined in the host society. In exile, the status of refugee becomes a hindrance rather than a resource in the resettlement process. Individuals begin to deny their status as asylum-seekers and refugees when the experience of exile fails to live up to expectations; when the status itself is viewed as a barrier in interacting with the host society; and when there is genuine fear for their own safety.[7] Such denial creates, for the individual, public and private spheres within their lives that are not easily reconciled and that have repercussions for individual self-esteem and identity.

The Asylum Process

The individual experience of the asylum process is both culturally and socially specific. Refugees bring into exile their own experiences, history, cultural background and expectations. While International Conventions govern host country asylum legislation, specific policy measures and available facilities vary widely from country to country. In Ireland, as in other countries, long delays in

---

[7] From country of origin Governments and their agents.

acquiring refugee status and insecurity and fear concerning the outcome of an application are among the factors that characterise the asylum process.

For the participants in this research, their dependence on the state welfare system is among the most important determinants of their experience as asylum-seekers.

Over time, though not infrequently at an early stage, individuals become conscious of the social stigma ordinarily attached to dependence on the state welfare system in Ireland. The temporary emergency accommodation that is initially provided for asylum-seekers is overcrowded, while its lack of privacy is experienced as particularly difficult, as are the restrictions imposed in such accommodation.[8] Guesthouse accommodation requires individuals to vacate the premises during daytime, leaving asylum-seekers with little option but to wander the streets. In the long term, asylum-seekers are expected to find their own accommodation within the private rented sector. While seeking accommodation, individuals become conscious of the limitations of the rent supplement and the additional difficulties of seeking accommodation when landlords do not accept the rent allowance provided by the Health Board.[9]

So, too, asylum-seekers become aware of hostility from members of Irish society to their dependence on social welfare. Such hostility is viewed as understandable but misplaced. Asylum-seekers note that their legally imposed status undermines their willingness to contribute to their host society as workers and taxpayers while confining them to the position of social welfare recipients, a position with which many are deeply uncomfortable. Mr D, who had no previous experience of a state welfare system, noted: "I feel as though I am taking something that does not belong to me . . ." None of the respondents in this research came from societies with an established welfare state system. Rather,

---

[8] For example, while some emergency accommodation does not allow visitors at all, others do so but only in a controlled and restricted manner.

[9] Regional Health Authorities who are responsible for the housing needs of social welfare recipients and the provision of emergency accommodation for all those who are homeless. Rent allowance is a secondary social welfare benefit and forms the main portion of an individual's rent.

they were familiar with the norm of self-sufficiency and its perceived dignity, neither of which was to be found within the state welfare system.

Well-educated professionals note the discrepancy between their previous lifestyle and that experienced as welfare recipients in Ireland. Dependence on state welfare is equated with forced unemployment, which is viewed as a dehumanising process. "How can you have a system which confines grown men to not working . . . it is not normal . . ." (Mr G) At the same time, highly skilled individuals were conscious of being de-skilled and of the long-term consequences. The status of asylum is experienced as resource-based restrictive inclusion in the host society as a consequence of which lives are wasted. Inability to work during the asylum phase and anticipated difficulties as refugees in getting educational qualifications recognised serves further to deny the individual's past and to devalue previous achievements. African asylum-seekers are particularly conscious of the lack of acceptance of their qualifications in Irish society. Mr K was a qualified accountant who had been in full-time employment in his country of origin. In Ireland, he enrolled on an accountancy course because as he said: "You see they think that qualifications from home are no good . . . you have to get an Irish qualification . . . that's why I'm doing this course."

In essence, the status of asylum is experienced as a normative order wherein the ability to meet one's own basic needs is withdrawn with a subsequent loss of dignity and self-esteem.

In exile, the prohibition on employment leads to role redefinition and to a perceived and associated loss of dignity and status within both the family and community. While dependence on the state welfare system is associated with a loss of social and economic status, it is equally associated with a loss of social roles. The asylum-seekers on which this work is based are predominantly from patrilineal systems within Africa where the role of male breadwinner is emphasised. Long periods of unemployment can and do translate into a loss of role with a resulting loss of dignity and status within the family unit and the wider community. Consequently, the asylum process involves much reference to the past and to a perceived loss of social status. Mr P spoke of the manner in which being in exile had destroyed his livelihood, saying: "Can you believe I used to work as an engineer, own a house and so on?"

Inability to fulfil role obligations in relation to the extended family further enhances the loss of individual status. Role redefinition and loss of social status is compounded when, in the host society, the label asylum-seeker emphasises materialistic pull factors. As Mr P further noted: "Can I really give up my house, my job and a salary for £60 per week?"

For individuals, the changes in status and identity as the outcome of exposure to a new socio-cultural environment is important, as is their marginalisation, which arises from the meanings attached to refugee and asylum status. But equally important is the manner in which the construction of the label *asylum-seeker* restricts the integration process and thereby limits the reestablishment of the individual's social world.

The Adaptation Process

As Ireland does not operate a system of detention centres for asylum-seekers, individuals interact with Irish society from the time of arrival. As a result, the process of learning about the new environment begins immediately and involves two separate but equally important types of information. Firstly, specific asylum knowledge is necessary to access the asylum process. Secondly, broad general knowledge of the new socio-cultural environment is perceived as an important component of the adaptation and integration process. At different points in time and in various combinations, government officials, the media, refugee networks and interaction with the general public are the main sources of both types of information.

Newly acquired knowledge about Irish society frequently gives rise to disappointment and frustration. Asylum-seekers are conscious that Ireland's colonial past and struggle for economic development is one shared with their countries of origin. Ireland's experience of emigration gives rise to the expectation that the causes of exile and refuge will be appreciated and understood in detail. A process of alienation begins when individual expectations are undermined by: the constant emphasis on pull factors as the cause of refugee movements; the negative portrayal of refugees by public figures and sections of the media;[10] the lack of access to a broader range of the host society's resources; and hostility from members of the public. In sum, frustration and alienation result from the perceived contradiction between Ireland's own past history and its current ambivalent response to those seeking refuge.

Asylum-seekers view the pre-1996 lack of legislation and policy measures governing asylum and refugee issues in Ireland in a historical context; namely, the lack of in-migration in the past. Equally, they are conscious of Ireland's "development history", the sudden arrival of asylum-seekers and the confusion this has caused at different levels in society. Mr T, who had come to Ireland in 1997, spoke of the ever-increasing numbers of asylum-seekers and the manner in which it can pose a dilemma for any host society population: ". . . quite frankly, I don't know how I would react if this was my country and you were the refugees coming in . . ."

While respondents appreciate Ireland's efforts to provide for them a place of safety, this does not mean that as participants they were uncritical of the manner in which the asylum process is being developed. Improvements such as the establishment of an independent appeals process and the opening of the one-stop-shop are acknowledged as positive developments in the asylum system. But the slow and ambivalent pace of change at the policy and administrative level symbolises for asylum-seekers a lack of commitment on the part of Government and by extension on the part of Irish society. The Government's failure to fully implement the Refugee Act (1996) and to provide clear and comprehensive policies on refugee resettlement further portray to those seeking refuge an ambivalent approach. That ambivalence is experienced as a lack of acceptance of the individual's situation and as a lack of urgency in response to refugee matters.

As asylum-seekers slowly become more familiar with Irish society, they begin to question facets of their host society. In particular, the nature and depth of Irish "hospitality" is questioned and equated more with curiosity than with acceptance or concern about the plight of those seeking refuge. Ms B who felt that it was

---

[10] Byrne (1997: 111)

unrealistic to expect the entire Irish population to behave in a similar manner noted: "It's like anywhere. . . . Some are friendly, some are not . . ." Mr S, who came to Ireland in 1998, had found people to be talkative and friendly but did not equate this with hospitality: "I don't know . . . this Irish hospitality . . . I think they are curious . . . you see Irish people want to know all about you but do not want to tell you anything about themselves."

At another level, asylum-seekers are conscious of emerging situations whereby sections of Irish society now benefit from their arrival. In particular, they note that it is Irish landlords who own the flats and emergency accommodation in which they stay and for which the Health Board pays. Referring to one such emergency accommodation, those housed there noted: ". . . you see that new Mercedes Benz out there, it belongs to the owner . . . they are making a lot of money on us . . ." As individual perceptions of the host society diverge from those held by the local population, asylum-seekers become apprehensive about Irish society. In essence, a wider knowledge of their host society combined with the social construction of the label *asylum-seeker* (therein) gives rise to a complex set of barriers to social interaction.

Barriers to social interaction exist for both the refugees and the host society population. The diverse ways in which individuals perceive their host society depends on factors such as past experiences, with whom and why they interact and consciousness of their position. In the Irish case, the initial point of contact is frequently a local social welfare office. The context of social interaction is thus within the confines of access to limited state resources and competition for these.

Contact with Irish people is viewed by asylum-seekers as essential to understanding the society and to the integration process. Yet asylum-seekers are conscious that their contact with Irish society is limited by the restrictions attached to their status. Social interaction is largely confined to the social welfare office, other social institutions such as schools and hospitals, together with shops and on some occasions social outlets (e.g. nightclubs). The legal prohibition on employment means that individuals cannot examine people's reactions to a range of work-related issues, while social welfare recipients are not viewed as representing the wider society.

At the same time, the establishment of primary networks consisting of other refugees and asylum-seekers takes place but is not unproblematic. Individuals bring into exile past experiences, most especially of other groups within their country of origin. Where such past experiences were negative in nature, individuals do not associate with some members of their own society. Indeed, the divisions brought from home may be so great that they are unable to interact at all with others from their country of origin. Such is the case with some Hutu and Tutsi refugees from Rwanda. While the causes of flight may act as a barrier to social interaction and network formation, language is also a barrier to interaction with those from other African countries. Finally,

> the negative label associated with asylum means that individuals seek to disassociate themselves from that label and from other refugees now portrayed as illegal immigrants (Zetter, 1991).

The small numbers of refugees in Ireland makes broader secondary social networks all the more essential if isolation is to be avoided and integration successful. For refugees, the development of social networks is hindered by a complex set of factors that include Government policies that keep them dependent on state and welfare agencies (Harrell-Bond, 1986). Individuals are conscious that the distrust generated by the meaning attached to *asylum* acts as a barrier to the formation of more extensive social networks within Irish society and ultimately as a barrier to integration. The repercussions are loneliness, feeling unwanted and generally excluded from their host society.

Re-establishing Self-esteem

Integration into the host society as an essential component of refugee resettlement is influenced by a host of structural and individual factors.

> While institutions have direct impact on the resettlement and integration process, refugees are ultimately the central agents in resettlement, and hence their own priorities and goals have influence upon their style of engagement with the surrounding society. (Valtonen, 1998: 41)

In seeking to re-establish their lives, asylum-seekers are at the same time re-establishing their self-esteem. At present, Ireland has no official integration policy for asylum-seekers and, as Ward (1998) notes, successive Irish Governments have learned very little from past experiences of dealing with programme refugees. Given the lengthy waiting periods, asylum-seekers begin to reconstruct their lives long before their refugee status is determined. They are active participants in constructing a life for themselves within the context of limited resources but are aided by interacting with their host society from the time of arrival.

In their efforts to restore self-esteem, maintain continuity with the past and with an emphasis on permanence, a number of strategies are employed. In dealing with the limitations of their status as asylum-seekers and the attendant uncertainty surrounding their position, individuals demonstrate a remarkable degree of resourcefulness. Firstly, and in particular in relation to those without the English language, they attend language classes. As there is no formal structure for language training provided by Government, individuals are dependent on that provided by the voluntary sector and specific refugee organisations such as the Irish Refugee Council (IRC). Secondly, individuals attempt to take forms of training (e.g. computer classes) that they feel will be of use to them in the future. Again, no formal training programmes are provided with the result that individuals attempt to finance such courses from the meagre social welfare payments they receive. Thirdly, the public library system is used for general reading and to access newspapers to enable individuals to keep in touch with events in their countries of origin. Fourthly, regular visits to the IRC enable the individual to interact with other asylum-seekers and to monitor the progress of their own application for refugee status. Fifthly, membership of a church provides the opportunity for the much-needed social interaction with the wider society.

Hirschon (1989) notes that:

> refugees try to establish familiar patterns and maintain continuity with their past in an attempt to overcome personal alienation and social disintegration.

A number of asylum-seekers engage in voluntary work for a host of agencies, which include the IRC, Comhlamh[11] and Concern.[12] However, opportunities for voluntary work are more open to men than women, who are constrained by childcare and childrearing responsibilities (Bloch, 1997). Among respondents those who engaged in voluntary work were men and unmarried women. Voluntary work re-establishes social roles and past work patterns and enables the individual to overcome the boredom and isolation associated with being dependent on state welfare. As asylum-seekers, men frequently continue their political and community activities, thus maintaining a link with their past while also re-establishing their role and status within the community. All of the above activities are seen as important for social interaction, which itself is viewed as an essential component of the process of permanent settlement in the host society. While forced migration destroys the individual's social world, asylum-seekers cannot be viewed as helpless individuals. Rather, they are active participants in re-establishing their lives and a sense of permanence for themselves, though the status of asylum can and does militate against this.

Equally, though asylum-seekers are victims of events in their countries of origin, they do not wish to become or to be seen as victims in their host society. Individuals are conscious of the lack of information on the causes of refugee movements in Irish society and the failure of Government to provide this information. In response and through the vehicle of refugee associations, they attempt to influence public perceptions through community group meetings, visits to schools, churches and other social institutions.

THE PROCESS OF CHANGE

Marx (1990) notes that an individual's social world consists of the individual's social relationships and the forces that shape his or her life. To satisfy the entire range of their social and economic

---

[11] Agency for returned Irish Development workers.

[12] Irish Non-Governmental Development Agency.

needs, individuals require a large and diverse set of social relationships.

> Such matters as finding work and a home, on one hand, and of establishing a secure and supportive environment for himself and his household on the other, can only be arranged with the help of a network of social relationships that include both simplex and multiplex relationships (Marx 1990: 196).

For refugees, their personal social worlds are disturbed and transformed as exile destroys livelihoods and removes the individual's social networks of family and friends. But social networks and the specific social and economic obligations of network membership do not cease because of physical distance. The duties and responsibilities of extended family membership continue to exist for the individual in exile.

In exile, an individual's primary social networks consist largely of family and friends at home (with whom they retain contact) and other asylum-seekers both in their host society and in other countries. Broader secondary social networks consist of members of Irish society.

For asylum-seekers, there is a tension and conflict between their perceptions of their status and the perceptions of Irish society. Resource-based restrictive inclusion, perceived hostility from host society members, the transition from refugee status to that of asylum-seeker and an ambivalent Government approach define the respondents' experiences of asylum. As the label *asylum-seeker* has, over time, taken on a negative meaning, it creates complex barriers to social interaction and network formation. For respondents, their primary and secondary social networks do not expand to any large extent during the long asylum process. Hence, network formation as an essential component in the reconstruction of the refugee's social world is hindered. As a consequence, individual social worlds remain incomplete and asylum-seekers are unable to satisfy all their social and economic needs. The repercussions are feelings of loneliness, exclusion and alienation within their host society. In this context, re-establishing self-esteem and identity together with successful social integration and resettlement are especially problematic for asylum-seekers.

References

Al-Rasheed, M. (1993), "The Meaning of Marriage and Status in Exile: The Experience of Iraqi Women", *Journal of Refugee Studies*, Vol. 6, No. 2.

Bloch, A. (1997), "Refugee Migration and Settlement: A Case Study of the London Borough of Newham", Unpublished PhD thesis, University of London.

Byrne, R. (1997), "On the Sliding Scale of Justice: The Status of Asylum-seekers and Refugees in Ireland" in R. Byrne and W. Duncan (eds.), *Developments in Discrimination Law in Ireland and Europe*, Trinity College Dublin, Irish Centre for European Law.

Department of Justice (2000), *Information Sheet: Applications for Asylum*, Dublin: Department of Justice.

Faughnan, P. (1999), *Refugees and Asylum-seekers in Ireland. Social Policy Dimensions*, Dublin: UCD, Social Science Research Centre.

Fuglerud, O. (1997), "Ambivalent Incorporation: Norwegian Policy towards Tamil Asylum-seekers from Sri Lanka", *Journal of Refugee Studies*, Vol. 10, No. 4.

Harrell-Bond, B.E. (1986), *Imposing Aid: Emergency Assistance to Refugees*. Oxford: OUP.

Hirschon, R. (1989), *Heirs of the Greek Catastrophe: The Social Life of Asia Minor Refugees in Piraeus*, Oxford: OUP.

Marx, E. (1990), "The Social World of Refugees: A Conceptual Framework", *Journal of Refugee Studies*, Vol. 3, No. 3.

O'Sullivan, E. (1997), *Homelessness, Housing Need and Asylum-seekers in Ireland – A Report for the Homeless Initiative*, Dublin: Homeless Initiative.

Roberts, A. (1998), "More Refugees, Less Asylum: A Regime in Transformation", *Journal of Refugee Studies*, Vol. 11, No. 4.

Refugee Agency (1997), *Information Bulletin*, Dublin: Refugee Agency.

Refugee Agency (1998), *Vietnamese Programme Refugees in Ireland*, Dublin: Refugee Agency (Information sheet).

Refugee Agency (1998), *Bosnian Programme Refugees in Ireland*, Dublin: Refugee Agency (Information sheet).

Refugee Agency (1998), *Annual Report 1998*, Dublin: Refugee Agency.

Refugee Agency (1999), *Kosovo Programme*, Dublin: Refugee Agency (Information sheet).

Refugee Agency (2000), *Information on Refugees in Ireland*, Dublin, Refugee Agency (Information sheet).

Shipsey, B. (1994), "Immigration Law and Refugees" in L. Heffernan (ed.), *Human Rights: A European Perspective*, Dublin: The Round Hall Press.

Valtonen, K. (1998) "Resettlement of Middle Eastern Refugees in Finland: The Elusiveness of Integration", *Journal of Refugee Studies*, Vol. 11, No.1.

Waldron, S. (1988), "Working in the Dark. Why Social Anthropological Research is Essential in Refugee Administration", *Journal of Refugee Studies*, Vol. 1, No. 2.

Ward, E. (1998), "Ireland's Refugee Policies: A Critical Overview" in D. O'Driscoll (ed.), *The Irish Human Rights Yearbook 1998*, Dublin, Sweet & Maxwell.

Zetter, R. (1988), "Refugees and Refugee Studies: A Label and an Agenda", *Journal of Refugee Studies*, Vol. 1, No. 1.

Zetter, R. (1991), "Labelling Refugees: Forming and Transforming a Bureaucratic Identity", *Journal of Refugee Studies*, Vol. 4, No. 1.

CHAPTER TWELVE

THE MAJORITY EXPERIENCE: AN INTERNATIONAL COMMENTARY

Stephen Bochner

In 1986, Adrian Furnham and I published a book on the psychology of culture contact, which we called *Culture Shock* (Furnham and Bochner, 1986). Most of the book was written during the preceding three or four years. It reflected the dominant model of culture contact driving research at that time, concentrating on the reactions of persons exposed to unfamiliar cultural environments. Any possible reciprocal effects on the receiving cultures of these strangers in their midst were largely ignored.

The admittedly somewhat snappy title of the book was partly chosen to make its spine more distinctive on crowded bookshop shelves. But it also summarised in plain English the results of decades of research: that life was not meant to be easy for the culture traveller, that second-culture exposure was stressful. And although the word "shock" featured in the title, much of the book in fact dealt with how sojourners, as they came to be called, cope with and adapt to unfamiliar cultures. My own contribution to that topic was to introduce the concept of *culture learning*, which regards the sojourn as a learning experience.

An associated general principle giving structure to the book was the concept of *culture distance*. This was used to account for individual differences between sojourners in how well they learnt their new culture and the ease of adjusting to it. Both theory and empirical findings indicated that the greater the cultural separation between the sojourners and their hosts, the more difficulties they would encounter in their personal and professional dealings with local individuals and institutions (Babiker, Cox and Miller, 1980; Dunbar, 1994; Furnham and Bochner, 1982; Searle and Ward, 1990; Torbiorn, 1982; Ward and Kennedy, 1999).

In the book, we distinguished culture contact that occurs between societies from inter-cultural relations within particular societies. We used the between-society classification to describe the experiences of various categories of persons who travel from their culture of origin to reside temporarily in another country in order to achieve a particular purpose. In the literature, these people came to be called sojourners (as distinct from settlers) because, in theory at any rate, they were supposed to return home after completing their assignment. This requirement also gave rise to the conceptual distinction between hosts and guests/visitors/strangers, an issue that has been of longstanding interest to sociologists (Gudykunst, 1983; Schild, 1962).

The main sojourner categories included overseas students, guest workers and expatriate business persons, military personnel, diplomats, international agency employees, Peace Corps personnel (a big topic in the 1970s but now superseded by various smaller Volunteer Abroad Programmes), missionaries (another dwindling lot), and tourists. It needs to be said that in many instances the culture travellers who started as sojourners ended up as settlers — that is, either did not return to their country of origin at the completion of their assignment, or went home and soon afterwards re-entered their host country as permanent residents. This was particularly the case with overseas students, many of whom found it difficult to re-adjust to the intellectual and professional life of their own countries, a process which was extensively investigated and given the name "brain drain" (Adams, 1968; Rao, 1979).

As indicated earlier, the major theoretical and empirical thrust of the early research was to investigate and account for the adjustment patterns of the sojourners. In our work, we identified four alternative psychological responses to second culture influences:

1. *Assimilation* or "*passing*", where individuals identify with and embrace the values and practices of the host society and re-

ject, abandon or greatly de-emphasise their culture of origin. Effects of this form of adaptation include cultural erosion and self-denigration.

2. What we called a *chauvinistic* response, where sojourners reject the salient aspects of the second culture and retreat into and exaggerate the virtues of their first culture. Effects that have been noted include xenophobia and international hostility. A good example of this process can be found in a book called *Disappointed Guests* (Tajfel and Dawson, 1965), which is an account of Commonwealth overseas students in Britain after the Second World War. As the title suggests, they were less than enthralled with their sojourn.

3. The classic *marginal* response first identified by Park (1928) and elaborated by Stonequist (1937), referring to persons vacillating between their first and second cultures, not fully identifying with nor accepted by either of their two groups. Effects include depression and identity conflict, but also high achievement as a way of dealing with these problems. Nehru captured the marginal syndrome with these words in his autobiography:

   > I have become a queer mixture of the East and the West, out of place everywhere, at home nowhere . . . I am a stranger and alien in the West. I cannot be of it. But in my own country also, sometimes, I have an exile's feeling (Nehru, 1936: 596).

4. What I called the "*mediating*" response (Bochner, 1981), where individuals are able to synthesise the best elements of both their first and second cultures and develop what today would be called bicultural identities (LaFromboise, Coleman and Gerton, 1993).

John Berry (1997) had proposed a similar scheme to classify changes that were observed in the behaviours, attitudes and cognitions of individuals in contact. His model also has four categories: assimilation, separation, marginalisation and integration respectively. Berry's special contribution has been to offer an empirical method for classifying individuals into these categories. The procedure consists of asking culture travellers two questions: "Is it considered to be of value to maintain one's cultural identity and characteristics?" and "Is it considered to be of value to maintain relationships with the larger society?". Respondents are then placed into one of the four categories depending on how they answer.

The reason why I have spent a little time in reviewing these theoretical models is that they reflect the received wisdom about culture contact current at the time in giving unequal weight to the two elements involved. Elsewhere, I have likened this to the notion of gravitational pull. Just as ocean levels cannot escape the moon's power but have no discernible effect on the lunar landscape, it was thought that newcomers would be unable to resist second-culture influences. It was considered that by necessity they would have to change and adapt — in one of the forms proposed by the model, to a fairly monolithic, unyielding mass called "mainstream culture". An underlying assumption, seldom questioned in the early days, was that most societies did in fact contain "mainstream" cultures. More on all this later.

The belief that the presence of the sojourners had very little effect on the structures and customs of the receiving societies shaped most of the empirical research. Basically, it was considered that there was not much point in studying sojourner impacts, because they were assumed to be minimal. This assumption began to wear thin with the expansion of global trade, initially captured by the phrase "cocacolonization" (Lambert, 1966: 170), and became quite threadbare with the advent of mass tourism. Nevertheless, an interactive model of culture contact, which assumes a mutual influence between sojourners and those segments of the host society in which they participate, is a fairly recent development.

We used the term "within-society" contact to describe relations between culturally diverse permanent residents of particular societies. The term "multicultural society" had not yet acquired the wide currency it enjoys (if that is the right word) today (Pedersen, 1999). Within-society culture contact refers to social transactions between relative newcomers such as immigrants and refugees on the one hand, and members of the so-called mainstream majority on the other. A corollary of this approach was to contrast the newcomers as members of a variety of "minority" groups. Within-society contact also included majority–minority relations in societies with an aboriginal population such as Australia, the United States and Canada.

The settlers were classified into adaptation categories similar to those employed in the between-cultures sojourner literature. In our own work, we used the term *assimilation* for the process whereby newcomers are melded into their host society, as in the "melting pot" analogy. *Segregation of out-groups* referred to the discriminatory treatment of minorities by the dominant in-group in many societies, instances being official and later unofficial apartheid policies in South Africa and the exclusion of black Americans in the USA. *Self-segregation* referred to proposals by minority out-groups to separate themselves from the mainstream, examples being attempts to establish tribal enclaves restricting entry to non-members in Alaska, the US South-West and Australia. *Integration* described the process by which societies become increasingly culturally diverse, one analogy being that of a mosaic where each segment retains its distinctive identity while creating a new overall pattern (de Lacey and Poole, 1979).

Here again, the dominant expectation until quite recently was that newcomers would assimilate to the values and practices of the societies they were joining. The official policy of most receiving countries was to encourage migrants to develop a core mono-cultural identity which closely resembled that of their hosts. The corollary of that policy was the assumption that the receiving societies would absorb the newcomers without themselves undergoing any significant changes. That assumption, too, is now unsustainable, with the huge post-war increase in the mass movement of various categories of people settling abroad. A major contributing factor underlying the increase in human relocation has been the gradual elimination of race as a criterion for admitting or excluding immigrants.

Australia is a case in point. For the first 150 years of its existence, Australia was a mono-cultural Anglo-Celt society (with the "Celt" referring to the large number of Irish arrivals, not all of them voluntary). In the 50 or so years since the Second World War, Australia has become a nation that now contains 140 different ethnic groups. One in three of its 20 million citizens were born overseas or are the children of parents born overseas in non-English-speaking countries (McLennan, 1996). Until relatively recently, Australia had an explicit White Australia policy. The relevant Act was repealed in 1966, but many of its practices continued until 1972 when a Labor Government was elected (Department of Labour and Immigration, 1975; Grassby, 1973). Succeeding Australian governments have progressively enacted non-discriminatory immigration legislation, leading over the years to a substantial presence of ethnic Chinese, Vietnamese, Indian and other non-European communities.

Other receiving countries in the past who tended to favour immigrants from European countries over migrants from Asia and Africa have now also adopted (or been forced into adopting) a non-discriminatory stance. France accepts about 60,000 immigrants each year (Schnapper, 1995) and Britain about 50,000 (Coleman, 1995). Many of these settlers would have originated in countries that previously were not regarded as an appropriate source. Germany, too, has a large, non-traditional immigrant population, although some of the figures are inflated by a movement from what used to be East Germany to the West (United Nations, 1994). The official statistics underestimate the actual number of migrants present because all receiving countries harbour a large number of illegal immigrants who do not show up in the count (Bierbrauer and Pedersen, 1996).

The practical consequences of these changes in immigration policy has been to foster the development of large Southeast and East Asian communities in urban centres in Australia, Canada, the United States, some European cities, and now also apparently in Ireland. As well, there are now large Hispanic settlements in parts of the United States, and African and Caribbean communities in Britain.

We have just completed the revision of a new edition of *Culture Shock* (Ward, Bochner and Furnham, in press). The research for this book was conducted between 1998 and 2000. The new edition reflects the developments that have occurred since the appearance of the original book in 1986. Of particular significance in the present context is the emergence of a literature explicitly acknowledging that sojourners and new settlers have a major impact on the societies that invite them (as in the case of overseas students), tolerate them (as in the case of guest workers and expatriate executives) and accept them, in theory at least (as in the case of immigrants and refugees).

The sheer number of culture travellers worldwide provides an international perspective to current developments in Ireland. At any time, there are an estimated 1.3 million students and scholars attending institutions of higher learning abroad (Hayes, 1998; Koretz, 1998). The United States has the largest number, with 450,000 overseas students in 1996 (Witherell, 1996). In the major receiving countries such as the United States, Britain, Canada and Australia, overseas students have become part of the export industry. In countries roughly comparable to Ireland, foreign students contribute A$2 billion annually to the Australian economy, C$2.3 billion to Canada, and NZ$530 million to New Zealand. The figure for the United States is US$7.5 billion (Hayes, 1998). World "trade" in international education has been estimated at US$28 billion, and many universities throughout the world now depend on the income they derive from this source (Bochner, 1999; Smith, 1997).

The response of many institutions of higher education has been to openly embrace a commercial perspective. Leading universities now speak of competing for market share and have adapted some of their procedures, courses and teaching methods to attract overseas "customers". This is beginning to create resentment among some academics as well as local students, who do not like to see higher education traditions commercialised in this way. But there is no turning back because many universities have now become hooked on the income they receive from their overseas "clients", and all the talk is of further expansion. What this will do to host–student interactions at the personal level remains to be seen.

The number of overseas expatriate assignments is also expanding. For instance, data for British business sojourns overseas shows that between 1978 and 1990 there was a 700 per cent increase in visits to Japan, a 200 per cent increase to the United States and a 100 per cent increase to the Caribbean. United States companies have about 350,000 expatriates located overseas. (Solomon, 1999). The actual number of expatriate-linked individuals living abroad would be greater, because many international workers are accompanied by their families. The same pattern is repeated worldwide, indicating that a very large number of individuals are involved. The response of the local population to these visitors ranges from acceptance to resentment, depending on the relative wealth and sophistication of the two cultures represented.

There has also been a huge increase in international recreational travel. World Tourism Organisation projections suggest that by the year 2010 a total of 940 million people will travel abroad as tourists each year (Vellas and Becherel, 1995). Undoubtedly, Ireland will get its share of this onslaught. Host-country attitudes towards tourism tend to be ambivalent. On the one hand, tourism is big business, employing about 125 million people directly, and the economies of many countries have become highly dependent on this source of income (Alzua, O'Leary and Morrison, 1998; Baldacchino, 1997; Campbell, 1999). On the other hand, there is indisputable evidence that tourists have a profound effect on the physical, social and cultural manifestations of the visited countries, producing changes that are not always for the better (Brunt and Courtney, 1999). Their presence alters the economy of the receiving societies by affecting the nature of employment, stimulating investment in commercial and residential building, airports, shipping terminals and highways (Smith and Eadington, 1992). Tourists also play a big role in subsidising the visual and performing arts, museums and art galleries.

In all of these areas, the tourist influence can have adverse consequences. The jobs created can be menial (Wilkinson and Pratiwi, 1995). In some parts of the world, tourism generates less salubrious commercial activities such as prostitution, and alcohol and substance abuse (Harrison, 1994; Leheny, 1995). The tourist-related building boom can lead to insensitive and inappropriate construction which destroys local amenities, creates traffic congestion and aircraft noise, and puts pressure on the water supply and sewage disposal (Hester, 1990).

Tourist demands on the arts can distort the production of indigenous art forms (Ryan, 1997). The crush of visitors can make life difficult for the local population, an example being Paris, which attracts 20 million tourists each year (Pearce, 1999). The great churches of the world have become tourist destinations for large groups of non-believers who stroll through these sacred places with little respect for their spiritual significance. Notre Dame, for instance, receives 12 million visitors annually, with 30,000 people entering the Cathedral on peak days (Pearce, 1997). Modern mass tourism is a mixed blessing, and the response of the local people is likewise mixed. Those individuals whose livelihood depends on tourism have a more positive attitude than those whose lives and values are disrupted (Faulkner and Tideswell, 1997; Husbands, 1986; Smith, 1989). Inevitably, Ireland will face some of these issues as it becomes an increasingly popular tourist destination.

Perhaps the biggest increase in the movement of people across cultural boundaries has occurred with respect to immigration and refugee resettlement. For instance, figures which are now almost certainly out of date have estimated that 100 million people live as permanent settlers outside of their country of origin (Russell and Teitelbaum, 1992). The United States alone accepts over one million immigrants *each* year (United States Immigration and Naturalization Service, 1999). The figures for countries roughly comparable to Ireland include Australia, with a population of 20 million which accepts about 70,000 immigrants per annum (Australian Department of Immigration and Multicultural Affairs, 1999); Canada, with a population of 30 million, 220,000 (Citizenship and Immigration Canada, 1999); and New Zealand, with a population of 3 million, 40,000 per year (New Zealand Immigration Service, 1999).

As was indicated earlier, in part this increase is due to a relaxation of restrictive immigration policies (Moghaddam, Taylor and Wright, 1993). But the main reason has been the relentless procession, worldwide, of both human and naturally caused disasters. These include civil wars, famine, floods, soil degradation, earthquakes, and modern versions of the plague such as the AIDS epidemic. Migration is conceptualised as consisting of "pull" and "push" factors. The majority of migrants are motivated by economic circumstances which "pull" them from poorer to richer countries. Refugees are strongly influenced by "push" factors, escaping from political, cultural and religious pressures that make life intolerable in their home countries. The odious term "ethnic cleansing" has come into the lexicon to succinctly summarise the essence of the biggest single source of refugee movement.

The number of refugees has steadily increased over the last 50 years, doubled between 1980 and 1990, and reached 19 million people in the early part of the last decade (Leopold and Harrell-

Bond, 1994; UNHCR, 1993). In 1996, the figure had risen to 26 million and current estimates have put the number at 27 million (Beiser, 1999). A persistent debate has been raging about the authenticity of these people — that is, whether they are "genuine" refugees or just "economic" ones. Even if some of the refugees are "bogus", this still leaves the world with a huge number of dispossessed persons seeking asylum. In this volume, Treasa Galvin provides a very comprehensive review of the theoretical literature in this area. Her chapter is complemented by Anna Keogh's empirical study showing that many of her respondents did not have a clear idea of the difference between immigrants and refugees. In this they are not alone.

Philip Curry's survey also suggests that there is a good deal of suspicion in Ireland about how genuine many refugees are. I am not qualified to comment as to whether there is any substance to these views, but they do seem to be quite widely held. Curry's measure of social distance can be interpreted as an index of perceived culture distance, and his findings mirror research conducted elsewhere about the relationship between education and prejudice. The main reason for this association, in my view, is that people who are less well-educated and have a lower income are more threatened by immigrants (who tend to be manual workers), because of the fear that these newcomers will take jobs away from them. Even so, the absolute levels of hostility in Curry's fairly large sample are not good news for those who would like Ireland to become a culturally heterogeneous society.

Although the Irish may feel that they are being swamped by refugees (as some of the contributions in this book suggest), in fact Africa, the Middle East and South Asia shelter over 90 per cent of the world's refugees. Europe has typically accepted only about 4 per cent, as has North America (UNHCR, 1998). In contrast, the refugee-to-community ratio in countries such as Croatia, Malawi, Belize and Armenia has at times exceeded 10 per cent of their respective total populations (Ajdukovic and Ajdukovic, 1993; UNHCR, 1993). The origins of the refugees mirror the main trouble spots in the contemporary world. Liberia, Somalia, Mozambique, Ethiopia, Rwanda, Bosnia-Herzegovina, Iraq, Burundi and Sierra Leone have *each* displaced between half a million and one million refugees respectively (UNHCR, 1993, 1996, 1998).

As I indicated, there has been a gradual shift from a unidirectional, visitor-centred construction of culture contact to an interactive one which looks at the reciprocal exchanges between host members and institutions on the one hand, and newcomers on the other. Recently, Bourhis et al. (1997) have elaborated their Interactive Acculturation Model, in which they distinguish between four state ideologies roughly located on a continuum from what they call "pluralism" to "ethnism". These are pluralist, civic, assimilation and ethnist ideologies respectively. Each has a distinct effect on the policies and legal, political and cultural practices that determine how immigrants are treated.

Pluralism anticipates that immigrants will adopt the public values of the country of settlement, but encourages them to maintain their private cultural and linguistic traditions. Ideological pluralism permits the state to offer financial support to immigrant groups.

Civic ideology also makes a distinction between public and private values. It too expects immigrants to adhere to public values, but is explicitly non-interventionist with respect to private cultural practices. State funds are not used to support such activities, although the rights of individuals to organise events promoting cultural maintenance are recognised.

Assimilation ideology counts on immigrants to abandon their cultural and linguistic distinctiveness and adopt the core values of the host community. It reserves the right of the state to intervene in regulating some private values. In some countries, it is anticipated that assimilation will occur voluntarily over time. Elsewhere, specific policies exist to hasten the process.

Ethnist ideology not only expects immigrants to adopt the public values of their host country but also actively regulates their private affairs. Another core aspect of ethnist ideology is that in some countries it will define who can become a citizen. For instance, immigrants in Australia and the US are encouraged to become naturalised citizens, upon which they assume the same rights and obligations as the native born. After the Second World War, immigrants to Australia were referred to as "New Australians", a term now no longer in use but quite effective in implying that anyone who wanted to and was eligible could become an Australian.

Not all nations have a naturalisation policy. In some countries, citizenship is defined in religious or ethnic terms. For instance, it is almost impossible for an outsider to become a Japanese citizen, and the few that do make it, in legal terms, are not embraced into the fold psychologically. The writer Lafcadio Hearn is a celebrated case of someone who tried to "become Japanese" and failed. After years of diligent striving to master the language, customs and soul of Japan, he had to admit total lack of success, not because he was unable to "feel" Japanese, but because the Japanese would not accept him as one of their own. He had this to say about the attitude of the Japanese to foreigners:

> The barriers of racial feeling, of emotional differentiation, of language, of manners and beliefs, are likely to remain insurmountable . . . under no ordinary circumstances need [the foreigner] expect to be treated like a Japanese . . . (Hearn, 1910: 134–135).

Where Ireland stands on the Bourhis ideology continuum is best answered by those working in the field. My impression from reading Cathal O'Regan's contribution is that Ireland is currently grappling with just that issue and its associated policy implications. However, although government policy does have some influence in shaping the attitudes and beliefs of members of host communities towards immigrants, the official line may not be universally endorsed. A particular problem seems to be the issue of employment. For instance, Australia, Canada and the United States all have explicit legislated multicultural policies. Nevertheless, Goot (1993) found that 44 per cent of Australians believe that immigration deprives Australians of jobs. Similarly, a recent poll in Canada revealed that 49 per cent believe that immigration increases unemployment (Esses, Jackson and Armstrong, 1998). And in the United States, a majority agree that immigrants burden the country because they take jobs.

Many economists argue that immigrants create jobs because their presence stimulates an increase in demands for goods and services. The psychological literature, on the other hand, tells us that people do not believe that assertion. Unemployment figures are strongly related to opposition to immigration. In a review of the Canadian literature spanning 20 years, Palmer (1996) found a significant correlation between higher unemployment rates and agreement with the proposition that immigration should be decreased. The same association between the threat of job loss and anti-immigration attitudes was reported in the United States by Espenshade and Hempstead (1966) and Stephan, Ybarra and Bachman (1999); in Canada (Esses, Jackson and Armstrong, 1998); and in Spain (Stephan et al., 1998). The results of Philip Curry's survey are consistent with this literature.

Acceptance of immigrants by host members is also a function of a perception of culture distance. For instance, it has been shown that in the United States, light-skinned immigrants are treated more favourably than immigrants with darker complexions (Espin, 1987). In Singapore, expatriates from the United States are held in higher esteem than professionals from mainland China (Lim and Ward, 1999). In Australia, various surveys have found that migrants from Britain and Europe were favoured over newcomers from Asia and the Middle East (Ho et al., 1994; McAllister and Moore, 1991).

Finally, social identity theory (Tajfel, 1978, 1981; Tajfel and Turner, 1986) can be used to explain (although not justify) the negative behaviour of members of receiving societies towards immigrants and refugees. Countless studies have shown that one means by which people increase their own and their group's self-esteem is by devaluing and derogating minority out-groups (Deaux, 1996; Moghaddam, 1998). Two strategies in particular are employed in this regard: negative stereotyping of the outgroup and the misattribution of their behaviour. An example of the latter is describing in-group frugal acts as prudent while exactly the same behaviour by out-group members is labelled as mean. The female respondents in Anna Keogh's study provide an example of misattribution that is closer to home.

Furthermore, out-group vilification increases when the person's own social identity is under threat (Branscombe and Wann, 1994). One of the effects of non-discriminatory immigration policies is that it leads to the establishment in receiving countries of visible communities of what might be called non-traditional newcomers. This in turn has the effect of increasing the perceived cultural distance between the host and immigrant groups, particularly in metropolitan centres. For instance, since the end of the Second World War, Australia in general and Sydney and Melbourne in particular absorbed a steady flow of European migrants from Britain, Poland, Yugoslavia, Holland, Greece and Italy. This was a relatively painless process, because the appearance and practices of these migrants did not differ significantly from the characteristics of the largely Anglo mainstream, particularly with respect to immigrants from Northern Europe.

However, in the past few years, large numbers of newcomers from Vietnam, China, Indonesia, Hong Kong and other Asian countries have established themselves in the larger cities. They constitute a highly distinctive group judged to be culturally distant from the mainstream. Social identity theory implies that this may constitute a threat to some of the less secure members of mainstream society. The presence of these migrants makes explicit what was previously only a hint: that the ethnic composition of Australian society is irrevocably changing. In particular, it leads to the realisation that the so-called heritage groups which used to define national ethnic identity, are now sharing their homeland with an increasing number of people whose cultures differ significantly from their own.

This trend is replicated in most of the countries that accept non-traditional immigrants. Many citizens are comfortable with these developments, and see them as diversifying and enriching society, acknowledging what has been called "the mutuality of accommodation" (Beiser, 1999) between host and newcomer values. Others fear that their nation may be swamped by unwanted and inappropriate social and cultural practices. The respondents in Anna Keogh's study provide a good example of that attitude. There is evidence, including the material in this book, that in many receiving countries the "mainstream" is beginning to actively resist any further transformation of their societies. This is true not just in Europe but also in Asian countries alarmed at the spread of Western values that threaten their Confucian base.

Officialdom also has a stake in this process, because changes in the ethnic composition of societies have implications for core state institutions such as the education and health systems, industrial and organisational practices, and the administration of law and order. It is much easier to administer a country that has a clear homogeneous mainstream than the culturally diverse societies that are currently emerging worldwide, including Ireland. David Walsh's contribution, describing the culturally related problems of the Irish police service, provides a good example. Until recently, the Garda Síochána were operating in a culturally very homogenous environment. Dealing with minority groups was not a very frequent occurrence. All that apparently is now changing, with over half of the police he interviewed reporting that they had professional contact with persons whose ethnic background was not Irish. As David Walsh indicates, this raises issues of organisational change and development, supervision and mentoring, training, and recruiting.

However, before we become too downhearted, let us view the situation in Ireland from a global perspective. Since the end of the Second World War, technically the world has been at peace. Nevertheless, millions of people have perished in a series of nasty civil wars. A partial listing of places where murder and mayhem are or have been a frequent part of the daily scene include the former Yugoslavia, the former Soviet Union, India, Pakistan, Sri Lanka, parts of Africa and South America, Northern Island, the Middle East, Spain, Cyprus and Indonesia. Isajiw (2000) in a recent review of the literature on inter-ethnic conflict, estimates that since the end of the War, between 233 and 295 groups were caught up in serious hostilities directly related to cultural divisions. Acrimonious within-society inter-group relations have been the major cause of the flood of refugees. The minor difficulties of relatively successful multicultural societies such as Australia, Canada, the United States and Singapore pale into insignificance when contrasted against the inter-ethnic violence that has cast a blight on so many countries.

Let me conclude by referring to one further major cultural dimension which may of relevance in understanding majority–minority relations in Ireland. Societies can be differentiated on the extent to which their cultures are "tight" or "loose" (Pelto, 1968; Triandis, Kurowski and Gelfand, 1994). Countries with tight cultures tend to be ethnically homogeneous, have a history of relative isolation from the rest of the world, exhibit a unitary set of behavioural norms which are strongly supported and enforced, and value uniformity (and conformity). Often such countries are fairly densely populated, and their educational system and child-rearing practices are aimed at socialising people to behave in ways that are considered universally appropriate. Japan is usually invoked as an illustration of a typical tight culture. Loose cultures, on the other hand, may contain a variety of possibly conflicting ethnic and value systems. However, these are tolerated because of a belief in the value of diversity. There is also a much greater acceptance of deviant behaviour — deviant in the sense of diverging from a set of central norms. The United States is sometimes used to illustrate a society with a relatively loose cultural system. One implication of this structural distinction is that immigrants and particularly refugees would enjoy a better reception in loose than in tight cultures. I am unfamiliar with the relevant characteristics of contemporary Irish society, but I would hazard a guess that it would be located on the "tight" end of the continuum. If I am correct, then this aspect of Irish society would have to be taken into account in any systematic interventions directed at reducing the hostility reported in some of the chapters in this section.

References

Adams, W. (ed.) (1968), *The Brain Drain*, New York: Macmillan.

Ajdukovic, M. and D. Ajdukovic (1993), "Psychological Well-being of Refugee Children", *Child Abuse and Neglect*, Vol. 17, pp. 843–854.

Alzua, A., J.T. O'Leary and A. Morrison (1998), "Cultural Heritage Tourism: Identifying Niches for International Travelers", *The Journal of Tourism Studies*, Vol. 9, pp. 2–13.

Australian Department of Immigration and Multicultural Affairs (1999), *Immigration Statistics*, Available: http://www.immi.gov.au/statistics/migrant.htm.

Babiker, I.E., J.L. Cox and P. Miller (1980), "The Measurement of Cultural Distance and its Relationship to Medical Consultations, Symptomatology, and Examination Performance of Overseas Students at Edinburgh University", *Social Psychiatry*, Vol. 15, pp. 109–116.

Baldacchino, G. (1997), *Global Tourism and Informal Labour Relations: The Small-Scale Syndrome at Work*, London: Mansell.

Beiser (1999), *Strangers at the Gate: The "Boat People's" First Ten Years in Canada*, Toronto: University of Toronto Press.

Berry, J.W. (1997), "Immigration, Acculturation and Adaptation", *Applied Psychology: An International Review*, Vol. 46, pp. 5–34.

Bierbrauer, G. and P.B. Pedersen (1996), "Culture and Migration", in G.R. Semin and K. Fiedler (eds.), *Applied Social Psychology*, pp. 399–422, London: Sage.

Bochner, S. (1981), "The Social Psychology of Cultural Mediation", in S. Bochner (ed.), *The Mediating Person: Bridges Between Cultures*, pp. 6–36, Cambridge, MA: Schenkman.

Bochner, S. (1999), "Cultural Diversity within and between Societies: Implications for Multicultural Social Systems", in P.B. Pedersen (ed.), *Multiculturalism as a Fourth Force*, pp. 19–60, Washington, DC: Taylor and Francis.

Bourhis, R.Y., C. Moise, S. Perreault, and S. Senecal (1997), "Towards an Interactive Acculturation Model: A Social Psychological Approach", *International Journal of Psychology*, Vol. 32, pp. 369–386.

Branscombe, N.R. and D.L. Wann (1994), "Collective Self-esteem Consequences of Outgroup Derogation when a Valued Social Identity is on Trial", *European Journal of Social Psychology*, Vol. 24, pp. 641–657.

Brunt, P. and P. Courtney (1999), "Host Perception of Sociocultural Impacts", *Annals of Tourism Research*, Vol. 26, pp. 493–515.

Campbell, L.M. (1999), "Ecotourism in Rural Developing Communities", *Annals of Tourism Research*, Vol. 26, pp. 534–553.

Citizenship and Immigration Canada (1999), *Immigration Statistics*, Available: http://www.cicnet.ci.gc.ca/english/pub/anrep99e.html#plan10.

Coleman, D. (1995), "Immigration Policy in Great Britain", in F. Heckmann and W. Bosswick (eds.), *Migration Policies: A Comparative Perspective*, pp. 105–128, Stuttgart: Enke.

de Lacey, P.R. and M.E. Poole (1979), *Mosaic or Melting Pot: Cultural Evolution in Australia*, Sydney: Harcourt Brace Jovanovich.

Deaux, K. (1996), "Social Identification", in E.T. Higgins and A.W. Kruglanski (eds.), *Social Psychology: Handbook of Basic Principles*, pp. 777–798, New York: Guildford Press.

Department of Labour and Immigration, Committee on Community Relations (1975), *Final Report*, Canberra: Australian Government Publishing Service.

Dunbar, E. (1994), The German Executive in the US Work and Social Environment: Exploring Role Demands, *International Journal of Intercultural Relations*, Vol. 18, pp. 277–291.

Espenshade, T.J. and K. Hempstead (1996), "Contemporary American Attitudes toward US Immigration", *International Migration Review*, Vol. 30, pp. 533–570.

Espin, O.M. (1987), "Psychological Impact of migration on Latinas", *Psychology of Women Quarterly*, Vol. 11, pp. 489–503.

Esses, V.M., L. M. Jackson and T.L. Armstrong (1998), "Intergroup Competition and Attitudes toward Immigrants and Immigration", *Journal of Social Issues*, Vol. 54, pp. 699–724.

Faulkner, B. and C. Tideswell (1997), "A Framework for Monitoring Community Impacts of Tourism", *Journal of Sustainable Tourism*, Vol. 5, pp. 3–28.

Furnham, A. and S. Bochner (1982), "Social Difficulty in a Foreign Culture: an Empirical Analysis of Culture Shock", in S. Bochner (ed.), *Culture in Contact: Studies in Cross-cultural Interactions*, pp. 161–198, Oxford: Pergamon.

Furnham, A. and S. Bochner (1986), *Culture Shock: Psychological Reactions to Unfamiliar Environments*, London: Methuen.

Goot, M. (1993), "Multiculturalists, monoculturalists and the many in between: Attitudes to Cultural Diversity and Their Correlates", *Australian and New Zealand Journal of Sociology*, Vol. 99, pp. 226–253.

Grassby, A.J. (1973), *A Multicultural Society for the Future*, Canberra: Australian Government Publishing Service.

Gudykunst, W.B. (1983), "Toward a Typology of Stranger–Host Relationships", *International Journal of Intercultural Relations*, Vol. 7, pp. 401–415.

Harrison, D. (1994), "Tourism and Prostitution: Sleeping with the Enemy?", *Tourism Management*, Vol. 15, pp. 435–443.

Hayes, C. (1998), "World Class Learning", *Black Enterprise*, Vol. 28, pp. 85–90.

Hearn, L. (1910), *Kokoro: Hints and Echoes of Japanese Inner Life*, London: Gay and Hancock.

Hester, R.T. (1990), "The Sacred Structure of Small Towns: A Return to Manteo, North Carolina", *Small Town*, Vol. 20, pp. 5–21.

Ho, R., S. Niles, R. Penney and A. Thomas (1994), "Migrants and Multiculturalism: A Survey of Attitudes in Darwin", *Australian Psychologist*, Vol. 29, pp. 62–70.

Husbands, W.C. (1986), "Periphery Resort Tourism and Tourist–Resident Stress: An Example from Barbados", *Leisure Studies*, Vol. 5, pp. 175–188.

Isajiw, W.W. (2000), "Approaches to Ethnic Conflict Resolution: Paradigms and Principles", *International Journal of Intercultural Relations*, Vol. 24, pp. 105–124.

Koretz, G. (1998), "US Colleges Look Overseas", *Business Week*, Vol. 3609, December 21, pp. 22.

LaFromboise, T., H.L.K. Coleman and J. Gerton (1993), "Psychological Impact of Biculturalism: Evidence and Theory", *Psychological Bulletin*, Vol. 114, pp. 395–412.

Lambert, R.D. (1966), "Some Minor Pathologies in the American Presence in India", *Annals of the American Academy of Political and Social Science*, Vol. 368, pp. 157–170.

Leheny, D. (1995), "A Political Economy of Asian Sex Tourism", *Annals of Tourism Research*, Vol. 22, pp. 367–384.

Leopold, M. and B. Harrell-Bond (1994), "An Overview of the World Refugee Crisis", in A.J. Marsella, T. Bornemann, S. Ekblad and J. Orley (eds.), *Amidst the Peril and the Pain: The Mental Health and Well-being of the World's Refugees*, pp. 17–31, Washington, DC: American Psychological Association.

Lim, A., and C. Ward (1999), *The Effects of Nationality, Length of Residence and Type of Occupational Skills on the Perceptions of "Foreign Talent" in Singapore*, Paper presented at the Third Conference of the Asian Association of Social Psychology, Taipei.

McAllister, I. and R. Moore (1991), "The Development of Ethnic Prejudice: An Analysis of Australian Immigrants", *Ethnic and Racial Studies*, Vol. 14, pp. 127–151.

McLennan, W. (1996), *Yearbook Australia: Number 78*, Canberra: Australian Bureau of Statistics.

Moghaddam, F.M. (1998), *Social Psychology: Exploring Universals Across Cultures*, New York: Freeman.

Moghaddam, F.M., D.M. Taylor and S.C. Wright (1993), *Social Psychology in Cross-cultural Perspective*, New York: Freeman.

Nehru, J. (1936; Reprinted 1958), *An Autobiography*, London: Bodley Head.

New Zealand Immigration Service (1999), *People Approved for Residence by Region*, http://www.immigration.govt.nz/about/statistics/faq/resid_region.

Palmer, D.L. (1996), "Determinants of Canadian Attitudes toward Immigration: More than just Racism? *Canadian Journal of Behavioural Science*, Vol. 28, pp. 180–192.

Park, R.E. (1928), "Human Migration and the Marginal Man", *The American Journal of Sociology*, Vol. 33, pp. 881–893.

Pearce, D. (1997), "Analysing the Demand for Urban Tourism: Issues and Examples from Paris", *Tourism Analysis*, Vol. 1, pp. 5–18.

Pearce, D. (1999), "Tourism in Paris: Studies at the Microscale", *Annals of Tourism Research*, Vol. 26, pp. 77–97.

Pedersen, P.B. (ed.) (1999), *Multiculturalism as a Fourth Force*, Washington, DC: Taylor and Francis.

Pelto, P.J. (1968), "The Difference between 'Tight' and 'Loose' Societies", *Transaction*, Vol. 5, pp. 37–40.

Rao, G.L. (1979), *Brain Drain and Foreign Students*, St Lucia, Australia: University of Queensland Press.

Russel, S.S. and M. Teitelbaum (1992), *International Migration and International Trade*, Washington, DC: World Bank.

Ryan, C. (1997), "Maori and Tourism: A Relationship of History, Constitutions and Rites", *Journal of Sustainable Tourism*, Vol. 5, pp. 257–278.

Schild, E.O. (1962), "The Foreign Student as Stranger, Learning the Norms of the Host Culture", *Journal of Social Issues*, Vol. 18, pp. 41–54.

Schnapper, D. (1995), "The Significance of French Immigration and Integration Policy", in F. Heckmann and W. Bosswick (eds.), *Migration Policies: A Comparative Perspective*, pp. 91–103, Stuttgart: Enke.

Searle, W. and C. Ward (1990), "The Prediction of Psychological and Sociocultural Adjustment during Cross-cultural Transitions", *International Journal of Intercultural Relations*, Vol. 14, pp. 449–464.

Smith, G. (1997), *Building on Egerton Ryerson's Legacy: Bringing Education to the World*: Ottawa: Department of Foreign Affairs and International Trade.

Smith, V. (1989), "Introduction", in V. Smith (ed.), *Hosts and Guests: The Anthropology of Tourism*, Philadelphia: University of Pennsylvania Press.

Smith, V. and W. Eadington (eds.) (1992), *Tourism Alternatives: Potentials and Problems in the Development of Tourism*, Philadelphia: University of Pennsylvania Press.

Solomon, C.M. (1999), "Short-term Assignments and Other Solutions", *Global Workforce*, Vol. 4, pp. 38–40.

Stephan, W.G., O. Ybarra and G. Bachman (1999), "Prejudice towards Immigrants: An Integrated Threat Theory", *Journal of Applied Social Psychology*, Vol. 29, pp. 221–237.

Stephan, W.G., P. Ybarra, C.M. Martinez, J. Schwarzwald and M. Tur-Kaspa (1998), "Prejudice toward Immigrants to Spain and Israel: An Integrated Threat Theory Analysis", *Journal of Cross-cultural Psychology*, Vol. 29, pp. 559–576.

Stonequist, E.V. (1937), *The Marginal Man*, New York: Scribner.

Tajfel, H. (ed.) (1978), *Differentiation between Social Groups: Studies in the Psychology of Intergroup Relations*, London: Academic Press.

Tajfel, H. (1981), *Human Groups and Social Categories*, Cambridge: Cambridge University Press.

Tajfel, H. and J.L. Dawson (eds.) (1965), *Disappointed Guests*, London: Oxford University Press.

Tajfel, H. and J. Turner (1986), "The Social Identity Theory of Intergroup Behavior", in W. Austin and S. Worchel (eds.), *The Social Psychology of Intergroup Relations*, pp. 7–24, Chicago: Nelson-Hall.

Torbiorn, I. (1982), *Living Abroad: Personal Adjustment and Personnel Policy in the Overseas Setting*, Chichester: Wiley.

Triandis, H.C., L.L. Kurowski and M.J. Gelfand (1994), "Workplace Diversity", in H.C. Triandis, M.D. Dunnette and L.M. Hough (eds.), *Handbook of Industrial And Organizational Psychology, Second Edition, Volume 4*, pp. 769–827, Palo Alto, CA: Consulting Psychologists Press.

United Nations (1994), *International Migration Bulletin*, Vol. 4, No. 1.

United Nations High Commission on Refugees (UNHCR) (1993), *The State of the World's Refugees*, New York: Penguin.

United Nations High Commission on Refugees (UNHCR) (1996), *UNHCR by Numbers: Basic Facts*, Available: http://www.unhcr.ch.

United Nations High Commission on Refugees (UNHCR) (1998), *Statistics: Refugees and Others of Concern to UNHCR*, Available: http://www.unhcr.ch/statist/98oview/ch1.htm.

United Sates Immigration and Naturalization Service (1999), *Immigration Statistics*, http://www.ins.usdoj.gov/graphics/publicaffairs/newsrels/98Legal.pdf.

Vellas, F. and L. Becherel (1995), *International Tourism: An Economic Perspective*, London: Macmillan.

Ward, C., S. Bochner and A. Furnham (in press), *The Psychology of Culture Shock*, London: Routledge.

Ward, C. and A. Kennedy (1999), "The Measurement of Sociocultural Adaptation", *International Journal of Intercultural Relations*, Vol. 23, pp. 659–677.

Wilkinson, P. and W. Pratiwi (1995), "Gender and Tourism in an Indonesian Village", *Annals of Tourism Research*, Vol. 22, pp. 283–299.

Witherell, S. (1996), *Foreign Students in the US*, New York: Institute of International Education.

Part Three

THE SOJOURN EXPERIENCE

CHAPTER THIRTEEN

IRISH ACCULTURATION IDEOLOGIES: MIXING MULTICULTURALISM, ASSIMILATION AND DISCRIMINATION

Gerard W. Boucher

INTRODUCTION

This chapter examines the role of Irish "acculturation ideologies" (Horenczyk in Breakwell and Lyons, 1996: 243) from the perspective of a group of international students in Ireland. The concept of acculturation ideologies refers to migrants' or non-nationals' "attitudes towards acculturation . . . and their views regarding the expectations held by the receiving society with regard to their social and cultural integration"(ibid.). The sample of students is drawn from a qualitative survey on racism and international students conducted in the autumn of 1997 at three universities in the Republic of Ireland. A total of 48 international students were interviewed, all of whom had been studying in Ireland for at least one year prior to being interviewed for the study. The survey was published as an Irish Council for International Students' report called *The Irish are friendly, but . . .* (Boucher, 1998). This chapter re-analyses the interview results in the report from the students' perception of the different acculturation ideologies expressed by the Irish "civic culture" and the Irish state.

At the societal level, the international students focused particularly on the acculturation ideology expressed in Irish civic culture. The predominant acculturation ideology identified by the students was based upon friendliness and insularity. For the students, Irish cultural insularity was the main characteristic of Irish society. Insularity led to both Irish friendliness and discrimination towards non-nationals and ethnic minorities, revealing a contradiction in the predominant acculturation ideology. Irish friendliness markedly increased towards those students who adapted to Irish cultural values, beliefs and social norms, such as the tacit rules for conversation, privacy and sites for socialising involved in everyday interactions. Those students who expressed Irish values, beliefs and norms were socially included by Irish people into the local community. However, those students who did not express these values, beliefs or norms tended to be excluded by Irish social groups in the community, a result which many of the students interpreted as a type of discrimination. In this way, the international students perceived the mode of inclusion in the acculturation ideology of Irish civic culture to be based on "assimilationism", socially including non-nationals and ethnic minorities to the extent that they fully adopted the Irish values, beliefs and practices of the majority population.

For the international students, the Irish state was perceived as being both multicultural and discriminatory in its treatment of non-nationals. These individual perceptions of the Irish state's acculturation ideology towards non-nationals are reflected at the institutional level in the state's emerging policy framework, which mixes internal inclusion for Irish citizens and certain categories of migrants with the external exclusion from Ireland of specific groups of non-EU migrants. This mixture of inclusion and exclusion can be seen in the Irish state's recent attempts to create a non-discriminatory, multicultural society (Employment Equality Act, 1998; Equal Status Bill, 1999), while at the same time patrolling the borders of Ireland's Common Travel Area with Britain within the European Union's "Fortress Europe". In this way, the Irish state's acculturation ideology was perceived by the international students to be contradictory, proclaiming internal equality and non-discrimination while often practising discrimination against non-nationals and ethnic minorities within Ireland and at the country's borders.

The re-analysis of the interview results suggests that there are inherent contradictions within and between Irish acculturation ideologies at the state and civic levels of Irish society. There is a contradiction within the Irish civic culture's acculturation ideology with respect to friendliness and discrimination towards the non-Irish and minorities. This contradiction is reproduced in the Irish state's acculturation ideology, promoting multiculturalism while often practising discrimination against non-nationals and Irish ethnic minorities. Further, there is a contradiction between that part of the state's acculturation ideology which supports multi-culturalism and the civic culture's acculturation ideology of assimilationism. In this case, the state promotes equality and cultural diversity in Ireland while the civic culture excludes those who do not assimilate and assumes the cultural homogeneity of the Irish people.

The remainder of this chapter is divided into two parts. The first discusses the main concepts used to re-analyse the interview results with the international students. These concepts include acculturation ideologies, civic culture, modes of inclusion and exclusion, assimilation, pluralism, multiculturalism and discrimination. The second part applies these concepts to the students' perceptions of the acculturation ideologies expressed by Irish civic culture and the Irish state respectively.

DISCUSSING ACCULTURATION IDEOLOGIES AND RELATED CONCEPTS

In analysing identity conflicts in recent Russian migrants to Israel, Horenczyk uses the concept of "acculturation ideologies" to help explain the migrants' perceptions about becoming acculturated into Israeli culture and society (in Breakwell and Lyons, 1996: 241–50). Specifically, Horenczyk discusses acculturation ideologies in terms of

> . . . taking into account not only the migrants' own attitudes towards acculturation, but also their views regarding the expectations held by the receiving society with regard to their social and cultural integration. (243)

The usefulness of Horenczyk's concept of acculturation ideologies for our purposes is that it moves beyond the personal acculturation attitudes of migrants to an analysis of migrants' perceptions of societal expectations concerning their inclusion or exclusion from the host society. By societal expectations, we mean the cultural values, beliefs, everyday practices and policies which express the host society's acculturation ideologies. In this way, what the migrants or, in our case, a specific group of temporary migrants called international students, perceive about the acculturation attitudes of the host society becomes an important topic of study in itself, providing a perspective of national acculturation ideologies from a group who are experiencing the process of acculturation from inside the host society. While Horenczyk's study focuses on new migrants to a host society, the concept of acculturation ideologies can also be applied to a range of non-national groups such as international students, temporary workers, asylum-seekers and refugees, as well as to national groups like indigenous ethnic minorities.

Of course, the use of the plural "ideologies" suggests that there is more than one acculturation ideology within a national society at the particular time. These various acculturation ideologies may be "located" at different levels of the host society; for example, within the national state or a private sector company, a region or local community and a social class or ethnic group. Another possible location for a host society's acculturation ideology could be what Rex refers to as the "civic culture" or the values, beliefs and practises expressed in areas such as the "public morality, law and religion" of the national society (Rex in Guibernau and Rex, 1997: 209). Rex's discussion of the civic culture focuses on the societal development of "moral and legal systems of an abstract character" alongside the more concrete "folk morality, folk culture and folk religion" (ibid.). However, we prefer a broader concept of the civic culture, which incorporates the values and beliefs articulated in abstract national laws by lawyers as well the concrete norms expressed in interpersonal interactions between friends in a local community. In this way, the concept of a civic culture stresses the core elements of the national culture which are more or less common and which "make sense" to national citizens who have been socialised and live within the national society.

Further, the possibility of more than one acculturation ideology within a host society suggests that these ideologies may differ with respect to the acculturation expected of non-nationals and indigenous ethnic minorities. One way to discuss these differences in acculturation ideologies located at various levels of society is through the concepts of modes of inclusion and modes of exclusion. By modes of inclusion, we mean the various goals and the means to achieve those goals expressed by different acculturation ideologies with respect to the inclusion of non-nationals and ethnic minorities into the national society. In particular, we will focus on three common modes of inclusion, referred to as assimilationism, pluralism and multiculturalism. By modes of exclusion, we mean the various goals and the means to achieve those goals expressed by different acculturation ideologies with respect to the exclusion of non-nationals and ethnic minorities from the national society. There a number of modes of exclusion, such as genocide and forced mass relocation, which are fairly rare and extremist in their treatment of non-nationals and ethnic minorities. However, we will concentrate on one of the most common and everyday modes of exclusion within a national society, referred to as discrimination.

The meaning and application of the concepts of assimilation, pluralism, multiculturalism and discrimination are often hotly contested by academics, politicians and in public debates, particularly with regard to "multiculturalism" in the last few decades (see, for example, Castles and Miller, 1998: 248-50, 302; Rex in Guibernau and Rex, 1997: 206–20; Yuval-Davis in Torres et al., 1999: 115–20). Perhaps the least controversial of these concepts at present in terms of its meaning and application is assimilation.

For Castles and Miller,

> assimilation may be defined as the policy of incorporating migrants into society through a one-sided process of adaptation: immigrants are expected to give up their distinctive linguistic, cultural or social characteristics and become indistinguishable from the majority population. The role of the state is to create conditions favourable to this process (1998: 245).

As a mode of inclusion, then, assimilation expects non-nationals and ethnic minorities to fully acculturate to the values, beliefs and practices of the majority national group in the society, expressing an intolerant attitude towards cultural diversity or the preservation of minority cultures alongside the majority culture in the national society. The state can be actively involved in the assimilation process, for instance, on "migrant children" through the control of national education in schools (ibid.) or it can be more *laissez-faire*, leaving the process of assimilation largely to the marketplace and the civic culture.

Compared to assimilation, the concept of pluralism is more complex, varying in meaning depending on the type of society to which it is applied. Thus, Rex discusses the meaning of pluralism in a historical context with respect to colonial societies in the Netherlands India or the present day Indonesia (Furnivall, 1939) and the British West Indies (Smith, 1965). In general, these colonial societies were pluralistic in that "each ethnic group existed separately . . . living side by side but interacting only in the market place" (Rex in Guibernau and Rex, 1997: 207). Further, these separated "ethnic segments" were "bound together" only by the colonial state, which was dominated and led by members from the white coloniser group, creating a plural society based on a "model of racial domination" (208).

The other principal meaning of pluralism derives largely from settler immigrant societies, particularly the American application of pluralism in the USA prior to the end of the civil rights era in the mid-1960s. For Castles and Miller, American pluralism is based on a "*laissez-faire* approach" in which "cultural difference and the existence of ethnic communities are accepted, but it is not seen as the role of the state to ensure social justice or to support the maintenance of ethnic cultures" (1998: 248). In this American type of pluralism, the gradual inclusion of non-nationals and ethnic minorities into the society, especially the acculturation of their children and grandchildren, usually results in a "slower and gentler form of assimilation" (245) especially for white ethnic minorities.

As suggested above, the concept of multiculturalism is much debated in the contemporary period with respect to the concept's meaning and application as well as its limits as a mode of inclusion in national societies. For our purposes, we will not discuss the ideological or practical limits of multiculturalism as a mode of inclusion (see Yuval-Davis for a succinct summary of these limits in Torres et al., 1999: 215–20). Castles and Miller discuss three main categories of meanings located in the USA; Western Europe; and Canada, Australia and Sweden (302). In the United States, multiculturalism "mainly refers to demands for rethinking history and culture to include the role of minorities" including women (ibid.). The Western European category of meaning "is often used pejoratively to refer to a policy of ethnic separatism" (ibid.). More positively, multiculturalism in Canada, Australia and Sweden "usually denotes a certain type of government policy, combining cultural rights and social equality for minorities" (ibid.).

In this last case, the meaning and application of multiculturalism "implies both the willingness of the majority group to accept cultural difference, and state action to secure equal rights for minorities" (248) in the institutions of the public sphere, such as social welfare, education and the marketplace and those of the private sphere such as the family and the community (see also Rex in Guibernau and Rex, 1997: 214, 217–18). We will use the concept of multiculturalism in this latter sense in which the civic culture expresses values, beliefs and norms associated with cultural diversity, while the state promotes equal opportunities for all denizens of the society in the public sphere and acts to protect minority cultures particularly in the private sphere of the family and the local community.

Overall, the goal of assimilation is the full acculturation of nonnationals and ethnic minorities in the public and private spheres to the dominant culture of the majority group in the national society, whether or not actively supported by the state. Outside of colonial societies, the goal of pluralism is the acceptance of cultural diversity in the national society by the majority group without state intervention in either the public or private sphere. The goal of multiculturalism is both the acceptance of culture diversity in the society's civic culture and state intervention to ensure equality in the public sphere as well as the maintenance of minority cultures in the private sphere. In this way, acculturation ideologies with respect to these three modes of inclusion range from the total absorption of minority cultures to their preservation in the national society and from a laissez-faire state to state activism in support of the eradication or the protection of minority cultures.

Let us now discuss discrimination as a mode of exclusion expressed in acculturation ideologies. Discrimination is another contested concept whose meaning and application can vary between societies and over time. Over the last 30 years or so, one significant trend has been the "conceptual inflation" of the term racism to encompass both the meaning of discrimination and its application to various social groups based on nationality, ethnicity, class and gender (Miles, 1989: 41–68). In discussing this issue, though, Miles succumbs to his own conceptual inflation, defining a specific form of discrimination called racism in terms of the general category of discrimination or "all those activities and practices which, intentionally or not, result in the continued exclusion of a subordinate group . . . and which are intended to protect the advantages of a dominant group" (50) in a national society.

To deflate this conceptual inflation, we will define discrimination as a general concept which refers to direct, indirect, intentional and unintentional actions by individuals or institutions dominated by members of a majority group which result in the exclusion of non-nationals and ethnic minorities from the material benefits, political power, social status and cultural resources of the national society. Racism is a form of discrimination directed against racial minorities identified through perceived physical differences such as skin colour, just as ethnicism is a form of discrimination based on perceived cultural differences between majority and minority group members, and nationalist xenophobia is a form of discrimination directed against "foreigners" based on perceived national differences (see Boucher 1998: 21–8). The important point here is that discrimination, no matter in what form it is manifested, results in the exclusion of non-nationals and ethnic minorities in the national society to the benefit of majority group members.

While the modes of inclusion and exclusion expressed in acculturation ideologies can be discussed as analytically distinct, they are in practice usually mixed in a national society with, for example, proactive policies of multiculturalism sometimes coexisting with blatant forms of racial, ethnic and national discrimination. In particular, Castles and Miller discuss the ambivalence of certain "European immigration countries" in which "policies of assimilation in some areas (such as labour market or social policy) may coexist with pluralism in other sectors (for instance, education and cultural policy)" (246) alongside institutional discrimination, for example, in the police or immigration department. In this way, there may be contradictions between and within acculturation ideologies, particularly as expressed in their practice by individuals, social groups and institutions at different levels of a national society.

Finally, Castles and Miller note that in "some countries there has been an evolution, starting with differential exclusion, progressing to assimilationism . . . leading to pluralist models" (245) and in some cases to multiculturalism. As such, there may be changes in the ideological predominance of particular modes of inclusion and exclusion practised in a national society over time, along with contradictions between and within acculturation ideologies in the same time period.

This discussion suggests that in analysing the role of acculturation ideologies in a national society, we should expect complexity with respect to the number, location and relationship between acculturation ideologies as well as fluidity in terms of changes over time in the predominance of particular acculturation ideologies in the national society. The next section of the chapter applies the concepts discussed above to the international students' perceptions of acculturation ideologies in the Irish civic culture and state in the autumn of 1997, beginning with an analysis of the predominant Irish acculturation ideology identified by the students at the time of the interviews.

The International Students' Perceptions of Irish Acculturation Ideologies

Irish Civic Culture

From the perspective of the international students, the predominant Irish acculturation ideology was based upon a mixture of friendliness and insularity. This ideology of friendliness and insularity was rooted in the Irish civic culture, but permeated Irish society, including the institutions of the state. For the students, Irish friendliness was an abstract value in itself, a firm belief about Irish society and a norm which oriented everyday interactions as well as the practices of Irish institutions.

However, insularity was a more complex cultural characteristic of Irish society, with positive and negative features. On the one hand, insularity reflected the relative cultural homogeneity of Irish society, which, surprisingly, many of the international students valued over their more culturally diverse home countries and other societies in which they had lived (see Boucher, 1998: 71). In this way, Irish insularity could be a positive value for the students as well as a reflection of their experiential belief about the nature of Irish society. Further, Irish friendliness towards others — Irish and non-Irish people — as a norm for everyday interactions could in part be explained by insularity in that each person was treated as if they were a member of the local community "family".

On the other hand, insularity could easily lead to discrimination against others who appeared to be physically or culturally different from the majority Irish population. In this case, the norm or tacit rule resulting in the practice of discrimination drew on the value of protecting one's family of community from unknown and different outsiders, as well as the belief that these different outsiders were a threat to the cultural integrity of the community family of Ireland. For most of the students, these acts of insular discrimination could be explained away as an unintentional, almost spontaneous reaction to the reality of cultural diversity embodied in the person of the "foreigner" who was culturally different and possibly physically different too. For these students, the forms of discrimination which they experienced were not really intentional acts of, for instance, racism, but understandable results of an insular society whose people did not know any better yet.

From this perspective, the predominant Irish acculturation ideology was driven by the contradiction that Irish insularity could result in either friendliness towards or discrimination against non-nationals and ethnic minorities. Insularity was perceived to be the most significant single feature of Irish society compared to the students' own countries and those countries in which they had lived, a feature which both described Irish society and explained Irish behaviour towards outsiders. In figurative terms, Irish cultural insularity was the hinge between friendliness and discrimination, leading to Irish friendliness towards outsiders if the door opened one way, but to discrimination if the door opened the other way. Standing at this door in every social interaction in Ireland, the big question for the international students was whether it would be opened to Irish friendliness or discrimination.

While this contradiction in the Irish acculturation ideology posed one difficulty for the international students in terms of the unpredictability of Irish behaviour towards them, a second difficulty arose from Irish expectations of their assimilation to Irish culture. For the students, Irish insularity was premised on the assumption of cultural homogeneity of Irish people in the Republic of Ireland, whether or not this assumption was an accurate reflection of Irish social reality. To be fully included by Irish people in the extended community family of Irish society meant non-nationals and ethnic minorities had at least publicly to appear to homogenise or "Irishise" themselves to the values, beliefs and norms of the majority population. In this way, assimilationism was the primary mode of inclusion associated with the Irish acculturation ideology of friendliness and insularity rooted in Irish civic culture.

In general, the international students perceived that Irish people were more likely to be friendly the more the students adapted themselves to Irish culture. This was especially true for the Irish people whom they met in sites of recurring social interactions such as shops, coffee bars, pubs and student societies among others. In these sites of socialising, the students perceived that Irish culture was group-oriented with individual Irish people frequently travelling together in groups to sites or joining an already formed group once arriving at the socialising site. Within these groups, the students further perceived that there were tacit rules for conversation based largely around a public/private division in which individual "private" issues, experiences or beliefs were rarely discussed. Instead, the students perceived that Irish conversations were publicly directed around topics such as politics, sports, the weather and gossip, frequently interlaced with "slagging" matches and often interwoven by narrative story-telling. While perhaps interesting, the students interpreted these Irish public conversations as superficial and as a prelude to "real" private conversations, which never seemed to occur, unless the Irish person was "drunk". Of course, these interpretations may simply reflect the "student" lifestyle of younger people and as such may not be representative of all Irish cultural practices.

For the international students, the site of the pub and the ritual of drinking, followed by the occasional opening up of Irish people to their private selves, were an integral part of Irish culture and an important element of the assimilation of the non-Irish to Irishness. Those students who chose to adapt to this particular set of Irish practices set around the pub appeared to be the ones who were the most integrated into the Irish community family of Irish society, primarily through Irish student social groups within the university. However, those international students who chose not or could not adapt to the Irish "pub culture" seemed to be the ones who were the least integrated into Irish society.

This was particularly the case for Muslim students, especially those who would not frequent sites where drink was consumed. Many of the Muslim students noted the apparent lack of interest and effort made by Irish "friends" to include them in socialising after the Muslim students expressed their beliefs about the consumption of alcohol. As a result, the Muslim students and the international students in general largely saw themselves as faced with a stark choice — assimilate to Irish pub culture or be excluded from the Irish social life of their fellow students and of the wider Irish society. In this way, the assimilationist mode of inclusion within the acculturation ideology of friendliness and insularity centred around the pub was perceived by many of the international students as a type of indirect cultural discrimination or a mode of exclusion for those who did not assimilate to the Irish pub culture.

For another group of international students, the door of Irish friendliness had been closed, only to be opened up to direct discrimination, largely in the form of racism. These mainly black African students experienced a marked increase in racialised verbal abuse expressed towards them by Irish people after the arrival of relatively small numbers of refugees and asylum-seekers, mostly from Romania and parts of sub-Saharan Africa, in Ireland from the mid-1990s. For these students, the negative features of Irish insularity, such as the perception of a threat to Irish cultural homogeneity, were heightened by the apparent physical differences of many of the refugees and asylum-seekers from the majority Irish. These Irish people projected their fears onto the non-white and especially "black" international students, discriminating against them mostly through shouting a racial epithet, usually followed by a national xenophobic phrase such as "go home!". In these cases, the threat of physical difference to Irish cultural insularity appeared so grave to the members of the majority Irish group that their desired mode of exclusion seemed to be the voluntary removal or forced deportation of the non-white person from Ireland.

Overall, the international students perceived that the predominant Irish acculturation ideology was located in Irish civic culture and based on Irish friendliness and insularity. Of these two, insularity was the most important characteristic of the acculturation ideology, leading to the contradiction that Irish insularity explained both Irish acts of friendliness and discrimination towards non-nationals and ethnic minorities. This contradiction in Irish civic culture was heightened by the dominance of the assimilationist mode of inclusion, in which Irish friendliness appeared to be directly related to the outsiders' choice and ability to assimilate to the values, beliefs and norms of the majority group culture. The expectations of Irish assimilationism were most strongly felt by the international students in terms of Irish pub culture, with social exclusion in the form of indirect cultural discrimination resulting for those students who did not adapt to the norms of Irish pub life. Finally, Irish insularity led to direct discrimination in the form of racism against mainly black African students who seemed to be grouped with refugees and asylum-seekers as a perceived physical threat to Irish cultural homogeneity by some members of the majority Irish population. These results suggest that there are cultural and physical limits in the Irish civic culture's acculturation ideology with regard to what and, more significantly, whom is deemed to be worthy of assimilation by the majority Irish group.

The Irish State

The international students experienced the Irish state primarily through members of certain public organisations such as civil servants in the Department of Justice or Foreign Affairs, immigration officials and the local police. For the students, the Irish friendliness of the civic culture translated into equality of treatment or being treated as if they were native Irish people by public officials. Most of the students reported that they were treated equally most of the time by Irish public officials. The students perceived that this equality of treatment was an important part of the state's acculturation ideology as a value, belief and norm for interactions between Irish public officials and non-nationals as well as between these officials and indigenous ethnic minorities.

At the time of the interviews in late 1997, this equality of treatment had not been formalised into part of a multicultural policy of equality and non-discrimination. However, many of the students believed that — as promised — the Irish government would enact such a policy, formalising the practice of Irish friendliness into statutory law. Subsequently, the Irish government passed two Acts in 1998 and 1999 which addressed equality in employment and status respectively, making illegal a number of forms of discrimination and creating an Equality Authority to enforce the provisions of these acts (Employment Equality Act, 1998; Equal Status Act, 1999). In terms of multiculturalism, these Acts represent one part of a more comprehensive Irish multicultural policy which would require, among other policies, state activism in support of cultural diversity in the private sphere alongside the legal commitment to equality and non-discrimination in the public sphere.

However, many of the students also experienced what they perceived to be discrimination by Irish public officials, principally by immigration officials at airports and at the Aliens Registration Office in Dublin. In particular, a significant number of the non-white international students perceived a change in their treatment by immigration officials after the summer of 1997 from one of equality to racial discrimination. These students noted that, prior to autumn 1997, they had not been stopped by immigration officials at Irish airports and had been treated equally with Irish passengers. Yet, upon their return to Ireland for the beginning of the 1997/98 academic year, immigration officials at Irish airports seemed to stop and question only non-white passengers, allowing people who looked white to pass through immigration. Many of the same students also recorded perceived discriminatory treatment by Irish public officials over refusals to issue multiple entry visas, denials of work permits and difficulties over family visits.

For the international students, these instances of discrimination by public officials against non-nationals were in part explained by Irish cultural insularity or the perceived threat to Irish cultural homogeneity by foreigners who were too physically or culturally different from the majority Irish population. From this perspective, the Irish immigration officials patrolled Ireland's borders in the Common Travel Area with Britain within the EU's "Fortress Europe" to protect Irish cultural homogeneity by excluding non-white and culturally distinct foreigners, not simply to follow common legal agreements between Ireland and Britain or the EU.

Overall, the students perceived a contradiction in the Irish state's acculturation ideology between the emerging multicultural mode of inclusion based on internal state policies with respect to equality and non-discrimination and the discriminatory mode of exclusion practised particularly by Irish public officials at the borders of the country. The Irish friendliness of the civic culture appeared to buttress the internal equality of treatment by Irish state officials of non-nationals and ethnic minorities, leading to a mode of inclusion based on a developing multicultural policy at the state level instead of the assimilation into the community family at the societal level. On the other hand, Irish insularity (expressed as a threat to cultural homogeneity) led to a mode of exclusion based on internal discrimination against non-nationals and ethnic minorities with regard to Irish civic culture and to external discrimination against certain groups of non-nationals on Ireland's borders with respect to the Irish state.

Conclusion

The contradictions between and within the acculturation ideologies of the Irish civic culture and the Irish state appear to be related to the central role of Irish cultural insularity within these ideologies. In the civic culture, Irish insularity can lead to friendliness towards outsiders who attempt to assimilate to the majority culture and therefore may be viewed as part of the Irish community family. However, insularity can also result in discrimination against outsiders who do not assimilate or who seem to be too physically and culturally different from the majority population. At the state level, the friendliness which arises from Irish insularity may be translated into the practice of equal treatment towards outsiders as well as the abstract formalisation of this practice into the statutory law of a developing multicultural policy. At the same time, Irish insularity can result in the practice of discrimination at the borders of the country against outsiders who are perceived to be physical or cultural threats to Irish cultural homogeneity.

Of course, the results of this re-analysis of the interview results from the ICOS report in terms of Irish acculturation ideologies must remain suggestive, given the limitations of the sample to a group of international students in Ireland during the autumn of 1997. To move from suggestiveness to a potential explanation requires more empirical research into perceptions about Irish acculturation ideologies from a broad range of non-national, ethnic minority and majority Irish sample groups. Nonetheless, this discussion of Irish acculturation ideologies suggests that a narrow focus on the issue of racism and on the social groups of refugees and asylum-seekers, which has dominated Irish public debate from the mid-1990s, misses the complexity and fluidity of contemporary Irish social reality with respect to broader issues of the inclusion and exclusion of all non-nationals and ethnic minorities into Irish society.

References

Boucher, G. (1998), *The Irish are friendly, but . . .*, Dublin: Irish Council for International Students.

Breakwell, G. and E. Lyons (eds.) (1996), *Changing European Identities*, Oxford: Butterworth Heinemann.

Castles, S. and M. Miller (1998), *The Age of Migration*, London: Macmillan.

Furnivall, J. (1939), *Netherlands India*, Cambridge: Cambridge University Press.

Guibernau, M. and J. Rex (1997), *The Ethnicity Reader*, Cambridge: Polity Press.

Government of Ireland (1999), *Equal Status Act, 1999*, Dublin: Government Publications Sales Office.

Government of Ireland (1999), *Immigration Bill, 1999*, Dublin: Government Publications Sales Office.

Government of Ireland (1998), *Employment Equality Act, 1998*, Dublin: Government Publications Sales Office.

Government of Ireland (1996), *Refugee Act, 1996*, Dublin: Government Publications Sales Office.

Miles, R. (1989), *Racism*, London: Routledge.

Smith, M. (1965), *The Plural Society in the British West Indies*, Berkeley: University of California Press.

Torres, R. et al. (eds.) (1999), *Race, Identity and Citizenship*, Oxford: Blackwell.

CHAPTER FOURTEEN

STRESS, COPING AND ACCULTURATION OF INTERNATIONAL MEDICAL STUDENTS IN IRELAND

Sinead Glennon and Malcolm MacLachlan

"Acculturation" is a term that has been defined as change that results from "continuous first-hand contact between two distinct cultural groups" (Redfield, Linton and Herkovits, 1936). A typical acculturation situation involves an individual of a particular (often non-dominant) cultural background being in contact with another cultural group (usually dominant). The ways in which an acculturating individual (or group) wishes to relate to the dominant society have been termed "acculturative strategies" (Berry, 1990).

Berry (1997) describes how when an acculturating individual does not wish to maintain his/her own culture and identity and seeks daily interaction with the dominant society, then the *assimilation* path or strategy is defined. In contrast, when there is a value placed on holding onto one's original culture and a wish to avoid interaction with others, then the *separation* alternative is defined. When there is an interest in both maintaining one's original culture and in daily interactions with others, *integration* is the option; here there is some degree of cultural integrity maintained while moving to participate as an integral part of the larger social network. Integration is the strategy that attempts to "make the best of both worlds". Finally, when there is little possibility or interest in cultural maintenance (possibly for reasons of enforced cultural loss) and little possibility or interest in relations with others (possibly for reasons of exclusion or discrimination) then *marginalisation* is defined.

The concept of acculturative stress refers to one kind of stress, that in which stressors are identified as having their source in the process of acculturation. Berry and Kim (1988) attempted to identify the cultural and psychological factors that govern the relationship between acculturation and mental health. They concluded that mental health problems often do arise during acculturation; however, these problems are not inevitable and seem to depend on a variety of group and individual characteristics that enter into the acculturation process. Berry, Kim, Minde and Mok (1987) proposed that moderating factors include the phase of acculturation, the mode (strategy), the nature of the larger society, the type of acculturating group, and individual members. In particular, one's appraisal of the acculturation experience and one's skills in dealing with the stressors can affect the level of acculturative stress experienced.

Phases of Acculturation

As a process that takes place over time, acculturation may be considered as a series of phases. In the *pre-contact phase*, there are two independent cultural groups. In the *contact phase*, the groups meet, interact, and new stressors appear. Usually, but not inevitably, a *conflict phase* appears, in which tension builds up and pressures are experienced by the non-dominant group to change their way of life. If conflict and tension do appear, a highly stressful *crisis phase* may occur, in which the conflict comes to a head, and a resolution is required. Finally, an *adaptation phase* may take place, in which the group relations are stabilised in one form or another. These varieties of adaptation may or may not bring about an adequate solution to the conflict and crisis, or a reduction in stress (Berry, 1997).

Acculturation Strategy

Of the four acculturative strategies identified by Berry, three modes represent various forms of adaptation, while one (Marginalisation) tends to suspend the individual in a highly stressful crisis.

Of the other three, Separation tends to maintain the resistance to inter-group relations, and thus maintain the conflict to some extent, suggesting that mental health may be relatively poor in this mode as well. Also, because Assimilation represents cultural loss, mental health may be poorer there than in the Integration mode, where selective involvement in two cultural systems may provide the most supportive sociocultural base for the mental health of the individual (Berry et al., 1987).

Nature of the Larger Society

The society that exerts the acculturation influences may do so in a variety of ways. One important distinction is the degree of pluralism extant (Murphy, 1965). Culturally plural societies, in contrast to culturally monistic ones, are likely to be characterised by two important factors:

1. The availability of a network of social and cultural groups that may provide support for those entering into the experience of acculturation,
2. Greater tolerance for or acceptance of cultural diversity (termed "Multicultural Ideology" by Berry, Kalin and Taylor, 1977).

MacGréil's (1996) *Prejudice in Ireland Revisited* is based on a comprehensive survey of a random sample of adults in the Republic of Ireland on a wide range of attitudes and opinions toward ethnic, national, political, racial, religious and social groups and minorities. Racialism, or racism, was examined in the Irish population by means of the "Racialist Social Distance Scale" (MacGréil, 1988), measuring social distance against ten racial and ethnic-racial categories. A significant and substantial reduction in racialism in Ireland since 1972–73 was found. However, MacGréil makes the point, that while these findings record positive trends, they still show an undesirable level of dormant racialism in Irish society (see also Curry's chapter).

CHARACTERISTICS OF ACCULTURATING GROUPS

There are many social and cultural qualities of the acculturating group that may affect the degree to which acculturative stress is experienced by its members. This list of possible factors identified in the literature (Berry and Kim, 1988) is extremely long, thus only a selective overview is given here. Standard indicators, such as age and gender, may play a role; relatively older persons, and often females, have frequently been noted to experience more stress (Cox et al., 1987). Perhaps the most comprehensive variable in the literature is that of social supports (as suggested by Berry and Kim, 1988). This refers to the presence of social and cultural institutions for the support of the acculturating individual. Included here are such factors as ethnic associations (national or local), residential ethnic enclaves, extended families, availability of one's original group and more formal institutions such as agencies and clinics devoted to providing support.

Psychological Characteristics of the Acculturating Individual

Beyond the social factors numerous psychological variables may play a role in the mental health status of persons experiencing acculturation. For example, contact experiences may account for variations in acculturative stress. Whether one has many or few contacts with the larger society, whether the first encounters are viewed positively or not, may set the stage for all subsequent ones and ultimately affect mental health. A recurring view is that the congruence between contact expectations and actualities will affect mental health; individuals for whom there is a discrepancy may have greater acculturative stress than those who achieve some reasonable match between them. If sojourners are carefully introduced into a new society by close, sympathetic, host culture friends, the evidence indicates that they may encounter fewer problems than if they are left to fend for themselves (Sellitz and Cook, 1962; Shattuck, 1965).

Among factors that appear during acculturation are the attitudes toward various modes of acculturation. As noted already, individuals within a group do vary in their preference for assimilating, integrating or rejecting. These variations, along with experiences of marginalisation, are known to affect one's mental health status (Berry et al., 1987). Finally, a key psychological variable in dealing with acculturative stress is that of coping, to be discussed shortly.

Acculturative Stress and Foreign Students

Berry and Kim (1987) identified five different acculturating groups including Immigrants, Refugees, Native Peoples, Ethnic Groups and Sojourners, varying in the degree of voluntariness, movement, and permanence of contact. This study focuses on one particular group of sojourners, foreign students. The problems facing foreign students are threefold. Firstly, there are the stresses that confront anybody living in a foreign culture, such as racial discrimination, language problems, accommodation difficulties, separation reactions, dietary restrictions, financial stress, misunderstandings and loneliness (Oberg, 1960). Secondly, there are the difficulties that face all late adolescents and young people whether they are studying at home or abroad, as this is a time of considerable vulnerability, when young people attempt to become emotionally independent, self-supporting, productive, responsible members of society (Erikson, 1970). Thirdly, there are academic stresses when students are expected to work hard, often under poor conditions, with complex material.

While the mental health of native students has previously been explored in Ireland and elsewhere, no such research exists regarding the level of psychological distress experienced by foreign students while studying at university in Ireland. According to the Higher Education Authority 6 per cent of full-time undergraduates in Ireland for the academic year 1995/1996 were not Irish citizens. To date no research has been undertaken with regards to this student body, which numbers over 3,500. As in many studies conducted elsewhere, foreign students are reported to suffer poorer mental health than native students (Ebbin and Blakenship, 1988; Berry and Kostovick, 1983; Furnham and Treize, 1983; Gunn, 1970; Kinnell, 1990). Foreign students have been found to have significantly higher rates of severe suicidal ideation than their peers (Salmons and Harrington, 1984), and three out of four suicides at one British University involved foreign students (Manderson and Sclare, 1973).

Previous research in this area has focused on how foreign students were found to be over-represented in the attendance figures at college counselling services (Lewins, 1990; Maha, 1964). This research was stimulated by the thesis that foreign students "somatise" their problems to avoid "loss of face" and to permit attendance for medical rather than psychotherapeutic advice. Gunn (1970) writing on the digestive, dermatological, sexual and adjustment problems of foreign students in the United Kingdom buttressed the notion of a "Foreign Student Syndrome". However, the findings of O'Mahoney and O'Brien (1980) in Ireland and Cole, Allen and Green (1980) in Australia (that foreign students are not over-represented in attendance figures) questions the idea of a syndrome specific to foreign students. Researchers such as Kadri (1966) and Cole, Allen and Green (1980), suggest that the "Foreign Student Syndrome" may be no more than the inability of Western physicians to cope with the needs of members of a different culture, labelling normal behaviour as pathological.

Coping strategies were defined by Lazarus and Folkman (1984: 141) as "the cognitive and behavioural efforts to manage specific external and/or internal demands that are appraised as taxing or exceeding the resources of the person". There has been considerable research into coping strategies as mediators and moderators of stress (Folkman, 1980; Heady and Wearing, 1990; Hovanitz and Kozora, 1989; Moos and Billings, 1982). However, the coping strategies employed by foreign students to deal with the acculturative experience have not previously been investigated. The present research was therefore undertaken to assess the previously unexplored levels of psychological distress experienced by foreign students in Ireland, and also to examine the relationship between the mental health of foreign students, their coping and acculturation strategies.

In the present study, the mental health of foreign students was compared to a "control" group of Irish students. We hypothesised that the additional stresses placed on foreign students studying in Ireland would make them more vulnerable to psychological distress. It was also hypothesised that the use of different kinds of coping strategies would be related to mental health. Finally, it was hoped that it may be possible to identify factors associated with elevated levels of psychological distress using the framework proposed by Berry et al. (1987).

METHOD

Subjects

A total of 181 undergraduate medical students (mean age 20.6) attending the Royal College of Surgeons in Ireland (RCSI) completed questionnaires: 100 Foreign students (mean age 20.9) and 81 Irish students (mean age 20.0). Subjects were taken from Pre-Medical year (1st year), First Medical year (2nd year) and Second Medical year (3rd year). Furnham and Treize (1983) grouped different nationalities together so as to facilitate statistical analysis of results and these groupings were adopted in the present study. The following national groupings were included in the study: North American (N=10), South American (N=2), European (N=20), Australian (N=6), African (N=8), Chinese (N=2), Middle Eastern (N=9), Malaysian (N=36), Indian (N=7) and Irish (N=81).

Materials

Two separate questionnaires were formulated: the Foreign Student Questionnaire (FSQ) and the Irish Student Questionnaire (ISQ). Both forms of the questionnaires contained the General Health Questionnaire 28 (GHQ-28, Goldberg and Williams, 1988) and the Coping Strategies Indicator (CSI, Amirkhan, 1990) and a Demographic Information Questionnaire. The GHQ and CSI have been used with different cultural groups and found to have similar factors structures cross-culturally (Goldberg and Williams, 1988, Ager and MacLachlan, 1998). Demographic information was gathered regarding foreign and Irish subjects' age, sex, academic year, country of birth, marital status, religious orientation, social supports, attitude toward the dominant culture, aspects of acculturative experience and acculturative strategy chosen. Acculturation strategy was measured by asking subjects to rate along a visual analogue scale the extent to which they believed it was important to (1) maintain their identity and characteristics prior to coming to study at RCSI, and (2) maintain relationships with those they had met since coming to RCSI.

Procedure

Data was collected on three separate occasions, in the last week of the first term of the academic year. During the last ten minutes of a lecture period, subjects were asked to complete a questionnaire and return it to the researchers.

RESULTS

Psychological Distress

Twenty-seven per cent of Irish students and 57 per cent of foreign students scored above the threshold score of 5 on the GHQ-28, used to identify a significant level of clinical symptoms — "caseness" (Goldberg and Williams, 1988).

Table 14.1: Mean Number of Symptoms for Foreign and Irish Students on GHQ Subscales

GHQ Subscales	Mean Number of Symptoms		t value (df=178)
	Irish	*Foreign*	
Somatic	1.112	1.830	2.511*
Anxiety	1.288	2.030	2.406*
Social Dysfunction	1.000	1.920	3.423**
Depression	0.520	0.538	–.096
Total	3.914	6.340	2.869*

*p<0.05, **p<0.001.

As can be seen in Table 14.1, the mean number of reported symptoms of foreign and Irish students were significantly different for three of the subscales, with foreign students having a significantly greater mean number of symptoms on the Somatic, Anxiety and Social Dysfunction subscales but not, however, on the Depression sub-scale.

The mean GHQ-28 total score for foreign students was significantly greater than the mean total of Irish students. The GHQ-28 mean scores for the different national groupings were as follows: North American (3.4), Irish (3.9), Australian (4.3), European (5.5), Malaysian (6.4), African (7.0), Indian (7.2), Middle Eastern (9.0), South American (10.5) and Chinese (11.5). Further analysis indicated significant differences were found between the mean GHQ-28 score of Irish and Middle Eastern students and Irish and Malaysian students. Overall, the mean GHQ-28 score for female students (6.2) was significantly greater than male students (4.2). However, there was no significant correlation between age of subject and GHQ-28 score.

Using one-way ANOVAs, it was found that *foreign students* with lower GHQ scores differed significantly from those with higher GHQ scores, by feeling more accepted by the dominant culture, having made a voluntary choice to study in Ireland, reported experiencing less discrimination, having a good knowledge of English, and having previous travel experience (all $p < .05$).

Acculturation

In both foreign and Irish students, the acculturation strategy most commonly adopted was Integration, followed by Separation, Assimilation and Marginalisation respectively. Table 14.2 shows the mean GHQ scores for subjects categorised by their chosen acculturative strategy. Subjects were identified as scoring above or below the midway mark on each of the two acculturation strategy measures. Those scoring below midway on each were categorised as "Marginalisation", those scoring above on each as "Integration", and so on. Unfortunately, uneven cell sizes compromised the robustness of appropriate statistical analysis, but comparing the two largest groups showed that subjects overall who chose the Integration acculturative strategy had significantly lower GHQ scores than subjects who chose the Separation acculturative strategy.

Table 14.2: Mean GHQ Score for Subjects (Overall, Foreign or Irish) who Chose the Integration, Assimilation, Separation and Marginalisation Acculturative Strategies

Acculturative Strategy	**Mean GHQ score (and number of subjects)**		
	Students Overall	*Foreign Students*	*Irish Students*
Integration	4.899 (119)	6.433 (60)	3.339 (59)
Assimilation	5.000 (23)	4.714 (14)	5.500 (8)
Separation	7.200 (30)	7.000 (20)	7.600 (10)
Marginalisation	4.667 (9)	7.000 (6)	0.000 (3)

Coping

To complete the CSI, respondents must first identify a stressful event they have recently experienced, or are currently experiencing. Sources of stress identified by foreign students were as follows: exam/college (14 per cent), relationships (6 per cent), health (6 per cent), accommodation (6 per cent), homesickness (5 per cent), family (4 per cent), discrimination (4 per cent), financial worries (2 per cent) and problems with visas (2 per cent). Stressors identified by Irish students were as follows: exams/college (25 per cent), relationships (12 per cent), financial worries (5 per cent), family (4 per cent), part-time job (4 per cent), flatmate problems (2 per cent) and personal health (1 per cent).

The only significant difference between the mean Irish and foreign student CSI scores was for the Seeking Social Support coping strategy, with foreign students and Irish students having respective mean scores of 24.31 and 22.4 ($p < .05$).

Analysis of variance showed that mean scores for the Problem Solving coping strategy were significantly different depending on the acculturation strategy adopted. The mean score for the Problem Solving coping strategy of subjects who chose Assimilation (29.4) was significantly greater than that of subjects who chose Integration (26.4) and Separation (25.1) ($p < .01$).

It can be seen from Table 14.3 below that significant negative correlations were found between GHQ scores of students overall and foreign students, and their scores on the Problem Solving coping strategy; and significant positive correlations between GHQ scores and scores on the Avoidance coping strategy. However, no significant relationships were found between Irish students' GHQ scores and their scores on any of the three coping strategies.

Table 14.3: Correlations of GHQ Scores of Participants (Overall, Foreign Only and Irish Only) with their Scores on Problem Solving, Seeking Social Support, and Avoidance Coping Strategies

Coping Strategy	**Pearson r value**		
	Students Overall	*Foreign*	*Irish*
Problem Solving	-.179**	-.222*	-.136
Seeking Social Support	-.052	-.107	-.062
Avoidance	.234***	.299*	.202

*p<0.05; **p<0.01; ***p<0.001

Discussion

Psychological Distress

Thirty-eight per cent of the subjects in the sample scored above the threshold score for "caseness" of 5. This value of 38 per cent is similar to findings reported in surveys of students in Ireland (41 per cent, Tyrrell, 1993) and the United Kingdom (50 per cent, Surtees and Miller, 1990). However, when the proportions of foreign (51 per cent) and Irish students (27 per cent) in the present study are compared, it is clear that the proportion of "caseness" in foreign students (57 per cent) is much higher than for indigenous students in Ireland (27 per cent).

The significant difference in the mean number of symptoms for Irish and foreign students on the somatic subscale of the GHQ-28, could be taken to support the ideas of the existence of a "Foreign Student Syndrome". However, the overall patterning of scores on the subscales suggests that foreign students are also experiencing significantly more psychological disturbance overall. They are not restricting their expression of this disturbance to somatic symptoms only. This would suggest that foreign students are not "somatising" their problems to avoid "loss of face", and this therefore questions the validity of a "Foreign Student Syndrome", at least in the present sample.

Furthermore, foreign and Irish students had similarly low scores on the depression subscale, suggesting that neither group is suffering from depression in a substantial way and also neither group is suffering from depression significantly more than the other. Tyrrell (1993) found similarly low scores on the depression subscale of the GHQ-28 for a sample of Irish University students. These results conflict, however, with the findings of O'Neil and Mingle (1988) who found that depression was probably the most commonly reported mental health problem in the university setting in the USA.

Closer examination of the seven items on the GHQ-28 depression subscale indicates that four of these seven questions refer to suicidal thought. If a student felt depressed, but not suicidal, there would be only three suitable symptoms for him/her to endorse on this subscale. Suicidal thoughts are only one of a range of possible symptoms of depression, and are perhaps over-represented as potential symptoms of depression on the GHQ-28.

Acculturation

Berry et al. (1987) suggested that associations can be made between acculturative strategies and differential levels of mental health. Berry et al. (1987) propose that the highest level of mental health is to be found in individuals who choose the Integration acculturative strategy, followed by those who choose the Assimilation strategy, then the Separation strategy and lastly those who choose the Marginalisation strategy have the poorest mental health. In the present study, the Integration strategy was most frequently adopted, and it was associated with relatively low GHQ scores. It is possible that the overall results have been confounded by a "negative" response bias among three Irish students, who clearly gave "not at all" responses not only to the 28 GHQ questions, but also scored towards the end of the Visual Analogue Scales, resulting in them being classified as *marginalisation.*

Although the pattern of GHQ scores for either foreign or Irish students does not perfectly match the pattern suggested by Berry et al. (1987), where deviations are found, few subjects chose that acculturative strategy. Mean GHQ scores of these groups may, therefore, be unreliable due to the small number of subjects belonging to these groups. Furnham and Bochner (1986) carried out an investigation of the nature and extent of social difficulties that foreign students experience in England and how relations with host culture members help them to deal with these problems. The results of their investigation revealed that stress experienced by foreign students was largely due to their lacking the requisite social skills with which to negotiate specific social situations.

On both the Foreign Student and Irish Student versions of the questionnaire, subjects were asked about their preconceptions of their dominant culture and also instructed to give examples of such preconceptions. Most Irish students expected college life to be a highly enjoyable experience, with a busy social life and the opportunity to make new friends, and few (10 per cent) focused on negative aspects of their future academic career. On the other hand, over 60 per cent of foreign students' preconceptions of Irish culture/society were restricted to negative stereotypes of Irish people as being lazy, heavy drinkers, who put their social life before their work-life. The purpose of the foreign student's stay in Ireland is very much achievement-oriented and involves intensive study; it is therefore not surprising that stereotypes such as those above portray the ideology of Irish society as running counter to that of the foreign student.

Foreign students with considerable cultural knowledge may have found that the Irish culture was as they had expected it to be, and their negative expectations may have predisposed them to expect negative situations (similar to the effect of the Self-fulfilling Prophecy proposed by Snyder and Swann, 1978) and this could be a possible explanation for the high GHQ scores of this group. In accordance with the above proposition, little cultural knowledge could result in lower GHQ scores, as negative expectations may be less with less cultural knowledge. In the present study, those foreign students with less cultural knowledge did in fact have lower GHQ scores.

A common assumption is that previous cross-cultural experience with other cultures or prior exposure to the host culture (Berry et al., 1987) should facilitate adjustment. However, previous cultural exposure may serve only to reinforce stereotypes and defences, which inhibit adjustment (DuBois, 1956). Thus, the nature and quality — for example, the depth, intimacy (Amir, 1969), accuracy (Basu and Ames, 1970) and similarity (Bochner, 1972) — of the previous cultural experience or host culture may be more important than the quantitative amount of previous exposure, as is evidenced in the results of the present study.

Quite a high percentage of foreign students had experienced some form of discrimination (38 per cent) and this was found to significantly affect their mental health status. Those having experienced discrimination had a mean GHQ score of 7.6, compared to a mean GHQ score of 5.5 for those who hadn't had such experiences. Tajfel and Dawson (1966) found that the experience of discrimination is a vital factor in accelerating or inhibiting adjustment to a new culture and, as is evident from MacGréil's (1996) research, and the findings of the present study, certain national groupings are more likely to experience discrimination than others.

Coping

The finding that subjects who chose the Assimilation acculturative strategy had significantly higher scores on the Problem Solving coping strategy, than subjects who chose the Integration or Separation acculturative strategies, may indicate that the relinquishing of one's cultural identity and moving into the dominant society may make the acculturating individual highly problem-focused. The problem he/she faces is that of fitting into their new culture and severing ties with their old.

There are, as yet, unresolved issues concerning causal directionality when interpreting the results of coping strategy inventories. If, however, we assume that use of different coping strategies has a causal effect on mental health, as measured by the GHQ, the results of the present study (correlation analysis) suggest that for foreign students, high scores on the problem solving coping strategy are predictive of low scores on the GHQ (little psychological distress). Also, high scores on the avoidance coping strategy are predictive of high scores on the GHQ (high psychological distress). However, no significant correlation was found between use of these two coping strategies and Irish students' GHQ scores. From the results reported here, it seems that the correlations between coping strategy scores and GHQ scores, for students overall, are accounted for by foreign students' scores for both of these variables.

Scores on the Seeking Social Support coping strategy were not significantly correlated with GHQ scores for foreign students, Irish students or students overall. This result is surprising, as when the scores of Irish and foreign students were compared (using T-test) on all three coping strategies of the CSI, the only significant result found was that foreign students had higher scores on the Seeking Social Support coping strategy. This would suggest that, while social support was sought more by foreign students, the benefits of such support (if received) were insufficient to prevent the development of significant symptoms of distress.

It is important to point out that the coping scale used here determines whether a person used a particular strategy, but does not assess whether it was used successfully. For example, interaction with host culture members has been shown (Furnham and Bochner, 1982; Sellitz and Cook, 1962; Shattuck, 1965) to be one of the most useful and necessary strategies that a foreign student can use: spending all of one's time complaining to fellow foreign students about a problem but not necessarily trying to do something about it, may not be a useful strategy.

Summary

The Higher Education Authority figures, for the academic year 1995/1996, showed that 73 per cent of the 947 students studying at the RCSI were from countries other than Ireland. Foreign students at the RCSI are therefore surrounded by others who are similarly experiencing acculturation. It is possible that, for this very reason, their adaptation to Ireland has been inhibited. While foreign students' scores on the Seeking Social Support coping strategy only, were significantly higher than Irish students' scores, foreign students' GHQ scores were not significantly correlated with their scores on the Seeking Social Support coping strategy. One interpretation of these results is that foreign students seek social support more than Irish students but the social support they seek is from other foreign students due to the large numbers of foreign students at the RCSI. Thus, as Furnham and Bochner (1982) suggest, foreign students at the RCSI are not in a position to acquire the social skills appropriate to their new culture, which are facilitated by interactions with host culture members. Further support for this hypothesis comes from the fact that the greatest difference in mean number of symptoms between foreign and Irish students, is on the social dysfunction subscale of the GHQ-28.

However, a definitive explanation of the foreign students' experience of acculturative stress cannot be provided by social learning theory alone. The present study emphasises the individual differences in the acculturation process of foreign students by adopting Berry et al.'s (1987) conceptualisation.

Several consequences flow from adopting a culture learning model of the cross-cultural sojourn. Firstly, failures and problems experienced by the foreign student need not be regarded as symptoms of some underlying pathology, but rather due to a lack of the necessary cultural skills and knowledge. Consequently, remedial action may not involve treatment of "problems" as such, but rather imparting appropriate knowledge and skills through standard social skills training methods, such as instruction, modelling, role-playing, video feedback and homework (Argyle, 1979). Secondly, "adjusting" a person to a culture has connotations of cultural chauvinism, implying that the newcomer should abandon the culture of origin in favour of embracing the values and customs of the host society. On the other hand, learning a second culture, just like learning a second language, has no such pejorative overtones.

Future research could therefore map out empirically the nature and extent of social difficulties that foreign students experience in Ireland and investigate how interactions with host culture members facilitate the acquisition of culture appropriate skills. The present study recommends that third level institutions in Ireland, as well as providing foreign student support groups/associations, should also facilitate foreign students acquisition of culture-specific skills.

We support the cultural learning position since:

> . . . this construction of the problem takes away some of the stigma of being socially incompetent in a new culture, implying as it does opportunities for making up lost ground, rather than genetic inferiority or psychopathology, in turn increasing the likelihood that persons will seek or accept remedial treatment (Furnham and Bochner, 1982: 193).

References

Ager, A. and M. MacLachlan (1998), "Psychometric Properties of the Coping Strategy Indicator (CSI) in a Study of Coping Behaviour amongst Malawian Students", *Psychology and Health*, Vol. 13, pp. 399–409.

Amir, Y. (1969), "Contact Hypothesis in Ethnic Relations", *Psychological Bulletin*, Vol. 71, pp. 319–342.

Amirkhan, J.H. (1990), "A Factor Analytically Derived Measure of Coping: The Coping Strategy Indicator", *Journal of Personality and Social Psychology*, Vol. 59, pp. 1066–1074.

Argyle, M. (1979), in A. Wolfgang (ed.), *New Developments in the Analysis of Social Skills: Non-verbal Behaviour*, Academic Press.

Basu, A.K. and R.G. Ames (1970), "Cross-cultural Contact and Attitude Formation", *Sociology and Social Research*, Vol. 55, pp. 5–16.

Berry, J.W. (1990), "Psychology of Acculturation", in J. Berman (ed.), *Cross-cultural Perspectives: Nebraska Symposium on Motivation*, pp. 201–234, Lincoln: University of Nebraska Press.

Berry, J.W. (1997), "Immigration, Acculturation and Adaptation", *Applied Psychology: An International Review*, Vol. 46, No. 1, pp. 5–68.

Berry, J.W., R. Kalin and D. Taylor (1977), *Multiculturalism and Ethnic Attitudes in Canada*, Ottawa: Supply and Services.

Berry, J.W. and U. Kim (1988), "Acculturation and Mental Health", in P. Dasen, J.W. Berry and N. Sartorius (eds.), *Cross-cultural Psychology and Health: Towards Applications*, pp. 207–236, London: Sage.

Berry, J.W., U. Kim, T. Minde and D. Mok (1987), "Comparative Studies of Acculturative Stress", *International Migration Review*, Vol. 21, pp. 491–511.

Berry, J.W. and N. Kostovick (1983), "Psychological Adaptation of Malaysian Students in Canada", Paper presented at the third Asian regional conference of the International Association for Cross-Cultural Psychology, Bangi, Malaysia.

Bochner, S. (1972), "Problems in Culture Learning", in S. Bochner and P. Wick (eds.), *Overseas Students in Australia*, Ranwick, NSW: New South Wales University Press.

Cole, J.B., F.C.L. Allen and J.S. Green (1980), "Survey of Health Problems of Overseas Students", *Social Science and Medicine*, Vol. 14A, pp. 627–631.

Cox, B., M. Blaxter, A. Buckle, N.P. Fenner, J. Golding, M. Gore, F. Huppert, J. Nickson, M. Roth, J. Strak, M. Wadworth and M. Wichelow (1987), *The Health and Lifestyle Survey*, Cambridge: Health Promotion Research Trust.

DuBois, C.A. (1956), *Foreign Students and Higher Education in the United States*, Washington, DC: American Council on Education.

Ebbin, A.J. and E.S. Blakenship (1988), "Stress Related Diagnosis and Barriers to Health Care among Foreign Students, Results of a Survey", *Journal of American College Health, Special Issue: International Student Health*.

Erikson, E. (1970), "Introduction", in G.B. Blame and McArthur (eds.), *Emotional Problems of the Student*, pp. xix-xxx, London: Butterworths.

Folkman, S. (1980), "Making the Case for Coping", in B.N. Carpenter (ed.) *Personal Coping: Theory, Research and Applications*, pp. 31–46, Westport, CT: Praeger.

Furnham, A. and S. Bochner (1986), *Culture Shock: Psychological Reactions to Unfamiliar Environments*, London: Methuen.

Furnham, A. and L. Treize (1983), "The Mental Health of Foreign Students", *Social Science and Medicine*, Vol. 17, pp. 365–370.

Goldberg, D. and P. Williams (1988), *A User's Guide to the GHQ*, Windsor: NFER.

Gunn, A. (1970), *The Privileged Adolescent*, London: Aylesbury Medical and Technical Publications.

Heady, B.W. and A.J. Wearing (1990), "Subjective Well-being and Coping with Adversity", *Social Indicators Research*, Vol. 22, pp. 327–49.

Hewstone, M. and J. Jaspers (1982), "Explanations for Racial Discrimination: The Effect of Group Discussion on Intergroup Attributions", *European Journal of Social Psychology*, Vol. 12, pp 1–16.

Hovanitz, C.A. and E. Kozora (1989), "Life Stress and Clinically Elevated MMPI Scales: Gender Differences in the Moderating Influence of Coping", *Journal of Clinical Psychology, Special Issue: Post-Traumatic Stress Disorder*, Vol. 45, pp. 766–777.

Kadri, Z.N. (1966), "Personality Appraisal of S.E. Asian University Students", *Journal of America College Health*, Vol. 15, pp. 131.

Kinnell, M. (1990), *The Learning Experiences of Overseas Students*, Milton Keynes: Open University Press.

Lazarus, R.S and S. Folkman (1984), *Stress, Appraisal and Coping*, New York: Springer.

Lewins, H. (1990), "Living Needs" in M. Kinnell (ed.), *The Learning Experiences of Overseas Students*, pp. 82–106, Milton Keynes: Open University Press.

MacGréil, M. (1996), *Prejudice in Ireland Revisited*, Survey and Research Unit, St Patrick's College, Maynooth, Co Kildare.

Maha, G.E. (1964), "Health Survey of New Asian and African Students at the University of Illinois", *Journal of American College Health*, Vol. 12, pp. 303.

Manderson, W.G. and A.B. Sclare (1973), "Mental Health Problems in a Student Population", *Health Bulletin*, Vol. 23, pp. 1–7.

Moos and Billings (1982), "The Role of Coping Responses and Social Resources in Attenuating the Impact of Stressful Life Events", *Journal of Behavioural Medicine*, Vol. 4, pp. 139–157.

Oberg, K. (1960), "Cultural Shock: Adjustment to New Cultural Environments", *Practical Anthropology*, Vol. 7, pp. 177–182.

O'Mahoney, P. and S. O'Brien (1980), "Demographic and Social Characteristics of Students Attending a Psychiatrist", *British Journal of Psychiatry*, Vol. 137, pp. 547–50.

O'Neil, M.K. and P. Mingle (1988), "Life Stress and Depression in University Students: Clinical Illustrations of Recent Research", *Journal of American College Health*, Vol. 36, pp. 235–240.

Redfield, R., R. Linton and M.J. Herkovits (1936), "Memorandum on the Study of Acculturation", *American Psychologist*, Vol. 38, pp. 149–152.

Salmons, P.H. and R. Harrington (1984), "Suicidal Ideation in University Students and Other Groups", *International Journal of Social Psychiatry*, Vol. 30, pp. 201–205.

Sellitz, C. and S.W. Cook (1962), "Factors Influencing Attitudes of Foreign Students toward the Host Country", *Journal of Social Issues*, Vol. 18, pp. 7–23.

Shattuck, G.M. (1965), *Between Two Cultures: A Study of the Social Adaptation of Foreign Students to an American Academic Community*, Department of Rural Sociology, Cornell University, Ithaca, NY.

Snyder, M. and W.B. Swann, Jr. (1978), "Behavioural Confirmation in Social Interaction: From Social Perception to Social Reality", *Journal of Experimental Social Psychology*, Vol. 14, pp. 148–62.

Surtees, R.G. and P.M. Miller (1990), "The Interval General Health Questionnaire", *British Journal of Psychiatry*, Vol. 157, pp. 679–686.

Tajfel, H. and Dawson, J. (1966), *Disappointed Guests*, Oxford: Oxford University Press.

Tyrrell, J. (1993), "Sources of Stress Among Psychology Undergraduates. Special Issue: Psychology at Trinity College Dublin", *Irish Journal of Psychology*, Vol. 13, pp. 184–192.

CHAPTER FIFTEEN

SOCRATES IN IRELAND: FIELD DEPENDENCE AND HOMESICKNESS AMONG INTERNATIONAL STUDENTS

David Orr and Malcolm MacLachlan

Most foreigners coming to Ireland, whether long-term migrants, short-term sojourners, or those whose political and/or economic circumstances have led them to seek asylum or refugee status, experience a loss of and often a longing for what they have left behind. This longing can be described as "homesickness" (Fisher, 1989) and goes far beyond the caricature of whining for what is familiar, to prohibiting the ability to adapt and function effectively within a new country and context. Foreign students are coming in increasing numbers to study at Irish third-level institutions and represent both an enriching source of cultural exchange and a valuable income to the tertiary education sector. As has been argued in Chapter 14 (Glennon and MacLachlan, 2000) foreign students on average have been reported to suffer poorer mental health and to have significantly higher rates of suicidal ideation than do local students.

While there has been much research on the mental health correlates, coping mechanisms and social supports associated with cross-cultural transitions, few studies have considered the experience as an instance of homesickness. Fisher's (1989) book is the most in-depth treatment of homesickness to date. Her composite model, treating homesickness as a complex cognitive–motivational–emotional disturbance, suggests that compulsive ruminations about home compete for attentional resources with the demands for adaptation to the new environment, resulting in sub-optimal adjustment.

Uninterrupted and compulsive ruminations on the lost home are found on one extreme, while a full commitment to the new environment is found on the other. Clearly individuals are rarely located at one extreme, but vary in the extent to which one direction predominates over the other. The processes that influence the experience of transition have been suggested by Fisher to consist of grief or loss, interruption of lifestyle, loss of control, change of role, and approach-avoidance conflicts.

Loss

The grief of loss is one possible approach to viewing the reaction to leaving behind the familiar environment. According to this theory, the loss of a home is thought to have a similar effect on an individual as does the death of a loved one. The comparison between bereavement and other kinds of loss is not new and has previously been applied to such events as the loss of a limb (Bradbury, 1997) or, more relevant here, of country (Van der Veer, 1998). This approach is further developed by the application of attachment theory (Bowlby, 1969; Ainsworth et al., 1978; Weiss, 1975, 1978, 1982), which is based on the anxious and despairing behaviour shown by a young infant when the mother is absent. Experimental evidence has suggested that human adults show similar behaviour during uncontrollable separation from a loved one. Fisher subscribes to a biological account of this phenomenon, whereby the execution of certain behaviours should lead to a certain expected consequence, and when this consequence does not occur (due to the absence of the loved one), the individual suffers distress as a result of the discrepancy. However, the separation from home is a special case, as the home still exists, and may be contacted periodically, leading to a sort of "reversible bereavement" (Van Tilburg et al., 1996: 903).

Lifestyle

Interruption of lifestyle and resulting discontinuity is proposed to be a second possible mechanism leading to homesickness. This comes about due to the sudden break with past routines and procedures, which may nevertheless linger on in memory and dominate thoughts. Suggestive evidence for this comes from laboratory experiments (Mandler, 1975; Mandler and Watson, 1966), where subjects were interrupted in the performance of a task, and responded with increased arousal (and sometimes anxiety), and often persistence in trying to complete the task. More naturalistic evidence comes from the literature on social learning in migrant populations who may continue to act according to their old cultural norms when new ones could be seen as more ecologically appropriate (Aroian, 1990; Juthani, 1992; Bochner and Furnham, 1982; Van der Veer, 1998).

Control

Loss of control is suggested as another feature of transition to a new environment, although it is also related to the previous mechanism. Here the emphasis is not on the distress caused by the interruption of previous plans and routines, but instead on the reduced effectiveness resulting from this. The theory is akin to Karasek's (1979) "job stress" model, using its features of perceived control and perceived demand to account for the stress the individual undergoes. Bochner and Furnham (1982) developed a theory of "culture shock" which also runs along similar lines, proposing that the problems encountered by foreign students in a new milieu are mainly due to ignorance of the appropriate customs, procedures and responses. Such social restriction therefore hinders successful adjustment by depriving the student of opportunities to observe the appropriate behaviour of the host nationality and to acquire such behaviour through modelling. Fisher (1989) gave questionnaires to first-year university students and found that homesick students tended to perceive university life as more demanding than did the non-homesick, as well as rating their own effective control as being lower. Burt (1993), having found that intensity of homesickness among first-year students gradually diminishes over time, attributed this to the increasing control experienced as the student learns new routines and information. It is, however, not clear whether this loss of control is antecedent to homesickness, or vice versa, or whether each feeds into the other.

Role Change

Change of role and consequent increased self-consciousness are theorised to result in increased anxiety during adjustment. Transition between the home role and that taken on in the new environment leads to interim discrepancy between the desired role and that perceived by the self and by others. Unfortunately, Fisher seems to neglect this mechanism when trying to find experimental evidence for her theories.

Approach-Avoidance Conflicts

Finally, conflict between the desire to stay in the new environment, arising from career advancement or other benefits, on the one hand, and the desire to return home to comparative security and comfort, on the other hand, may lead to increased distress.

Fisher's (1989) proposed causal mechanisms are not mutually exclusive, and they most likely work in combination to bring about homesickness. Studies done on incidence level have found that it does not differ in prevalence between the sexes (Brewin et al., 1989; Burt, 1993; Fisher, 1989; Horstmanshof and Reddy, 1998), and affects all age-groups (Fisher, 1989).

Homesickness and Culture

Carden and Feicht (1991) found a significant difference between the incidence of homesickness in American female university students (19 per cent) and that in Turkish female university students (77 per cent), each attending college in their own countries. Horstmanshof and Reddy (1998) also found significant differences between the incidence levels of homesickness among different national groupings in the case of their study of Asians, foreign English speakers and foreign non-English speakers in Australia. This suggests that, at least in the case of certain cultures, the prevalence of homesickness may vary according to the cultural background of the sojourner. This is entirely consistent with the great variation in other forms of physical and psychological distress across cultures (MacLachlan, 1997). However, the limited number of cultures on which research into homesickness has been carried out and the increasing number of exchange students give rise to a need to further study the topic.

Many homesickness studies are carried out on student samples (Brewin et al., 1989; Burt, 1993; Carden and Feicht, 1991; Fisher, 1989; Horstmanshof and Reddy, 1998). This is partly because students are a convenient group for academic researchers to work with, but largely because they are, in comparison to other mobile groups, quite homogeneous in the features of their transition. They all arrive at more or less the same time; they stay in the new location for a similar length of time; they are mostly in the same age group; they all come for a similar primary reason, that is, academic study. However, although there have been many studies on the international student experience of transition, they have all tended to focus on those students who are making relatively large (trans-continental) cultural transitions.

A considerable body of international students has been ignored in favour of these more "exotic" sojourners. This is the large number of European students who each year undertake the SOCRATES exchange, a European Union funded university exchange scheme for students of member-states. Although homesickness among these students has been acknowledged by, for instance, the exchange staff in Trinity College Dublin (Office of International Student Affairs, 1998), the assumption is that it is limited to an initial reaction, and will pass within a few weeks. Such an attitude to a phenomenon that can cause a significant degree of academic underperformance (Burt, 1993) as well as acute psychological distress, is perhaps surprising considering the vast resources devoted by the European Union to this exchange programme.

While being primarily interested in these intracontinental exchange students in Ireland, the large number of US students in Ireland also presented an opportunity for comparison. These students had the added "control" attribute of having English as their first language, while still experiencing similar acculturation challenges.

FIELD-DEPENDENCE/INDEPENDENCE

An interesting aspect of Fisher's role change theory is that it implies that the homesick individual has a considerable regard for the opinions of those around them. The "feedback" arising from his/her social environment may be strong enough to cause distress when the role the sojourner perceives for him or herself does not match the role others perceive him/her to be occupying. The idea that sensitivity to feedback from the social environment — which would allow one to develop social skills appropriate to the culture and context — is related to the degree of homesickness, is an important aspect of Fisher's (1989) theory which has received virtually no experimental evidence either for or against it (Van Tilburg et al., 1996).

The Embedded Figures Test (EFT) (Witkin et al., 1971) provides a means for testing the degree to which individuals' behaviour is influenced by the context they are experiencing. At its most basic level, the EFT provides a means of measuring an individual's perceptual ability to pick out a certain aspect of an organised pattern. However, this relatively simple application has been shown (Witkin et al., 1962; Karp et al., 1969) to be only part of a much broader cognitive dimension referred to as field-dependence/independence. This dimension measures the extent of the sense of a self separate from the surrounding environment, and which, in the case of more field-independent individuals, is relatively independent of that environment. For such an individual, internal frames of reference have been developed which are relatively fixed, and which render them much less susceptible than the field-dependent individual to the influence of the opinions or attitudes of others.

In the present study, we sought to use the EFT to investigate the relationship between field-dependence/independence and homesickness in a sample of foreign students in Ireland. At a theoretical level, the finding that field-dependence is positively correlated with homesickness would provide supporting evidence for Fisher's role change concept, as it implies that those who are more easily influenced by the opinions of others are more likely to be homesick, at least in the short term. At the practical level, it could be beneficial to have a simple form of assessment which could be used to identify those at most risk of homesickness, and perhaps allow us to provide them with appropriate support so as to avert their own personal distress and the risk that they might drop out of an exchange programme.

METHOD

Subjects

Sixty-one foreign students were recruited by snowball sampling of known visiting students at Trinity College Dublin. Twenty-seven male and 34 female students comprised the sample. All of the students taking part were in their first year at Trinity, regardless of how many years they had previously studied in their home country. Foreign students who had studied at the college in previous years were excluded from the sample. Their mean age was 21 years 9 months (SD = 11.52 months). Due to the fact that the Embedded Figures Test (EFT) had to be administered individually, a procedure which takes some time, and to the students' varying timetables, they were tested at various points over a period from the beginning of November, 1998 to the beginning of February, 1999.

To avoid the problem posed by the small size of some of the national samples (the Dutch, the Swiss, etc.), it was decided to group separate nationalities into three broad categories. There is precedent for this; Bochner and Furnham (1982) used groupings corresponding to the Northern and Southern European categories used here, and found that the scores of the members of each category on a measure of social difficulty experienced while studying abroad followed a consistent pattern which justified their *a priori* classification. Each subject in the present study fell into one of three groupings of nationality:

a) 11 subjects from the USA (the American group);

b) 30 subjects, 13 of whom were from France, 10 from Germany, 1 from Sweden, 1 from Switzerland, 1 from Russia, 3 from Belgium, and 1 from Holland (the Northern European group);

c) 20 subjects, 9 of whom were from Italy, 7 from Spain, and 4 from Greece (the Southern European group).

Materials

The primary materials required for this study were the Embedded Figures Test (EFT) and the Dundee Relocation Inventory. Demographic details such as age, nationality and gender were also recorded, although in order to protect anonymity, names were not noted. Collins foreign language dictionaries were used when necessary, and a stopwatch was required for the EFT.

Embedded Figures Test (EFT)

The EFT came into use in 1950, but the edition used in this research dates from 1971. It was originally developed to measure performance on perceptual tasks requiring the subject to "disembed" a form from an organised field, an attribute given the name field-dependence/independence, but understanding of the underlying dimensions of this trait has grown, leading to expansion in the number of attributes it purports to examine. The original perceptual-based finding was found to be associated with performance on tasks that required identifying (or disembedding) one particular aspect of an intellectual problem. However, subsequent research extended this to the concept of self and the nature of an individual's psychological defences (see Witkin and Goodenough, 1981).

What is meant by the concept of the self in this context is the extent to which the subject is aware of himself/herself as an individual distinct from the surrounding environment, able to distinguish between "within-skin" and "outside-skin" stimuli, what may be expressed as a sense of separate identity. That is to say that highly differentiated individuals have an awareness of, and categorise, their feelings as their own and distinct from those of others, segregating the experience of self from that of non-self. Less differentiated individuals display more reliance on external sources for definition of their attitudes, judgements, sentiments and views of themselves.

The test consists of 24 cards depicting complex figures, and 8 cards depicting simple figures, as well as an example of each for practice. The task of the subject is to identify the location of the simple figure within the complex figure within the shortest time possible. Some simple figures may be used more than once. The 24 cards are divided into two test groups, of which the second is used for retests (this group was not used in this study). Scoring is done by summing the times taken in seconds to find each of the figures, and then dividing by 12 to obtain the mean time taken. If the subject fails to find a figure after 3 minutes, the attempt is abandoned and the time recorded as 180 seconds.

A full list of studies which have validated the use of the EFT to measure social identity is given in the EFT manual (Witkin et al., 1971). The reliability of the test for college students was found to be .82 for males and .79 for females. A small sex difference has been shown for this test, with males showing greater field-independence than females.

Dundee Relocation Inventory (DRI)

The DRI was generated by Fisher (1989) from the best selectors of a large 65-item pool to measure homesickness following transition from home to university. It consists of a 26-item questionnaire, of which the first two questions are dummy items. The subject must rate how often he experiences certain cognitions and feelings connected with homesickness: Never, Sometimes or Often. Scoring ranges from 0 to 2, with a higher score indicating a more negative feeling. The scoring is reversed in the case of positive items.

The test-retest reliability was 0.59 across two weeks and 0.21 across six months for the homesick, whereas the corresponding values for the non-homesick were 0.71 and 0.81 respectively. As Fisher points out, homesickness being a state rather than a trait, the test-retest reliability would be expected to vary within and between subjects.

While we recognised the difficulty that norms established for the culture of origin of the tests may not be applicable to an international sample, it would be exceedingly difficult to find single forms of tests standardised across the various nations of Europe as well as the United States. However, the EFT has been shown to be applicable across a wide range of cultures, for example, from Sierra Leone to the Canadian Inuit (Berry, 1966). The Dundee Relocation Inventory has previously been used in Germany (Smrcek and Stiksrud, 1994), Australia (Horstmanshof and Reddy, 1998; Burt, 1993) and New Zealand (Ward and Kennedy, 1993), as well as in its native Britain, and seems to adapt well to these different nationalities and contexts. In the absence of comprehensive norms across many different cultural groups for other measures of homesickness and field-dependence, the use of the DRI and EFT was considered justified in this research.

Procedure

The tests were first given to ten students as a pilot study. Being satisfied that it was practical, foreign students were then recruited through snowball sampling around Trinity College and asked to take part in research into "the SOCRATES experience in Trinity College Dublin". The focus on homesickness was not mentioned until afterwards so as to minimise the transparency of the testing. Each individual was tested separately. All questionnaires were completed in the presence of the researcher.

Language problems did arise, but, given the high level of English required to follow third-level courses in Trinity, they were invariably limited to uncertainty over the precise meaning of a particular word in the sentences presented. In these situations, the word was explained by resort to a bilingual dictionary, thus ensuring uniformity of translation for subjects within a language group, though not between language groups.

A crude measure of validity was obtained by asking the subjects at the end of the test if they would say that they were homesick or not.

Results

Homesickness

Eleven participants rated themselves as homesick, while 50 said that they were not. The mean score on the DRI for those rating themselves as homesick was 17.82 (SD = 2.52), while the mean score for those rating themselves as not homesick was 11.66 (SD = 1.95).

Gender and Homesickness

The mean homesickness score for males was 12.22 (SD = 2.54), while the mean homesickness score for females was 13.21 (SD = 3.55). No significant difference was found between these two scores ($t = -1.219$, $df = 59$, $p = 0.228$).

Nationality and Homesickness

The mean homesickness scores were 12.43 (SD = 2.71) for the Northern European group, 14.15 (SD = 3.39) for the Southern European group, and 11.18 (SD = 3.03) for the American group. Analysis of Variance found no significant difference between the Northern European group and the Southern European group, or between the Northern European group and the American group. However, the Southern European group was found to be significantly more homesick than the American group ($f = 3.835$, $df = 2$, $p < 0.05$). No significant effect was found for the interaction between gender and national grouping ($f = 1.060$, $df = 2$, $p = 0.353$).

Embedded Figures Test and Homesickness

Subjects' scores on the EFT were found to correlate strongly and significantly with their scores on the DRI (Pearson r value = .660, $p < 0.01$). There was also found to be a significant difference between the genders on EFT score ($t = -3.328$, $df = 59$, $p < 0.01$), with females obtaining scores which indicated higher field-dependence than males. The average total time for males on the EFT was 235.63 secs (SD = 53.30), while the average total time for females was 294.75 secs (SD = 79.07).

A partial correlation was carried out on the relationship between homesickness and EFT, using gender as the controlling factor. The outcome showed that a significant correlation remained between homesickness and EFT scores ($r = .64$, $df = 58$, $p < .000$).

Discussion

The results of this study confirm that elevated levels of homesickness do occur in a significant minority of subjects. The overall mean of DRI scores for the non-homesick (11.66) is higher than that reported by Fisher for the original standardisation of the test, who found that the non-homesick had a mean score of 5.3, but this is perhaps to be expected in a population who have not just travelled within their own country, but have come to another country to study. The score for the homesick (17.82) was very close to Fisher's finding of 17.5. The finding that there is no significant difference between the genders concurs with the findings of Fisher (1989), Burt (1993), and Brewin (1989), and suggests that this lack of differentiation between the sexes is general across Western cultures.

It appears from these findings that students from different regions of Europe have a fairly uniform level of reaction to the transition to Ireland. The finding that the level of homesickness found in the Southern European group is significantly higher than that found in the American group suggests that "cultural distance" may play a part in reaction to transition. This difference clearly cannot be due to the language difference alone, as the Northern European group would have similar difficulties to the Southern European group if this were so. This may imply a sliding scale of cultural distance, on which the Americans are closest to Irish culture; the Northern Europeans are close enough to show no statistically significant difference when compared to the American group but also distant enough to show no significant difference when compared to the Southern Europeans; and the Southern Europeans are furthest away.

An alternative explanation for this finding could lie in the different natures of the university experience in America and Europe. It is the rule for American students to move away from home to attend university, while this is less common for Northern European students and extremely unusual for Southern European students. Fisher (1989) found that previous experience away from home may reduce homesickness, provided that the previous experience was of a similar nature. Thus, while having spent some time staying with relations in a student's youth would not help them adjust to life in a foreign university, the experience of having left home to attend university before would.

The correlation shown between the EFT and homesickness in this study is significant. The finding that more highly differentiated, or field-independent, individuals tend to be less homesick is interesting in the light of Witkin's (1981) claim that less differentiated individuals are more sociable, make friends more easily, and are easier to get on with. Ordinarily, one would expect that the more sociable (field-dependent) students would find the transition easier as they are more capable of making new friends and interacting, but this appears not to be the case. The field-independent students, on the other hand, who are less influenced by, and pay less attention to, the opinions of others seem to adjust better psychologically to their new environment.

Fisher's role change theory may be an appropriate explanation for this finding, as it is precisely those people who are most influenced by other people's perceptions of them and their roles who adapt badly to the transition. This finding can also be interpreted as supporting Bochner and Furnham's (1982) social skills model of culture shock. They suggest that it is caused by an inadequate knowledge of the norms and routines of the new environment, which may lead the sojourner to apply the norms of his previous environment and experience humiliation and/or rejection when they are found to be inappropriate. This could explain how the supposedly more socially aware field-dependent subjects are less comfortable in the new environment; having been used to relying on social norms which they have learned very adequately in their home environment, they are bewildered when confronted with new and different ones after transition. Field-independent subjects, however, may rely less on external cues to determine behaviour or cognition, and so find it much easier to deal with a sudden transformation of those cues. It would be interesting to investigate whether or not this continues to be the case: one might suppose that the field-dependent students would, given time, learn the new norms more effectively and become better adjusted than the field-independent students without this ability.

The finding that the EFT had a significant correlation with homesickness has intriguing implications for cultural exchange. It suggests that innate personal characteristics may have as significant an effect on homesickness and adjustment as do more situational factors such as the company found in the new environment or liking for the culture (of course, the quality and quantity of company found in the new environment may be influenced by feelings of homesickness rather than causing them). While it would be rash to extend this judgement to more extreme cultural transitions (for example, from China to Ireland) it may hold true for the comparatively lesser cultural transitions involved in coming from continental Europe or the United States to Ireland. This implies that trying to match individuals to their exchange may be as, or more, profitable than attempting to modify the situation in which they find themselves.

While we are not recommending a form of screening to determine who is allowed to take part in these exchanges, the EFT could form the basis for a means of identifying those individuals who are more likely to find the exchange experience more distressing, enabling co-ordinators to discuss with the prospective participants their reasons for applying, provide them with detailed information on acculturation and perhaps offer the opportunity for counselling on adaptation to their prospective new environment. This might help reduce the incidence of students abandoning their exchange programme before the end of its period, thus wasting resources, depriving someone who might have gained more from the experience, and not least causing themselves a great deal of anguish and misery.

Our study has been limited by several factors. The main difficulty was our inability to conduct a longitudinal study in the timeframe available to us, which lessens the certainty of any conclusions that can be drawn due to the instability of homesickness as a state. It is quite probable that the situations of the SOCRATES students will change somewhat over the year, as they make new friends, get to know Ireland better, become more proficient in the language, and even (for Southern students) find that the weather gets a little closer to what they are used to. Nevertheless, the study has still covered a period lasting over half the Trinity academic year, and even if things were to change over the coming months, this information is still valuable for what it tells us about the initial period of the stay. Furthermore, the EFT has been demonstrated to be stable over time, so even if homesickness levels change, over time the more homesick individuals identified here should continue to be overall the most homesick.

An intriguing finding was that the average time taken for these subjects to "disembed" the EFT figures was much shorter than that given in other student norms (Witkin et al., 1971). It would seem that either the student sample in this study was unusually field-independent (and perhaps this is related to their choice to enter the SOCRATES programme), or that the norms given with the test have become outdated. Either way, this sounds a cautionary note in our evaluation of the results; for whatever reason, the subjects may not constitute a representative sample, as they all seem to be clustered towards one end of the differentiation scale. Ultimately, this means that the difference between them in field-dependence is much smaller than might be the case for a contemporary sample of undergraduate students in general. It may also be the case that with a less restricted range of scores on the EFT, a stronger correlation coefficient would more accurately represent the relationship between homesickness and field-dependence.

Finally, the modest size of our sample limits the general conclusions that may be drawn. Furthermore, severely homesick students may withdraw more than most, and thus the chances of contacting them to participate in any such study are much reduced. The amount of sample bias introduced in this way may be small, as most students will still attend classes, but it is a problem of which to be aware.

This study has taken the first step in filling a gap in an understanding of the SOCRATES experience. Furthermore, to our knowledge, this is the first study to demonstrate a relationship between field-dependence (as measured by the EFT) and homesickness (as measured by the DRI), either among international exchange students, or any other group undergoing a cultural transition. We hope these results will encourage others to consider homesickness and field-dependence as important factors in understanding and alleviating acculturation stress.

References

Ainsworth, M.D.S., M.C. Blehar, E. Waters and S. Wall (1978), *Patterns of Attachment: A Psychological Study of the Strange Situation*, Hillsdale, NJ: Erlbaum.

Aroian, K.J. (1990), "A Model of Psychological Adaptation to Migration and Resettlement", *Nursing Research*, Vol. 39, pp. 5–10.

Berry, J.W. (1966), "Temne and Eskimo Perceptual Skills", *International Journal of Psychology*, Vol. 1, pp. 207–229.

Bochner, S. and A. Furnham (1982), "Social Difficulty in a Foreign Culture: An Empirical Analysis of Culture Shock", in S. Bochner (ed.) *Cultures in Contact: Studies in Cross-cultural Interaction*, Oxford: Pergamon Press.

Bowlby, J. (1969), *Attachment and Loss, Volume 1: Attachment*, New York: Basic Books.

Bradbury, E. (1997), "Understanding the Problems", in R. Lansdown, N. Rumsey, E. Bradbury, T. Carr and J. Partridge (eds.), *Visibly Different: Coping with Disfigurement*, Oxford: Butterworth-Heinemann.

Brewin, C.R., A. Furnham and M. Howes (1989), "Demographic and Psychological Determinants of Homesickness and Confiding among Students", *British Journal of Psychology*, Vol. 80, pp. 467–477.

Burt, C.D.B. (1993), "Concentration and Academic Ability Following Transition to University: An Investigation of the Effects of Homesickness", *Journal of Environmental Psychology*, Vol. 13, pp. 333–342.

Carden, A.I. and R. Feicht (1991), "Homesickness among American and Turkish College Students", *Journal of Cross-cultural Psychology*, Vol. 22, pp. 418–28.

Fisher, S. (1989), *Homesickness, Cognition and Health*, London: Erlbaum.

Horstmanshof, L. and P. Reddy (1998), "Homesickness among Overseas Sojourners in Australia", *Asian Journal of Social Psychology*, Vol. 1, No. 1, pp. 345–355.

Juthani, N.V. (1992), "Immigrant Mental Health: Conflicts and Concerns of Indian Immigrants in the USA", *Psychology and Developing Societies*, Vol. 4, pp. 134–148.

Karasek, R.A. (1979), "Job Demands, Job Decision Latitude and Mental Strain: Implications for Job Redesign", *Administrative Science Quarterly*, Vol. 24, pp. 285–309.

Karp, S.A., L. Silberman and S. Winters (1969), "Psychological Differentiation and Socioeconomic Status", *Perceptual and Motor Skills*, Vol. 28, pp. 55–60.

MacLachlan, M. (1997), *Culture and Health*, Chichester: Wiley.

Mandler, G. (1975), *Mind and Emotion*, New York: John Wiley and Sons.

Mandler, G. and D.L. Watson (1966), "Anxiety and the Interruption of Behaviour", in C.D. Spielberger (ed.), *Anxiety and Behaviour*, New York: Academic Press.

Office of International Student Affairs (1998), *Welcome Guide to Trinity for International Students*, Dublin: Trinity College.

Smrcek, A. and C.R. Stiksrud (1994), "Commitment and Homesickness During Post-adolescence", *Studia Psychologica*, Vol. 36, No. 3, pp. 211–221.

Van der Veer, G. (1998), *Counselling and Therapy with Refugees and Victims of Trauma*, 2nd edition, John Wiley and Sons.

Van Tilburg, M.A.L., A.J.J. Vingerhoets and G.L. Van Heck (1996), "Homesickness: A Review of the Literature", *Psychological Medicine*, Vol. 26, pp. 899–912.

Ward, C. and A. Kennedy (1993), "Psychological and Socio-cultural Adjustment During Cross-cultural Transitions: A Comparison of Secondary School Students Overseas and at Home", *International Journal of Psychology*, Vol. 28, No. 2, pp. 129–147.

Weiss, R. (1975), *Marital Separation*, New York: Basic Books.

Weiss, R. (1978), "Couples' Relationships", in M. Corbin (ed.), *The Couple*, New York: Penguin.

Weiss, R. (1982), "Attachment in Adult Life", in C.M. Parkes and J. Stevenson-Hinde (eds.), *The Place of Attachment and Loss in Human Behaviour*, London: Tavistock Press.

Witkin, H.A. and D.R. Goodenough (1981), *Cognitive Styles: Essence and Origins: Field Dependence and Field Independence*, New York: International Universities Press.

Witkin, H.A., R. Dyk, H.F. Faterson, D.R. Goodenough and S.A. Karp (1962), *Psychological Differentiation*, New York: John Wiley and Sons.

Witkin, H.A., P.K. Oltman, E. Raskin and S.A. Karp (1971), *Embedded Figures Test*, Palo Alto, CA: Consulting Psychologists Press, Inc.

CHAPTER SIXTEEN

THE SOJOURN EXPERIENCE: AN INTERNATIONAL COMMENTARY

John Berry

The three chapters in this section provide an account of stress and adaptation of sojourners, specifically international students, in Irish surroundings. However, although this provides a unifying theme, clearly the methodology, sample background and activities of the students are all quite diverse. What is required is a conceptual frame of reference to draw them together for the reader and to cohere them as a set of studies around the same social question. Theories and models originating in the research tradition of cross-cultural psychology provide an overarching paradigm within which one common interpretation of these studies can be provided.

It has been noted that cross-cultural psychology has an interest in two domains. The first and dominant tradition is that of linking "variations in individual behaviour to cultural and ecological contexts by way of general enculturation and specific socialization" (Berry, 1995; 457). The other, more novel approach is to examine changes in individual behaviours that are related to the meeting (or clash?) of separate cultures especially visible in the phenomenon of acculturation. With increasing geographical dislocation of certain groups as well as the growth of globalisation, the process of acculturation gains ever more importance. The ways in which people from one culture deal with and negotiate life in another culture clearly has more than just theoretical interest (but is nonetheless theoretically interesting). A number of factors have been identified through research as contributing to the ease or difficulty which people experience during acculturation. One of these is the type of group and it is clear that although generalisations have been made about the effects of acculturation, clearly these effects can vary depending on certain characteristics. Berry and Kim (1988) have outlined five different types of acculturating groups: immigrants, refugees, native peoples, ethnic groups and sojourners. Immigrants and refugees are both first-generation arrivals into the population by way of migration from elsewhere and thus face some similar problems. Sojourners are temporary immigrants who reside for a specific purpose and time period and return to their home country. The three articles in this section clearly deal with this group and while some of the challenges facing them may be less difficult than permanent immigrants because their stay is ultimately short-term, they may also have additional problems because of the lack of permanent supports and may experience, for example, more severe health problems.

Another factor is the acculturation attitude or orientation of the individual. These attitudes arise as the product of an interaction between one's commitment to the way one has been previously (one's culture, language, way of life and identity) and one's views on the dominant society and the willingness to have interactions in this new culture. Four permutations of acculturation arise and these have been labelled:

a) *Integration*: a set of attitudes where one wishes to continue to value one's cultural identity while also have interactions with groups within the new dominant culture;

b) *Assimilation*: a set of attitudes where an individual wishes to have relations with the new culture but no longer values (older) cultural maintenance;

c) *Separation*: maintaining the older culture and avoiding or withdrawing from the new; and

d) *Marginalisation*: avoiding the new culture but also separating from the old.

These are largely in correspondence with other terms such as the decision to move towards (adjustment), against (reaction) or away from (withdrawal) a new culture. It has been proposed and largely confirmed that each of these varieties of acculturation attitude implies different levels of stress and that integration is the healthiest, since one has a supportive base in two camps; while assimilation and its inevitable cultural loss may mean higher levels of stress. Separation and especially marginalisation are thought to undermine mental health to the greatest degree because an individual is in conflict with the new culture and possibly also with the old (in the case of marginalisation).

Another obvious factor influencing acculturation is the dominant culture itself and the problems faced by those undergoing acculturation will clearly depend in part on demographic factors such as religious, linguistic, dietary and economic characteristics. More subtle issues though (and perhaps not so subtle when dealing with them) may be to do with the culture of the country, its pluralism and openness to multiculturalism. This feeds directly into issues such as racism and xenophobia but it may also have an impact on how valued cultural difference and diversity are in general to the host country.

The final issue relevant to the examination of the experience of sojourners in Ireland raised in these chapters is that of individual psychological style. It may be the case that an individual's cognitive style can be described as more or less differentiated or showing more or less field dependence. Field-dependence/independence at a very basic level may mean the ability to pick out certain shapes from a different context as a perceptual task but is also relates more broadly to "the separation of cognitive structures into discrete units". In the widest terms, such as social functioning, it might be anticipated that highly field-independent individuals can function with little guidance from others, and maintain their own views in the face of contradiction from others. It also seems feasible that field-independence might work as an insulating psychological factor against acculturative stressors.

These articles can all be viewed as contributing to different aspects of the acculturation model in an Irish context. The study by Glennon and MacLachlan is most explicitly located in that framework and looks at the relationship between acculturation strategy (integration, assimilation, separation and marginalisation) and levels of psychological well-being, as measured by the GHQ in a group of overseas medical students studying in Ireland. A substantial difference in the proportion of Irish compared to foreign students (27 per cent versus 57 per cent) scored above the threshold score with the difference especially high on the social dysfunction subscale of the GHQ. For the majority of foreign students, the researchers found that integration was the dominant acculturation strategy. As expected, the smaller numbers pursuing strategies of separation and marginalisation scored more highly on the GHQ (indicating lower levels of psychological well-being). The assimilation strategy was associated with far lower scores (and better psychological well-being — see comments below on the article by Boucher for possible reasons for this). The potential for practical intervention with students dealing with acculturative stresses is also highlighted in this study — those students whose coping style was based primarily on problem-solving had significantly lower GHQ scores than those seeking social support or showing an avoidance strategy.

The study by Orr and MacLachlan confirms the importance of personal psychological style in mediating the stresses of acculturation. The benefit of using a fairly homogeneous group, at one level, such as SOCRATES students is that so much situational variation is controlled for, allowing for a closer examination in individual differences with regard to acculturation. Taking homesickness as one consequence of acculturation for sojourners, the authors avoid the problem of generalisation by comparing the participants according to broad geographical categories as well as assessing their field independence/dependence levels through the EFT (Embedded Figures Test). Both variables, geographical and psychological, as expected, have an impact on the outcome measure, with more field-dependent respondents displaying higher levels of homesickness and difficulty in adapting to a new culture.

Finally, the chapter by Boucher is interesting in that it moves away from the sojourners' experiences *per se* as the topic of analysis and examines instead their perceptions of the host country and the ease with which acculturation might take place. As Boucher skilfully shows, these perceptions are quite subtle and reveal a pattern of interaction between acculturation strategy and acceptance. More specifically, the interviews revealed that if the sojourners were willing to assimilate totally and lose their own cultural identity, they were warmly accepted by members of the host country. But attempts to maintain their own cultural identity meant they were excluded from mainstream interaction. Thus the pattern uncovered in these views tells us a lot about the host country and the importance of the ideologies there. In a country like Ireland, where insularity is dominant, assimilation appears to be the only way into the society. This contrasts with the *laissez-faire* pattern of the US and much slower assimilation where cultural difference is accepted. So while African-American may be an acceptable term to most Americans, Irish society may be too insular for people to be comfortable with an integrationist (as opposed to assimilationist) term such as African-Irish or Afro-Celt. By broadening the concept of civic culture to include not just social norms but also legal ones, the authors also reveal the perception of increasing state discrimination at the level of officialdom sharply in contrast to its egalitarian rhetoric.

In sum, these chapters provide in the broadest sense a picture of the way in which ecological, cultural, behavioural and psychological dimensions have to be understood in their correct context and not in isolation from one another. They contribute to the ongoing programme to capture intellectually the multi-layered process of acculturation. And they make available the research background to potentially enable practical intervention to benefit the lives of sojourners in Ireland.

References

Berry, J.W. (1995), "Psychology of Acculturation" in N. Goldberger and J.B. Veroff (eds.), *The Culture and Psychology Reader*, New York: New York University Press.

Berry, J.W. (1997), "Immigration, Acculturation and Adaptation", *Applied Psychology: An International Review*, Vol. 46, No. 1, pp. 5–68.

Berry, J.W. and U. Kim (1988), "Acculturation and Mental Health", in P. Dasen, J.W. Berry, and N. Sartorius (eds.), *Health and Cross-Cultural Psychology*, London: Sage.

Reflection

CHAPTER SEVENTEEN

"REWRITING YOU": RESEARCHING AND WRITING ABOUT ETHNIC MINORITIES

Katrina Goldstone

> "Yet the point is not so much about belonging and not belonging on the basis of identity/identities, but about the relationships of power that ultimately decide whose version of reality becomes the dominant representation."
> — Magdalene Ang-Lygate in *Representing the Other*

> "There is always more to learn, always more than one Story about anything — despite the fact that for the most part, the academy's raison d'être has been to discover and write the One Story." — Elizabeth Ellsworth in *Multicultural Research*

> "Our stories were untold and, therefore, invisible or distorted." — Joyce E. King in *Multicultural Research*

The focus of this chapter is to discuss the ethics and methodologies involved in researching ethnic minorities and to question the nature of the research agenda as it appears to be developing in an Irish context. Special attention is paid to the issue of the attitudes and motives of those researchers who are not from the minority group they are studying. In addition, the issue of perpetuating racist or supremacist attitudes through thoughtless research is also addressed. The aim of the article is to intervene in the torrent of research currently being produced on refugee and minority issues, or at least to provoke some thought about the legitimacy of some of the projects being undertaken.

This article is written from a growing concern and sense of ill ease about the way ethnic minorities are being represented in Irish academic circles. I write from my own experience of researching Jewish history and culture and from being asked to participate or "help" with research projects, TV programmes and newspaper articles on minorities and on refugees. I believe there are no shortcuts to studying ethnic minorities in whatever academic discipline. I want simply to put the bluntest of arguments, to plead the case, paraphrasing what Karen Henwood has said about feminism: "It should be possible to do research that is for ethnic minorities (or refugees) rather than on them." As R. Ruth Linden has stated in the context of writing about studying Holocaust survivors:

> I can ask no less of myself than I ask of my ethnographic subjects. I must be prepared to be at least as vulnerable and honest as I ask them to be. I must be willing to stand beside them, not to speak for them but to speak for myself and with them.

Otherwise one risks perpetuating misrepresentation while at the same time professing to be impartial. In addition, I might make the suggestion that it should be made difficult to conduct such research and some component of lobbying or practical work should also be compulsory with it. Otherwise, there is too much scope for the people in the race relations or antiracism industry to become parasitic and researchers who forge reputations on the study of ethnic minorities — and who are not from those groups — are not exempt from this possibility. We all need to evaluate — and keep evaluating — the motivations we have for doing the work we do.

Concerns about the ethics of researching other groups have been long discussed in American academic circles and in the fields of psychology, sociology and feminist theory (McCready, 1983; Stanfield and Dennis, 1993; Kitzinger and Wilkinson, 1996; Grant, 1999). The awareness of the construction of Woman as Other has made women's studies academics acutely aware of the pitfalls of studying other women across the boundaries of class, race and sexual orientation. In a volume dedicated to the theme of representing the other, editors Celia Kitzinger and Sue Wilkinson set out their motivation for such a volume:

> Discussing a wide range of different Others, the authors as a group draw the attention of the reader to a set of complex but vital questions. These questions include: Who is the Other, and who are "we"? Along what shifting lines of power and powerlessness is Otherness constructed? What are the costs and benefits of "including" or of "excluding" the Other from our research, and on what terms? Should we speak only for ourselves? Should we act simply as "conduits" through which the voices of Others can be heard? . . .

Broadly speaking, these questions can act as beacons or guidelines for researching minorities across a broad spectrum of academic disciplines.

Looking at the essays in Carl A. Grant's volume on multicultural research, it is striking how many researchers from minorities started from or engaged with history, be it personal or social, as a way of seeking to understand what it was that gave one set of people permission to ridicule, denigrate and murder people from other cultures (Hudson: 128; Gomez, 81–2; Thornton, 135, all in Grant, 1999). I have been working on historical research about Jewish refugees, and the images of Jews in Irish society, for five years. I have subsequently become more interested in the way history is written — and who is written out of history or written about in a certain way — than I am in the study of history *tout court*. That is because I have realised that it is different in Ireland if you want to write history about ethnic minorities and it is different again if you're from an ethnic minority trying to write that history.

I came to write this article as the result of an uncomfortable feeling that lingered in the aftermath of writing and researching my thesis on the treatment of Jewish refugees by Irish officialdom during World War II. It was an experience at once searing and formative, for many reasons, but partly because I conducted the research in a predominantly male and Christian environment. Thus the ways of thinking, asking questions, framing research and analysing data that were imparted to me was influenced by this. As I was a mature student and anxious to please, I quashed any doubts I had about the tone of thesis and carried on. I read voraciously about the Holocaust as background to the thesis but it soon became an overwhelming presence.

The difficulty I had in completing the thesis was not just about the emotive nature of the research but it was also about issues concerning how the majority culture wants minorities to write their own stories. Through this realisation, I became aware of other perspectives, and the writings of Anglo-Jewish academics confirmed to me that there were other perspectives and theories, different to the ones being presented to me as "the norm". Thus I came to think more deeply about the implications — or some of the implications — for minorities who want to write within a dominant and sometimes hostile cultural tradition and also to ponder the ambiguities and motives of those from the majority culture who decide they want to write about ethnic minorities. It became clear that serious responsibilities face researchers and writers on minority issues — provided, that is, they themselves take seriously what they're doing, not just regarding it as trendy or righteous. It involves steering a fine course, what Bryan Cheyette, in another but related context, has described as "finding a critical vocabulary which neither reinforces nor reproduces the racialized exclusions of the past" (Cheyette, 1996: 14). This also means negotiating the tricky business of approaching the subject of study with either an unrecognised or unacknowledged ambivalence or indeed an unquestioning over-empathy. Listening to testimonies from minorities requires one to be vigilant, not just to the distortions created by your own prejudices, but also to be watchful for the distortions which may have been wrought by internal self-perception.

In my experience, many people from religious or ethnic minorities function in a multi-layered way and often have different levels of communicating with those from a dominant culture and will relate on a more honest level only within their own peer group or after a long period where trust has been established with the majority person.

Where Are the Real Jews?

In the historical field, there has been more written on anti-Semitism in Ireland than about real-life Jews. Whilst anti-Semitism and the study of it is critically important, nonetheless it is frequently — though not always — the study of fantasies and stereotypes. Therefore it says something quite distinct about Irish society and the public perceptions about Jews that there is a disproportionate amount of research into fantasy as opposed to the facts and multifaceted reality of Jewish life in Ireland. For me, reading the monographs on Irish anti-Semitism provoked discomfort or anger. The fact that much of the historical writing was written in a semi-apologetic tone was almost as disturbing as the discovery that some of the writers didn't recognise good old-fashioned stereotypes when confronted with them and they actually presented them as true reflections of reality.

In addition, there was the issue of Jewish denial or rebuttal of Irish anti-Semitism. Despite ample evidence to the contrary, the loudest affirmations of Irish tolerance have frequently been uttered by rabbis and communal leaders. Without the insights offered by a number of Anglo-Jewish academics, I would not have gained any understanding of this complex conundrum. The work of a number of historians in England highlighted the complex role of Jewish leaders in relation to the state and to authority and described the dilemmas which Jews faced when trying to counter anti-Semitism. Not only did the work of Tony Kushner, David Cesarani and Bill Williams give intellectual insights, it provided me with a sense of community with scholars on issues from a Jewish perspective.

The fact that the majority of non-Jewish writers in Ireland referred to "the Jewish community" as one amorphous mass was also problematic. The majority of writers have ignored differences along lines of gender, class or orthodox versus secular. This "totalised" Jewish experience, reducing it to a limited and one-dimensional account. Few writers have seemed to want to find out how Jews coped with anti-Semitism in their day-to-day lives — perhaps because to do that, one would have to grant Jews a sense of autonomy and agency in their own affairs. So busy were many of the writers being self-righteous or guilty about anti-Semitism that they in fact reified or objectified the Jews whose lives were blighted by such prejudice. Writing from this sort of perspective tells us more about Christian attitudes to Jews than it does about the multi-faceted experience of Jews in Irish society. In *Representing the Other*, a similar argument is posited about the representations of blacks:

> Amina Mama makes the . . . point about psychology's representations of black people. Psychological constructions of "the African" in the colonies and "the Negro" in Britain and North America also tell us more about the subjectivity of Europeans than about what it meant to be black and Other under a colonial or racist order. (Kitzinger and Wilkinson, 1996:10)

Writing about anti-Semitism in a regretful way can perpetuate attitudes of superiority and risks painting Jews only as victims. Similarly, writing about racism also carries within it the danger of perpetuating the image of minorities only as oppressed or victimised and thus in one stroke wiping out or eradicating the nuances and realities of life. bell hooks, cultural commentator and distinguished academic, has written extensively about the perniciousness of the victim role. Talking about the development of militant black resistance at the time of the civil rights movement in America, she writes:

> There was a great difference between a civil rights struggle that worked primarily to end discrimination and radical commitment to black self-determination. Ironically, many whites who had struggled side by side with black folks responded positively to images of black victimisation. . . . The image of blacks as victims had an accepted place in the consciousness of every white person; it was the image of black folks as equals, as self-determining that had no place — that could evoke no sympathetic response. (hooks, 1996: 54)

Anyone in Ireland engaged in anti-racism work or the study of minorities must ask themselves searching questions about the legacy and influence on the consciousness of white Irish people of decades of missionary and development work, which reduces the black experience solely to that of victim or potential convert to Christianity.

I cite these examples to show how it is possible for differing perspectives to alter research. Of course, every single researcher has a unique perspective but the onus is firmly on the majority person researching minority issues to fully acquaint themselves with the culture involved. Many researchers do not seem to realise how fundamentally insulting it is to approach a minority group and then display absolute ignorance of their beliefs, rituals or customs. I was consulted a few years ago by a student who intended to "do something about anti-Semitism". She rang me up in a panic because she was encountering problems in her methodology. I asked her how much time she had spent gaining the confidence and trust of her interviewees. This seemed a novel idea to her. "It's only a minor thesis," she said. I found her lack of sensitivity breathtaking, but then the blame should actually be attached to her supervisor. It was irresponsible to encourage a young student to tackle a complex subject like anti-Semitism and then give her no guidance as to how to approach the subject. What exactly did either of them expect? That if they simply presented themselves to Jewish people and said, "tell me about your experiences of anti-Semitism", their respondents would just open up and speak? Within this assumption there is no acknowledgement whatsoever that anti-Semitism is a painful or thorny issue. Persuading people to relate their experiences of prejudice is not the same as interviewing respondents on their consumer habits. Whilst one does not want to suggest that the interviewers of minorities overdo the empathy, at the same time is it too much to ask for a little sensitivity?

This is one of the many reasons to reiterate that everyone studying minorities — but most particularly those not from them — must thoroughly question their motives. If a Christian or a white person feels guilty about the appalling history of Jews or blacks, then they should think again. It is obvious that too much shoddy or mediocre work appears about minorities simply because feeling guilty or feeling sorry for them is not a good point of departure for trenchant study. As bell hooks has commented, ". . . goodwill can co-exist with racist thinking and white supremacist attitudes" (hooks, 1996: 16). Work conducted in an unquestioning manner, underpinned by an assumption of tolerance and sympathy, will end by just being about the researcher rather than the researched. If this is the underlying or subconscious motivation for study, then it only continues the pernicious practice of exoticisation or objectification — turning minorities into exhibits or quaint objects of anthropological curiosity. Most of us don't wish to be turned into what Henry Louis Gates Jr has called "an already read text", and that is what stereotyping is all about.

I have been lobbying for asylum rights for some years now and in that time scarcely a week has gone by that someone doesn't contact refugee organisations or their allies wanting "to do something on refugees". Or something on racism. There is no doubt that from the point of view of reporters, programme makers, journalists and researchers, this is a hot topic. Unfortunately, in the clamour to climb on board this particular bandwagon, it is evident that some — though not all — have not for one minute thought about the impact their questions will have on their subjects (or is it objects?); no thought that, in the hellish period of uncertainty imposed by our government, asylum-seekers might not welcome such attention, and that it is not necessarily going to improve their situation one iota, though it may well bestow plenty of benefits on the person doing the interviewing.

We must be on our guard, too, that in the cultural arena we resist all simplifications and reductionist versions of other cultures. Increasingly, the Holocaust is being used by a majority and populist culture and there is a growing sense that people do not want to hear the part of the story that is disturbing. There may be a clamouring for the evidence of the pain that some minorities have suffered but there appears to be no will to hand them the power to tell the stories in their own words. The overwhelming acclaim granted to Roberto Benigni's film *Life is Beautiful* is part of a more pernicious trend. We are, at the start of the twenty-first century, with the death of the survivors imminent, in great danger of turning the Holocaust into nothing more than a character-building exercise. As the triumph over tragedy ethos dominates the media, we are less and less able to hear the darker version of events and crave an upbeat ending to even the most grotesque catastrophes. As Lawrence Langer has stated:

> . . . the pretence that from the wreckage of mass murder we can salvage a tribute to the victory of the human spirit is a version of Holocaust reality more necessary than true. (quoted in Belton, 1999: 135)

It was only in 1995 that the Irish government, following the orgy of end-of-the-war commemorations in England, held a State ceremony to commemorate those murdered in the Holocaust. Even so, the day was clouded by controversy as the day originally chosen was picked without prior consultation with Irish Jews and was in fact a high holy day (*Irish Times*, April 1995).

History, memory, images, writing — academic or popular — all can be used as a means of legitimising continued oppression or condoning past injustices. Therefore to combat that through research projects, we must be alert to the chameleon-like quality of such distortions. If we consider any kind of writing or imagery at all, be it popular, literary or academic, and invest it with the significance that western Eurocentric culture has accorded it, we will merely be creating new versions of distortion. If representation and the control of images, including everything from TV screen to doctoral thesis, were not so important, would "political correctness" be demonised the way it is? And why would the relatively few inroads on cultural imperialism be so virulently resisted? Bryan Cheyette has referred to the fact that all texts in some way reflect and encode structures of power and domination. The colonisation of the images and experiences of blacks, Jews, Muslims or any group outside of the golden circle of western Eurocentrism contributes to continued subjugation. It annihilates and erases the experiences of Others. If one chooses to conduct the sort of research that is intended to undo the harm of such colonisation, one must be humble without being abject and ever-critical and questioning of motives — one's own and others — and ever-wary of recreating or reinforcing distortions. In other words, to reach a place that is "beyond guilt and atonement". bell hooks has summarised this most powerfully:

> I am waiting for them to stop talking about the "Other", to stop even describing how important it is to be able to speak about difference. It is not just important what we speak about, but how and why we speak. . . . Often this speech about the "Other" annihilates, erases. "No need to hear your voice when I can talk about you better than you can speak about yourself. No need to hear your voice. Only tell me about your pain. I want to know your story. And then I will tell it back to you in a new way. Tell it back to you in

> such a way that it has become mine, my own." Re-writing you, I write myself anew. I am still author, authority. I am still the colonizer, the speaking subject, and you are now at the centre of my talk. (hooks, 1991: 151–2)

hooks comes to a simple conclusion, and one with which I am inclined to agree: Stop.

References

Belton, N. (1999), *The Good Listener*, London: Weidenfield and Nicholson.

Cheyette, B. (1996), "Unanswered Questions: An Introduction" in B. Cheyette (ed.), *Between "Race" and Culture*, Stanford, CA: Stanford University Press.

Ellsworth, E. (1999), "Multiculture in the Making", in Carl A. Grant (ed.), *Multicultural Research: A Reflective Engagement with Race, Class, Gender and Sexual Orientation*, London: Falmer Press.

Gomez, M.L. (1999), "Narrating My Life", in Carl A. Grant (ed.), *Multicultural Research: A Reflective Engagement with Race, Class, Gender and Sexual Orientation*, London: Falmer Press.

Grant, Carl A. (ed.) (1999), *Multicultural Research: A Reflective Engagement with Race, Class, Gender and Sexual Orientation*, London: Sage.

Henwood, K. (1994), "Resisting Racism and Sexism in Academic Psychology: A Personal/Political View", in K. Bhavnani and A. Phoenix (eds.), *Shifting Identities, Shifting Racisms*, London: Sage.

hooks, b. (1991), *Yearning: Race, Gender and Cultural Politics*, London: Turnaround.

hooks, b. (1996), *Killing Rage: Ending Racism*, London: Penguin.

Hudson, M. (1999), "Finding My Life's Work", in Carl A. Grant (ed.), *Multicultural Research: A Reflective Engagement with Race, Class, Gender and Sexual Orientation*, London: Falmer Press.

Kitzinger, C. and S. Wilkinson (1996), "Theorising Representing the Other", in Celia Kitzinger and S. Wilkinson (eds.), *Representing the Other*, London: Sage.

Linden, R. Ruth (1993), *Making Stories, Making Selves: Feminist Reflections on the Holocaust*, Columbus: Ohio State University.

Thornton, M. (1999), in Carl A. Grant (ed.), *Multicultural Research: A Reflective Engagement with Race, Class, Gender and Sexual Orientation*, London: Sage.

Glossary

Compiled by Treasa Galvin

Acculturation

The process that occurs when people from one culture encounter and react to another culture. Acculturation may occur at a group level (for instance, a change in the values of a group of immigrants) and/or at an individual level, where encountering a different culture changes the psychology of the individual. The degree and type of group and individual acculturation may differ significantly. Berry's Acculturation Framework is particularly relevant to the experience of migrants. *(See Assimilation, Integration, Marginalisation and Separation below.)*

Assimilation

One of four strategies in Berry's Acculturation Framework. Assimilation occurs when it is not considered to be of value to maintain one's identity and characteristics derived from the culture of origin, but it is considered to be of value to establish and maintain relationships with the culture that characterises mainstream society.

Asylum-seeker

Any individual who has applied for refugee status under the criteria stipulated in the 1951 Geneva Convention (*see Refugee*). The United Nations High Commission for Refugees defines an asylum-seeker as:

> A person who requests refugee status in another state, normally on the grounds that they have a well-founded fear of persecution in their country of origin, or because their life and liberty is threatened by armed conflict and violence. (UNHCR, 1997)

Asylum-seeker is a temporary status conferred on the individual while their host Government determines their right to full Convention refugee status. As asylum-seekers have notified the relevant authorities of their presence in the state and have lodged a claim for refugee status, they are not illegal immigrants.

Convention Refugee

Any individual who, having sought refuge in a host society, is granted refugee status in terms of the criteria stipulated in the 1951 Geneva Convention.

Culture Shock

Anxiety, disorientation and stress that an individual may experience when in a new or unfamiliar cultural environment.

Expatriate

An individual who undertakes a voluntary or compulsory period of residence outside their own country of origin.

Humanitarian Leave to Remain

The status granted to an individual whose personal circumstances do not fully meet the criteria for refugee status stipulated in the 1951 Geneva Convention, but whom the relevant authorities decide should be allowed to remain in the host society on humanitarian grounds. The criteria used to grant Humanitarian Leave to Remain are not stipulated in The (Irish) Refugee Act, 1996. As a consequence, this status is granted at the discretion of the Minister for Justice, Equality and Law Reform.

Integration

One of four strategies in Berry's Acculturation Framework. Integration occurs when it is considered to be of value to maintain one's identity and characteristics derived from the culture of origin, but it is also considered to be of value to establish and maintain relationships with the culture that characterises mainstream society.

Marginalisation

One of four strategies in Berry's Acculturation Framework. Marginalisation occurs when it is not considered to be of value to maintain one's identity and characteristics derived from the culture of origin, nor is it considered to be of value to establish and maintain relationships with the culture that characterises mainstream society.

Migration

In relation to population groups, migration refers to the voluntary or involuntary movement of people on a permanent or semi-permanent basis in response to a set of complex factors. People may migrate within their own country or to another country.

Mono-cultural

The situation where a society is portrayed as having one unified and dominant set of cultural practices irrespective of the existence in that society of differential social and cultural traits.

Multicultural

The situation where a society is portrayed as having a diverse and heterogeneous set of cultural practices, as a result of the existence in that society of differential social and cultural traits.

Prejudice

A favourable or unfavourable judgement or opinion about a person or thing that is not based on actual experience or accurate knowledge.

Pluralism

(See Socio-cultural Pluralism below.)

Programme Refugee

Section 24 of the (Irish) Refugee Act, 1996 defines a programme refugee as:

> . . . a person to whom leave to enter and remain in the state for temporary protection or resettlement as part of a group of persons has been given by the Government . . . whether or not such a person is a refugee within the meaning of the definition of "refugee" of section 2 [of the Refugee Act 1996].

Racial/Ethnic Discrimination

Negative or positive actions toward an individual based on prejudicial beliefs.

Racism

A set of beliefs and practices based on inaccurate linkages (between personality, cultural traits and hereditary characteristics) as a consequence of which one group of people is defined as inherently inferior or superior to another.

Refugee

A legal status conferred (by the relevant host society authorities) on an individual whose personal circumstances meet the criteria stipulated in the 1951 Geneva Convention. Section 2 of the (Irish) Refugee Act, 1996, quotes this Convention, which defines a refugee as:

> A person who owing to well-founded fear of being persecuted for reasons of race, religion, nationality, membership of a particular social group or political opinion is outside the country of his nationality and is unable or, owing to such fear, is unwilling to avail himself of the protection of that country; or who, not having a nationality and being outside the country of his former habitual residence as a result of such events, is unable or, owing to such fear, is unwilling to return to it.

Separation

One of four strategies in Berry's Acculturation Framework. Separation occurs when it is considered to be of value to maintain one's identity and characteristics derived from the culture of origin, but it is not considered to be of value to establish and maintain relationships with the culture that characterises mainstream society. This category also describes Segregation, where the choice of separation is not voluntary but imposed by larger society.

Social Distance

> "The level of intimacy of social interaction that individuals find acceptable between themselves and members of particular social categories." (Brewer and Crano, 1994)

Socio-cultural Pluralism

The recognition that there exists in society multiple and different types of social relations, social institutions, cultural practices and identities.

Sojourn/sojourners

A sojourn is a period of temporary residence outside an individual's own country of origin. A sojourner is an individual who undertakes such a period of residence.

References

Berry, J.W. (1997), "Immigration, Acculturation and Adaptation", *Applied Psychology: An International Review*, Vol. 46, No. 1, pp. 5–68.

Brewer, M.B. and W.D. Crano (1994), *Social Psychology*, New York: West.

UNHCR (1997), *The State of the World's Refugees: A Humanitarian Agenda*, Oxford: Oxford University Press.

INDEX